The Rise of Arnold Schwarzenegger

The Fall of Gray Davis

Recall Elections in the United States

By Donald Musch

ISBN 0-9743501-6-8

Dedicated to
Benjamin Lawrence

"Recall is a procedure by which it is the voters themselves who make the ultimate determination as to whether an official should retain his or her office for the duration of the term to which he or she was elected."

63C AmJur 2d, Sec. 202

Introduction

The recall of California Governor Gray Davis, and his replacement by actor Arnold Schwarzenegger, focused the attention of millions on a unique vehicle for expressing political dissatisfaction – the recall of an elected official. Though this tactic has been used extensively at the local level, it has seldom been effective to displace state elected officers. It was the first time since Governor Lynn Frazier of North Dakota was recalled in 1921 that a governor was replaced in such fashion. And, taking place in the most populace state in the United States which has one of the world's largest economies (not to mention that it spotlighted a neophyte politician who is an actor immortalized as "The Terminator") only increased interest in the race.

A recall election for state officials is nothing new to America, or to California where it was first introduced through a constitutional amendment in 1911. The rationale for inserting such a procedure is also nothing new. Discussions leading up to the formation of the constitution of the United States included arguments for recall as a tool for the electorate to control elected or appointed officials. In California , Governor Hiram Johnson pushed through a constitutional amendment in 1911 which authorized recall arguing in part that it could forestall graft and corruption amongst government officials.

This work describes the background for recall elections, details the recall in California with an emphasis on the recall of Governor Gray Davis, covers the main elements in a recall with observations on potential improvements, and includes the text of recall provisions in those states authorizing the tactic for replacing state-wide officers.

"OKAY ARNOLD, SHE'S ALL YOURS..."

TABLE OF CONTENTS

APPENDICES

WHAT DEFICIT?
I DON'T SEE
ANYTHING. NOPE.
NO DEFICIT HERE...
CALIFORNIA
DAVIS
SPENDING

CHAPTER 1

The Evolution of Recall Elections

According to historian Joshua Spivak who has concentrated on the history of the recall:

> "While the first instance of the recall can be found in the laws of the General Court of the Massachusetts Bay Colony of 1631, and again in the Massachusetts Charter of 1691, the recall gained a firm footing in American politics with the democratic ideals that burst forth from the American Revolution. After declaring their independence, 11 of the 13 colonies wrote new constitutions, and many of these documents showed the new spirit of democracy... Some opened up the right to vote to a larger portion of the population. And a few states wrote the recall into law as a method of controlling their elected representatives... Unlike its modern day counterpart, the seventeenth and eighteenth century versions of the recall involved the removal of an official by another elected body..." (in History News Network - online, 9/01/03)

The early concept for recall is aptly described in The Recall of Public Officers by Frederick L. Bird and Frances M. Ryan (Macmillan, 1930) at page 3, where they point out that Article V of the Articles of Confederation permitted the States to recall their delegates, saying:

> "For the more convenient management of the general interests of the United States, delegates shall be annually appointed in such manner as the legislature of each state shall direct, to meet in Congress on the first Monday of November, in every year, with a power reserved to each state to recall its delegates, or any of them, at any time within the year and to send others in their stead, for the remainder of the year.

The appeal of a recall was that it offered the electorate an opportunity to displace an elected official before the end of his or her term of office. From inception it was viewed, certainly by its proponents, as a necessary vehicle to rebut the narrow interests who often controlled the government (and the people). And that is the way it was used in several of the early recalls – coping with elected officials who were at the beck and call of private interests. As pointed out by Bird, opponents consistently maintained that:

- The recall was simply a method to subvert the general concept of direct elections.
- It would be used for strictly personal purposes.
- It would provide a vehicle for petty bickering amongst political factions leading to political demoralization.
- Political timidity and time-serving would become the primary attribute of elected officials. Officials would be dependent on the public moods, and unable or unwilling to risk making a decision for the public good.
- It would deter competent candidates from running for office by endangering tenure. And it involved a false interpretation of the American form of representative government and of the proper relation of an elected representative to his constituency.

The proponents argued to the contrary that recall was:

- A means of continuous popular control over men in public office.
- A way to correct mistakes in nominating persons for elected office and to check the "deliberate betrayal of the people's will."

- A method to free elected officials from bosses and corporations who nominated or financed them.

- To be seldom used so its potential for spreading uncertainty would be minimal. The mere knowledge of the recall potential keeps officials aware of their responsibility to the public.

- A way of ensuring that public officials stand or fall on their merits as a public officer.

Interestingly, Bird points out that the "real question" for recall narrowed down to whether there exists "a public opinion ready and able to pass intelligent judgment upon the issues which might be raised in recall elections involving the honesty, the faithfulness, the legality, and the efficiency of the conduct of holders of public office?" (at page 11)

Rather than using the legal system as is done for an impeachment, the recall requires an election, giving the same constituents who voted the official into office the opportunity to vote him out. And, contrary to the requirements for an impeachment, recall can usually be instituted for much less reason. In some jurisdictions this means the recall can be set merely because the electorate dislikes actions taken by the official, even though that official might be acting legally, fulfilling a campaign promise, or acting in concert with his political party. In a sense, circumstances totally out of his or her control at the time might well be the basis for the recall election (as is partially the case in the Davis recall election).

The ease with which a public official can sometimes be recalled, and its impact on the normal functioning of government has engendered particularly acute criticism of the very concept. Depending on the jurisdiction involved, the recall can apply to elected officers, (local or state), appointed officials, or judges. Over the years since it was first introduced in 1903 at the municipal level in California, the tool has been used more extensively at the local level, much less at the State level, and in only two instances has it been successful in replacing a sitting Governor. Oregon led the way in authorizing a state-wide recall of its Governor in 1908, but North Dakota was the first to replace its Governor by recall in 1921. According to Jerome Tweton, a retired University of North Dakota history professor, "...the whole atmosphere in the state at the time was very chaotic and rancorous. You just look at the newspapers for that period of time, and my God, there is all kinds of libelous stuff in there." But, striking a chord similar to California in 2003, the Kansas City Star in an article dated September 22, 2003 about the recall of Governor Frazier in North Dakota stated "...his popularity fell with the state's economic fortunes and growing disillusionment over a farm relief program..."

As of September of 2003, eighteen states and the District of Columbia permit the recall of state officers.

Though the following excerpt from The Recall of Public Offers emphasizes the California experience, its conclusions and observations are relevant to the overall concept of recall as practiced throughout the United States.

"...II. The recall, in its operation, has given illustration of the full range of both the virtues and the vices forecast of it at the time of its original adoption. Based on the principle that a public official is a continuously responsible agent of the electorate, and that a fixed term of office does not always secure from him the proper regard for the opinions of his constituents, the recall has developed as a check upon unrepresentative officials and as a method of popular impeachment when the processes of criminal law, judicial removal, and legislative address have failed, or when the pressure of public opinion has proved insufficient to avoid the betrayal of the public trust or to secure the observance of a desired policy. While situations do sometimes arise which make desirable the removal of officials before the expiration of their terms, the electorate generally has not as yet learned to be any more judicious and discriminating in the recall of officials than in the election of officials. Unnecessary political turmoil has sometimes been aroused, needless election expenses incurred, and competent officials seriously embarrassed by shortsighted criticism and self-seeking factionalism.

In considering the justifiable and unjustifiable results of the operation of the recall it is significant that it has been applied almost entirely to political or quasi-political officials. The application of the recall to technical officers on questions of efficiency, while theoretically of questionable desirability, calls for little consideration here, because in the few areas in which such officers are subject to recall the provision has been practically a dead letter. Only one appointive official has been thus removed. This single instance, the recall of a city manager of Long Beach, is far from being a convincing example of the appropriate use of the plan.

Although the judiciary of the state is subject to recall, the public has never presumed upon its prerogative to influence judicial decisions, to dictate to judges engaged in the proper performance of their duty, or to interfere in any way with the stability and independence of the judiciary. The only three judicial officials above the rank of justice of the peace whose recall has been effected – three municipal judges of San Francisco – were summarily removed with ample justification. In each case a clear-cut moral issue was involved upon which the public competently based its decision.

It is absurd for an electorate to have to suffer for years from an unsatisfactory public servant because he has been elected to office for a fixed term. If there were no means for the control of such officials, the lengthening of terms of office to four years or more would be too dangerous to tolerate. No private business could be run on any such theory. It seems reasonable that if an official has acted dishonestly or illegally, if he has proved inefficient or incompetent, or if he has failed to represent his constituency he should be removed from office.

When an official is guilty of corruption which can be clearly proved his removal from office is not the proper function of the recall. It is not incumbent upon the public to usurp the prerogative of the courts in such matters, and it has not done so. The court is in a better position to get at the facts in a case of this kind and is less likely to be influenced by irrational factors. But the judicial process is somewhat cumbersome, and corruption is difficult to prove in a court of law. An official's conduct may have been so subject to suspicion as to undermine public confidence in his integrity and services without the possibility of legally proving malfeasance. Since the danger of injury to the public should take priority over an official's personal benefit from his office, such cases would seem to be fit subjects for the application of the recall. As Judge Oster said in the famous Davenport case, "The difficulty of proving official turpitude or malfeasance is in itself sufficient reason for a remedy which, while perhaps assuming some form of malfeasance, does not involve the necessity of proving it." In several instances, notably those of the recall of a councilman and a mayor in Los Angeles, and of three municipal judges in San Francisco, the recall has been used most effectively to secure the removal of officials of doubtful integrity who could not be reached by the courts.

The question of the inefficiency or incompetency of an elective political or executive official is one which must be treated with a fair degree of leniency and consideration. Such officials are much more frequently stupid bunglers than they are shrewd corruptionists; but it must be born in mind that mediocre, well-meaning novices are often placed in office by the public themselves to deal with highly involved situations and problems. The recall of more officials has been sought on the grounds of "inefficiency and incompetency" than on any other charge; but the public has not been intentionally overcritical or severe. This expression, on a recall petition, is usually nothing but a generic term of disapproval for high taxes, for too many or too few public improvements, or for whatever policy the proponents of the recall dislike. The expression is safe because it is almost certain to be measurably true, and convenient because it avoids the necessity of detailed indictments. Careful, expert study and analysis of official policies and a closer and more continuous scrutiny of the activities of local legislative bodies by interested citizens, especially in rapidly growing localities, would not infrequently bring to light inexcusable conditions which would both justify and dignify movements for recall on the grounds of incompetency. In the comparatively few instances in which this has been done by the promoters of a recall, the movement has been successful either in removing the offending official or in securing an improvement in conditions. As pointed out incisively by Arnold Bennett Hall in his Popular Government, the determination of the guilt or innocence of an official accused of corruption or inefficiency is likely to demand information which is beyond the ability and opportunity of the average voter to obtain. But within a limited range the public is quite competent to detect malfeasance and incompetency by observation of the general results of official action. It does not, for instance, take an expert to determine the existence of both when a patented paving material, liberally spread about a town by a favored contractor, begins to deteriorate within a year of its installation.

The recall has found its most satisfactory application, however, in making possible the retirement of political officials who have arbitrarily run counter to the opinion and wishes of their constituencies. While there are many official activities upon which the average voter is not competent to pass judgment, there are numerous matters of public policy which come within the scope of his knowledge and observation, which vitally affect his welfare, and with regard to which he is entitled to honest co-operation from his elective representatives. If, for example, a mayor permits the maintenance of a wide-open town, if a council installs expensive public improvements against the wishes of those who have to pay the bill, or if a legislative body favors one section or group of its constituency at the expense of another, there is a sound basis for the use of the recall.

The recall has proven more generally useful in California for the admonishing or removing of "misrepresentative" officials than for any other purpose. When thus used, it has in the great majority of cases, been directed against officials elected for four-year terms in areas blessed with a comparatively short ballot. During so long a term in office there is abundant opportunity and incentive for an official to follow the wishes of his local boss, the vice interests, the public utility interests, or the paving and other public improvement interests, to the detriment of the interest of the public. In fact, it is exceedingly difficult for him to avoid favoring the ingratiating crew of lobbyists that are constantly insinuating themselves into his good graces. The busy citizen, with his right of election once in four years is no match for these public relations specialists who daily haunt city halls in behalf of their presumptuous employers. But the recall is as practical a means as can be placed at his disposal for preventing these interests from gaining free range and for keeping the harried official mindful of his public responsibility. When the electorate realizes more fully that it is frequently preyed upon, through its government, by certain classes of corporations, it will find even more effective use for the recall. "Speaking of ocean-going submarines," said a councilman of a certain beach city, a veteran of numerous recall campaigns, "they can't compare in their menace with the land-going corporation submarines that cruise around our city government. They attack below the surface; suddenly a bomb goes off without warning; and the public is 'blowed up.' But if you know how to keep your eyes open you can see their periscopes."

Watching out for their periscopes, however, is not always practical for the average voter unacquainted with the intricacies of public business. In a democratic Utopia where every citizen was alert and informed, the recall would be a much more formidable weapons. Under actual conditions, however, it is sometimes possible for the recall to be used against the public by the interests that seek to use government for the promotion of selfish or sordid ends, in the same way that they frequently control elections. But because the people are sometimes vanquished by their own weapon is no justification for depriving them of so desirable a potential means of protection.

Corporate interests have much at stake in the securing of favorable action by legislative bodies, and with the aid of their adroit lobbyists are ready to turn any opening to their own advantage either in the election or in the recall of an official. Professional politicians have much the same vantage ground, and by controlling the sources of information and manipulating popular impulses, they can frequently control a situation. The recall has sometimes been misused for too trivial an issue, or has been employed on occasion by a disgruntled candidate for office or by a dismissed job-holder. The flexibility necessary for the useful functioning of any democratic instrument makes the abuse of those instruments possible. No system has ever been devised which will perfectly protect the electorate from its own lack of judgment and discrimination. It will probably continue to elect inferior men to office at times and by the same token may be deceived by a recall election with all the earmarks of respectability but which conceals varied purposes and selfish motives.

Failure to recognize the existence of defects and mistakes in the ways in which the recall has been employed will weaken its possibilities for future effectiveness. Although the public cannot be expected to attain complete rationality and good judgment in the employment of so trenchant a weapon, it can learn, and is learning, to be more discriminating than in the past. Before any citizen signs a recall petition he should raise and seek answer to several always pertinent questions. Who started the recall movement and for what actual purpose?

What interests are financing and promoting the campaign? Why does this newspaper favor the recall and that one oppose it? Are conditions such as to demand drastic correction? If a real grievance exists is the assailed official responsible? Have other less expensive and less formidable methods of correction been exhausted? What assurance is there that the recall will provide a remedy? While no citizen is going to find a complete answer for these searching questions, the mere consideration of them should stimulate a rational attitude toward the movement that will guard against undue gullibility, haste, and impulsiveness.

Certain general charges made against the principle of the recall deserve recognition. It has been contended that the recall suppresses the desirable qualities of courage and independence, results in official timidity and time serving, and discourages the candidacy for office of men of high caliber. There is no doubt that threat of recall is very frequently used as a club over the actions and policies of public officials. There is evidence, moreover, that such threats are frequently productive of the desired results. When the effect has been to influence an official who has attempted to repudiate his constituents, it can hardly be branded as undesirable. The danger of resulting timorousness depends entirely on the courage and independence of the official himself, and there have been very few instances in which a public official courageously performing his duty to the satisfaction of a majority of the people has been allowed to lose a recall election through public apathy or misunderstanding. While the recall has, on occasion, been employed as a means of intimidation, there is no evidence that it has in this way seriously handicapped constructive public service, or discouraged the candidacy of able and fearless men for public office.

Those advantages of the recall which are perhaps the most constructive and significant are too intangible for more than general comment and appraisal. It has permitted the lengthening of terms of office without the risk of the establishment of official bureaucracies. Under the existence of the recall no public officer can take advantage of his four-year term to repudiate his constituency with impunity. It has established the principle of responsibility and responsiveness with a value limited only by the capacity of the public to understand it and benefit thereby. Finally it serves a useful purpose in helping to maintain public interest and confidence. The knowledge on the part of the public that it does possess a potential weapon to prevent government from slipping entirely beyond popular control tends to stimulate both an interest in its processes and a feeling of political security.

III. Recall campaigns and elections are far from being the conventional, stereotyped proceedings that are characteristic of the general political routine. While they are subject to most of the shortcomings that accompany ordinary elections they frequently overstep the bounds of deadly political conventionality and develop a colorful spontaneity, a popular enthusiasm, and an active participation of the electorate that is almost unique in this day of popular indifference and declining political interest. Under such conditions the average citizen is fully as susceptible to the devices of artful politicians as in ordinary elections, and even more likely to be swayed by his feelings in the making of decisions; but he does act with a vigor that shows he has not lost his interest in the functioning of representative government when real issues are involved. This is especially true of small cities and of rural areas, where recall politics sometimes become intensely personal and arouse factional bitterness that requires some time to subside. Judged by the percentage of votes polled in recall elections the participation is greater than that for other types of special elections, rarely falls below the average for general elections, and frequently runs to a much higher figure. In hotly contested recalls in the smaller cities the vote polled has risen as high as ninety-three per cent of the total registration, and on several occasions has ranged from seventy-five to eight-five per cent.

V. It should be borne in mind, finally, that the recall is still in the experimental stage of development. Its operation, over the brief period in which it has been in existence, has revealed great potentialities for civic betterment when it is judiciously employed. There is a growing tendency for the recall in its use to become self-corrective of its weaknesses, for in those areas in which it has been too lightly applied sentiment is developing against its employment except as a last resort. The disquieting problems brought to light in the operation of the recall are mainly the general problems related to the functioning of all democratic government. Any expectation of an intelligence developing about the use of the recall superior to that reflected in the election of officials and the exercise of other electoral functions could arise only from an exaggerated concept of the intellectuality of mankind. While many critics express their irritation with its operation and urge the rigid curtailment of its use, there is little advocacy of the abandonment of the plan. The public is too well satisfied with the sense of security which the existence of the recall conveys to permit it to be discarded. As a defensive weapon of democracy it apparently has come to stay."

(From: The Recall of Public Officers, Frederick L. Bird and Frances M. Ryan. The MacMillan Company, New York, 1930. pages 346-354 and page 362 – footnotes omitted)

CHAPTER 2

Background of Recalls in California

The recall was born in California when it became part of the Los Angeles city charter in 1903. Though it reflected the spread of progressive thought throughout the greater western part of the United States, it was more specifically attributed to countering the influence of the Southern Pacific Railroad. As often happens, social conditions influenced the push for this change but without the intensive efforts of Dr. John R. Haynes, described as a "...tireless advocate of the initiative and referendum, and father of the recall provision in the United States." it would never have been adopted. Acting on an appointed Committee of Legislation, Haynes successfully worked behind the scenes so that eventually the recall was passed by the electorate as the law for the City of Los Angeles.

At the state level a new personality led the fight for the recall, Governor Hiram Johnson. (See Appendix A for biographical information on Johnson) Though he apparently didn't wish to run for Governor, once elected, he proposed this tool "as a way for the populace to fight back against political corruption and the powerful railroads and banks, which had enormous influence over state governments..." (Wikipedia.org). Johnson achieved notoriety earlier when he took over as a special prosecutor in a San Francisco graft trial after the chief prosecutor was shot dead in the courtroom. Elected as Governor of California, he served with distinction and later was elected as a United States Senator from California where he served until 1945. A reading of his first inaugural speech (See Appendix B for the full text of this speech) of January 3, 1911 highlights his views on the need to fight corruption and pressure from private interests and the need for recall:

"...I take it, therefore, that the first duty that is mine to perform is to eliminate every private interest from the government, and to make the public service of the State responsive solely to the people..."

"...How best can we arm the people to protect themselves hereafter?...while I do not by any means believe the initiative, the referendum, and the recall are the panacea for all our political ills, yet they do give to the electorate the power of action when desired, and they do place in the hands of the people the means by which they may protect themselves. I recommend to you, therefore, and I most strongly urge, that the first step in our design to preserve and perpetuate popular government shall be the adoption of the initiative, referendum, and the recall...if the people have the right, the ability, and the intelligence to elect, they have as well the right, ability, and intelligence to reject or to recall..."

In the end, the California legislature voted 106-14 for the recall and when this measure was brought before the California voters for approval it passed, gathering the second largest vote total of the 22 amendments which were approved by the public. In Bird's history is the statement attributed to Franklin Hichborn in his account of the legislature of 1911 that "Probably never before had a measure before the California Legislature been so thoroughly studied and considered...In the legislature interest had been so intense that every member of both houses voted for or against the measure." On the other hand, the Los Angeles Times of October 10, 1911 enjoined voters to reject the measure, saying:

"A vote of "NO" is a rebuke to those who would upset established representative government for whim or caprice or malice, and is a dignified demand for a constitutional convention if the organic law is to be overhauled."

Recall efforts against State-wide officials was tried shortly after the new amendment was approved. Senator Marshall Black was caught up in the failure of the Palo Alto Building and Loan Association. An investigation revealed he was involved in illegal transactions (he was Treasurer of the Association), he was arrested, and though pressured to resign, he refused. A recall petition was circulated and in the ensuing election of January 2, 1913 Black was recalled and Herbert C. Jones was elected. Black subsequently pleaded guilty and was sentenced to ten years in the state penitentiary.

The second recall involved Senator James C. Owens who had made specific campaign promises to labor groups in California and then, after entering office, either voted against these issues or failed to vote at all. Bird and Ryan point out in their treatise on Recall that progressives pointed out that "Owens had voted consistently against every bill in the interest of the general public when the public's interests conflicted in the slightest degree with those of the Standard Oil Company, the railroads, and other big interests..." (at page 274). It is interesting to note the wording of the petition circulated to recall Owens which said, in part:

> "Senator Owens repeatedly violated his pledges as a Democrat; broke his written promises to Labor; and assisted Big Business at crucial moments by his vote or by staying away..." (Bird and Ryan at page 273)

The foregoing was followed by a description of the inconsistencies between his platform and voting record. Labor in the end did not prevail and the recall failed with Owens getting support from the Democratic Party (the party of Senator Owens), farmers, Republicans and the press.

Perhaps the most colorful recall election was that of Senator Edwin E. Grant, an aggressive foe of prostitution and vice. The original impetus for his recall was his sponsorship of the Redlight Abatement Act, but historians argue that opponents recognized that it would be untenable to ask for recall against one fighting against vice. In the event, the initial petition stated he "had voted to make the World's Fair 'dry,'" and that he had voted against a bill to prevent the solemnizing of marriages until at least five days after the issuance of the license, and that he had opposed a measure giving California authors and publishers preference in the publication of school books. (The Recall, Tribunal of the People, by Joseph F. Zimmerman, Praeger, Westport, Connecticut, 1997) On the third attempt to get a valid petition, those opposed to Grant succeeded and in his recall election on October 8, 1914 he was defeated by Senator "Eddie" Wolfe.

The next successful recall for a state office didn't occur until 1995 with the recall of Assemblyman Paul Horcher, a Republican who changed to an Independent. Horcher incurred the wrath of the Republican Party when he cast a key vote for Democratic Assembly Speaker Willie Brown, Jr. Republicans at the time held a 41-39 edge in the Assembly and they had anticipated naming their own Speaker to replace Brown. In an article in the California Journal of July, 1995 by Laureen Lazarovici the basis for the recall is described as follows:

> "The visceral and emotional appeal of the Horcher recall was based on the belief that the two-term legislator had betrayed voters in his district. "Legislators sometimes do cast votes that are unpopular," said Assembly Republican Leader Jim Brulte (R-Rancho Cucamonga), whose speakership dreams were dashed last December by Horner's vote. However, "Horcher conspired with Willie Brown to deceive the voters," he said, referring to the oft-repeated story that the Republican assemblyman went to the speaker last year to seek advice on whether he should run as an independent. Brown reportedly cautioned him that such a switch prior to the election would be political suicide..."

It appears that Horcher had, for some time, cooperated with Brown in the Assembly engendering deep antipathy among Republicans. The end for Horcher came on May 16, 1995 when he was recalled and Republican Gary Miller was elected as his replacement.

The second successful recall election in California during 1995 involved another member of the Assembly, Doris Allen, who ran unsuccessfully for the Senate against the wishes of the State Republican Party. Once again, the oft heard motive of "revenge" is paramount in this recall effort.

After describing how Allen was elected over two other Republicans in a hotly contested newly formed district in California, A. G. Block states in the California Journal of January, 1996:

> "Her relationship with caucus leaders dissolved completely early in 1995 when she ran for the state Senate in a bare-knuckles special election that also featured one of the grand poohbahs of Orange County conservatism – Assemblyman Ross Johnson (R-Fullerton)...backed by a powerful clique of Orange County conservatives...In addition, a good chunk of the GOP Caucus weighed in on behalf of Johnson. As a result, his eventual victory left Allen feeling bitter and abused, but she soon found an avenue for her wrath."

The act which Allen took was to accept the Speakership of the Assembly with the support of detested Democratic leader Willie Brown. According to Block:

> "Allen never had a chance. Nearly every Republican who is any Republican backed her ouster...Given this kind of support, Republicans who may have opposed the recall...were silenced by fears for their own political safety..."

Allen was recalled by a 2-1 margin, and as pointed out by Block "This marked a stunning turn-around for a veteran law-maker who only one year before had won re-election to a seventh term with 73 percent of the vote. Historian Joshua Spivak, commenting on these California recalls stated:

> "...it appears that the conditions that result in a successful recall are either a corrupt official, like Black, or some mix of partisan betrayal and a specific issue around which to rally the voters.."
>
> "As opposed to defeating a candidate in a general election, voters recall a candidate because they feel betrayed. By running as Republicans and then switching to support Brown, Allen and Horcher were seen as betraying the voters, who elected Republicans and reasonably expected their legislators to vote accordingly..." (History News Network, online September 29, 2003).

Eight years later the voters of California engaged in their historical recall of Gray Davis.

CHAPTER 3

THE RECALL OF GOVERNOR GRAY DAVIS

There are almost as many theories about the downfall of Governor Gray Davis as there were candidates in his recall election. And, based on past political experience in California, only a political earthquake would make an impression. But the mix of immense funding, the proliferation of candidates, the economic disasters which befell California, and not the least the arrival of "The Terminator", resulted in a change which could be of immense importance to California and to America. What prompted the recall of Gray Davis?

The Personality Factor:

"Gray" is probably the least offensive description attached to the California Governor when assessing his personality. Throughout the recall campaign writers dwelt on the fact that Governor Davis served the public in a series of positions without ever comprehending that his personality might well cause his eventual downfall. As David S. Broder, Washington Post Staff Writer stated on September 28th, 2003:

> "As he (Governor Davis) faces this climactic political challenge after three decades during which he doggedly climbed the ladder from staffer to assemblyman to a succession of higher statewide posts, Davis as always is showing a stoic face to the public..."

Other writers have described Davis as "Least Objectionable Politician", or "The Perfect Political Bureaucrat" with one astrologer going so far as to suggest the initial mistake was naming him "Gray" (his full name at birth was Joseph Graham Davis, Jr.) rather than "Joe" which has a much stronger connotation! If pundits can be believed, Davis worked his way up the political ladder with "...a slavish attention to detail, getting jobs done by the book..." and is "...devoid of charisma and considered aloof even by those closest to him." One writer states that "Again and again, Davis was able to size up opponents and tailor a campaign to fit the need..." and many would point to his re-election campaign as proving the accuracy of the last statement. He beat Bill Simon who, at best, is described as a weak candidate and who some would contend was instrumental in his own defeat.

If personality was a major factor in the election, and if the foregoing opinions accurately reflect the Davis personality, one could not have asked for a starker contrast than presented by his major opponent, Arnold Schwarzenegger. In an online opinion column (October 5, 2003, updated October 9, 2003) in Epinions.com the Governor-elect is described as "an obvious authoritarian" who has some of the same traits as Davis (goal oriented and totally dedicated to achieving success). He is also a household name (even though most can't spell it), a symbol of power and strength (even in an unworldly context), and he has the distinct advantage of financial independence and (following his marriage) a direct entre into the best political circles. There were "blips" on the political landscape late in the election when Schwarzenegger was named by several women for sexual indiscretions (he didn't deny the possibility these claims were true).

In the event, the recall presented voters with the prospect of seeing "Gray" for the remainder of his term, or embracing an entirely new personality who promised new directions, energetic action, clear-cut policies, and the prospect (no matter how difficult to achieve) of a balanced budget with no substantial increases in taxes.

Money and the Intangibles

The financial condition of California has been a deep concern for much of the past three years. Though Davis inherited a booming economy and a large surplus when he first entered the Statehouse, a series of events (many outside his control) converged to make Californians believe that bankruptcy might be just around the corner.

- The national dip in the economy was, in many instances, led by the dot.com free fall and that industry was a major part of the economic backbone of California.

- The energy crisis of 2001 hit California with power failures and immediate increases in the cost for energy.

- Fees (another word for taxes) which had been rescinded when there was a surplus have now been reinstated.

- Davis signed a bill authorizing illegal aliens to obtain drivers licenses.

Against the backdrop of such factors, Governor Davis was unable to effectively communicate the successes of his administration and the progress he had made to better the lives of Californians by improving education, transportation, and the environment.

The recall supporters and candidate Schwarzenegger entered the fray with not only commitment, but with a war chest of significant proportions. The recall itself was initially started by an anti-tax organization which was led by Republican backers. In May of 2003 the movement to replace Davis received a financial and organizational boost when Congressman Darrell Issa launched his recall effort, backing it with a major financial commitment. Once the Secretary of State for California had announced the requirement for valid signatures had been met there was an open field for prospective candidates who needed only 65 nomination signatures and $3,500 or 10,000 signatures with no cash deposit. What happened next was either a comedy or tragedy, depending on one's view of the political process but, in the end, 135 candidates were certified. One by one, prominent Republicans dropped out of the race following the withdrawal of Issa, with both Bill Simon and Peter Ueberroth stepping down, and independent Arianna Huffington ultimately withdrawing (asking her supporters to vote against the recall), leaving the field to Lieutenant Governor Bustamante, Schwarzenegger, and Republican State Senator Tom McClintock as the only major competitors.

According to a report in The Oakland Tribune of October 8, 2003, Arnold Schwarzenegger raised over $21 million, while Davis raised over $18 million. The recall passed with 55.4% voting to recall Governor Davis. Arnold Schwarzenegger was elected as the successor receiving 48.7% of the vote, more than both Bustamante and McClintock combined (45%). As evidenced by this election, the availability of large sums of money not only triggered the successful petition process, but it also contributed heavily to the ultimate downfall of Gray Davis.

Taxes and the Economy

Californians appear to be no different than their millions of American counterparts in being extremely sensitive over any actions which might increase taxes. To a large extent, Gray Davis and his administration took every measure possible to avoid imposing new taxes on their constituents. Unfortunately for Davis, the decline of the California economy (not his fault, but a mere reflection of the national decline) coupled with the pervasive and unprecedented energy crisis in California (See Appendix C), brought the economy in that State to the point where drastic measures were required. In coping with a budget deficit Davis was forced to agree to extended borrowing to bring down the current deficit, while he negotiated agreements with the energy sector which appeared to be costly to the consumers, and in one relatively minor action (in terms of overall impact) he was forced to reinstate a license fee on vehicles which he had originally dropped. This latter action involved a provision which permitted Davis to roll back license fees so long as there was a budget surplus in California. When the surplus was wiped out, the license fees were reinstated. As stated on Epinions.com on October 5, 2003:

> "...he has been forced to exercise a safety provision of the Motor Vehicle Licensing Law, which requires him to eliminate the cuts in car license fees he made when there was a budget surplus...the fees are now much higher for many car owners than they were over three years ago, when he lowered the taxes..."

One of the first acts of newly installed Governor Schwarzenegger was to issue Executive Order S-1-03 to repeal the car tax retroactive to October 1, 2003. According to The Mercury News website (www.MercuryNews.com): "The order directs the Department of Motor Vehicles to issue refunds to drivers who have paid the higher rate since it went into effect Oct. 1..."

Davis attempted to point out in his campaign that many of the economic problems, and certainly the energy crisis, were not of his doing but reflected either the decline of a national economy or in the case of energy, were driven by deregulation passed by the California legislature under his predecessor, and by private sector practices which were either wrong, too late, or perhaps illegal. But these major problems increased unease and dissatisfaction among voters which turned into outright opposition to Davis and all he stood for when he reinstated the vehicle fees. In looking at Davis the electorate didn't seem to be saying "what have you done for me recently?" as a candidate would encounter in most elections but "look what you did to me recently!" and the result contributed to his downfall.

Immigration

It is difficult to measure the extent to which immigration policies affected the downfall of Gray Davis, but most observers would agree it was a major factor. At minimum, the Governor appears to have miscalculated the deep seated fear, or anger, within the electorate which was increased with his unpopular decision to grant illegal aliens the opportunity to obtain legal drivers licenses. This was a bill which Governor Davis had vetoed twice before. The emotional reactions and total opposition to current policies toward immigrants can be discerned from the platform material issued by candidate for Governor Joe Guzzardi which includes, inter alia:

> "...I will work to remove every magnet that the government of California now provides to entice illegal aliens to enter California..."
>
> "...Davis has mocked those of us who argue that the U.S. immigration laws should be obeyed. Instead Davis...has worked tirelessly to promote illegal immigration..."
>
> "...Instead of responding to financial and social consequences of the illegal alien invasion, Davis feeds it..." *(See Appendix D for the full text of this campaign statement.)*

Other observers, with more objectivity on the topic, agree that Davis made distinct mistakes, as seen in the following quotation from an article by David Broder of The Washington Post on September 28, 2003:

> "Democratic consultant Bill Carrick points to Davis's struggle to solidify the Latino vote as an example (of mobilizing Democratic constituencies to beat the recall). A year ago, Davis vetoed a Democratic bill to allow illegal immigrants to obtain drivers' licenses. A few weeks ago, he signed a similar bill—but one lacking some of the security safeguards included in the original measure. 'For over a year, he was being beat up in Spanish-language media,' Carrick said, 'and now he's trying to repair the damage in a few weeks.'"

CNN published another indication how Davis attempted to parley his approval of the drivers' license bill into Hispanic support on September 8, 2003 when it pointed out that "Davis appeared at Sunday's Mexican Independence Day parade in predominantly Hispanic East Los Angeles, where he touted his signing of a controversial bill that would allow illegal immigrants to obtain drivers' licenses.."

It is entirely possible this issue – illegal immigrants – was a major force in the massive support for Schwarzenegger in southern California, to include San Diego and Orange County. This view is supported by the fact that in San Francisco where such an issue would not make as great an impact, a majority voted against the recall. In exit polls immediately after the election it was clear that a large majority of those voting opposed granting illegal immigrants state drivers' licenses (69% said "no" and 25% said "yes") and it was also clear that those voting for the recall were largely opposed to the action. (69% to 31%) As pointed out in another poll published by The Sacramento Bee on October 9, 2003 "...The governor also reversed position on a bill allowing illegal immigrants to get a California drivers' license...only a quarter of voters agreed with that position..." The Sacramento Bee added in its coverage that "...nearly half of Hispanics and a similar proportion of union members voted to recall the governor, according to exit polls..."

Summarizing, it appears Gray Davis made a miscalculation when he thought signing the drivers license bill would gain him support. It is also apparent that California voters are willing to vote against those who appear to be encouraging benefits of any kind for illegal immigrants, and with a new Governor in California who consistently stated that he opposes bills such as the drivers license measure, immigration as an issue will probably be in the forefront of all forthcoming state or national elections in California. In fact, the newly elected Governor has already asked the legislature to overturn the drivers license measure. The earlier passage of Proposition 187 initiated wide-spread controversy in California and the Davis approval of the drivers' license bill built upon that controversy to the point where immigration is now linked with a number of other vital topics, to include education, transportation and security. An article dealing with the importance of immigration in California in The Mercury News, dated October 1, 2003 is carried as Appendix E .

Impact of the Results

Polls taken after the election clearly indicated approval for the recall process, provided changes were introduced which would make it more difficult to force the recall, and for steps which would decrease the number of potential candidates should the recall succeed. According to the San Francisco Chronicle, on October 16, 2003, "Six in 10 of those surveyed during the final week of the recall election believe the process should be used only when there is an illegal or unethical activity by an officeholder, according to a new poll by the Public Policy Institute of California." Another commentary on the recall in California, Epinions.com on October 9, 2003 opined: "The (recall) law needs to have a bill of particulars added to it, so that it cannot be used on a whim, as a "dirty trick," or as a conspiratorial manipulation. The present California Recall provision stresses personality over experience and qualification."

As pointed out elsewhere in this work, Gray Davis suffered from the defection of large numbers of Hispanics and Democrats, those who gave him resounding support in his earlier win for the governorship. It is too early to tell whether many of these losses will prove permanent, giving Schwarzenegger a broader base within the California electorate, and whether these voters will support other candidates who have previously received their support.

There is also a potential benefit for the Republican Party, not only in California but across the land in the Schwarzenegger victory. The President remained aloof from the California recall but he, along with his Republican supporters are elated to have the State House in the hands of a Republican (albeit a moderate one). Aiming toward the 2004 national elections the new Governor can expect much more support from the Federal government than was garnered by his Democratic predecessor and, in the hopes of the Republicans, this added interest (translated into actual dollars for California) could transform the State's voting pattern in 2004 and assist in returning President Bush to office.

There appears to be little likelihood that recalls will proliferate around the country. Noises were made immediately after the California election that Democrats were going to organize a recall of Schwarzenegger as soon as possible, but little has been said since the initial comments. Recall of Governors in other States are being mentioned but they are generally being proposed by fringe elements having little financial support, and less chance for success.

CHAPTER 4

California Recall Provisions

In 1911, California voters first approved an Amendment to their Constitution permitting recall of state officials which stated:

> "Every elective public officer of the State of California may be removed from office at any time by the electors entitled to vote for a successor of such incumbent, through the procedure and in the manner herein provided for, which procedure shall be known as the Recall, and is in addition to any other method of removal provided by law."

That subject is now covered by Article 2 (Voting, Initiative and Referendum, and Recall) of the California Constitution which has the following provisions specifically covering recalls. Comprehensive coverage of the statutory Elections Code on recall is included in Appendix F.

> "Section 1. All political power is inherent in the people. Government is instituted for their protection, security, and benefit, and they have the right to alter or reform it when the public good may require."

> "Section 3. The Legislature shall define residence and provide for registration and free elections."

> "Section 13. Recall is the power of the electors to remove an elective officer."

> "Section 14. (a) Recall of a state officer is initiated by delivering to the Secretary of State a petition alleging reason for recall. Sufficiency of reason is not reviewable. Proponents have 160 days to file signed petitions.

(b) A petition to recall a statewide officer must be signed by electors equal in number to 12 percent of the last vote for the office, with signatures from each of 5 counties equal in number to 1 percent of the last vote for the office in the county. Signatures to recall Senators, members of the Assembly, members of the Board of Equalization, and judges of courts of appeal and trial courts must equal in number 20 percent of the last vote for the office.
(c) The Secretary of State shall maintain a continuous count of the signatures certified to that office."

"Section 15. (a) An election to determine whether to recall an officer and, if appropriate, to elect a successor shall be called by the Governor and held not less than 60 days nor more than 80 days from the date of certification of sufficient signatures.
(b) A recall election may be conducted within 180 days from the date of certification of sufficient signatures in order that the election may be consolidated with the next regularly scheduled election occurring wholly or partially within the same jurisdiction in which the recall election is held, if the number of voters eligible to vote at that next regularly scheduled election equal at least 50 percent of all the voters eligible to vote at the recall election.
(c) If the majority vote on the question is to recall, the officer is removed and, if there is a candidate, the candidate who receives a plurality is the successor. The officer may not be a candidate, nor shall there be any candidacy for an office filled pursuant to subdivision (d) of Section 16 of Article VI."

"Section 16. The Legislature shall provide for circulation, filing, and certification of petitions, nomination of candidates, and the recall election."

"Section 17. If recall of the Governor or Secretary of State is initiated, the recall duties of that office shall be

> performed by the Lieutenant Governor or Controller, respectively."
>
> "Section 18. A state officer who is not recalled shall be reimbursed by the State for the officer's recall election expenses legally and personally incurred. Another recall may not be initiated against the officer until six months after the election."

A unique feature of the California recall procedure is the coupling of the recall ballot with the ballot for a successor, offering the opportunity for a successor to be elected with a plurality of the votes. This practice was, according to an account in The Green Papers, online, dated August 15, 2003 contained in the ballot form for a recall election which originally read:

> "Form of ballot. There shall be printed on the Recall ballot, as to every officer whose recall is to be voted on thereat, the following question: "Shall (name of person against whom the recall petition is filed) be recalled from the office of (title of office)?" following which question shall be the words "Yes" and "No" in separate lines... in which the voter shall indicate...his vote for or against such recall. On such ballots, under each such question, there shall be printed the names of those persons who have been nominated as candidates to succeed the person recalled, in case he shall be removed from office by said recall election; but no vote cast shall be counted for any candidate for said office unless the voter also voted on said question of the recall of the person sought to be recalled from said office..."

Article II, Section 15 (see above) simplifies this wording and the California Election Code (See Appendix F) covers the recall in more detail, but the primary provisions in the Constitution permitting both recall and election of a successor on the same ballot still prevails.

An important provision of the California Elections Code was declared unconstitutional on July 29, 2003 (Partnoy v. Shelley, Case No. 03CV1460 BTM (JFS), RJN, Exh. S.). U.S. Federal District Court Judge Barry Moskowitz struck down the portion of Section 11382 which states that "no vote cast in the recall election shall be counted for any candidate unless the voter also voted for or against the recall of the officer sought to be recalled." In his ruling the Judge stated that: "...what is at stake is the right of a voter to decide who shall succeed the governor, if recalled. Every voter, whether they voted for or against that recall, has a paramount interest in choosing the person who will govern them..." The Secretary of State of California indicated the State would not appeal that decision.

CHAPTER 5

Elements in Recalling State Officials

The Grounds for Recall

The California constitution permits the recall of a state officer "alleging reason for recall" and it states that "Sufficiency of reason is not reviewable." (Article 2, Section 14(a)). The grounds described in this provision constitute one of the broadest in the United States, offering the electorate the opportunity to replace an elected official for ANY reason they choose to select. Thus, the recall petition submitted to recall Governor Gray Davis stated:

> "The grounds for the recall are as follows: Gross mismanagement of California's Finances by overspending taxpayers' money, threatening public Safety by cutting funds to local governments, failing to account for the exorbitant cost of the energy fiasco, and failing in general to deal with the state's major problems until they get to the crisis stage..."

The full text of this petition is in *Appendix G*

Other states, such as Kansas, require the conviction for a felony, misconduct in office, incompetence, or failure to perform duties prescribed by law which is a much stricter test to meet. As pointed out in *The Recall* at page 37:

> "...However, performance of a discretionary act is proscribed as a ground for the recall of a public officer. In this respect, the Kansas Supreme Court in 1987 said:
>
> 'The grounds stated in a recall petition must be specific enough to allow the official an opportunity to prepare a statement in justification of his or her conduct in office.

> Here, the charge is merely a general allegation that Unger and Temple violated the Open Meetings Act... The petitions for recall of Unger and Temple do not contain a clear Statement of the alleged act or acts constituting the grounds for recall.'"

Yet, a Kansas court in 1995 indicated it agreed with the prior statement of the Kansas Court of Appeals that the truth or falsity of recall grounds is up to the voters to decide.

Such views are similar to the opinion of the Louisiana Superior Court in 1981, as described in *The Recall* (at page 36):

> "The Louisiana Superior Court in 1981 opined that the power of voters to recall public officers does not have to be based on malfeasance because the voters have the absolute right to recall a public officer for any reason or no reason because the state constitution stipulates that "the sole issue at a recall election shall be whether the official shall be recalled."

Zimmerman, in *The Recall* makes the distinction between those jurisdictions which view recall as a political process and those which believe it is a legal issue. California is clearly in the former category with its Constitutional statement that the grounds listed in a recall petition are NOT reviewable by the courts.

Following is a listing giving the grounds for recall in each of the eighteen states which permit the recall of State officials:

Alaska

"The grounds for recall are (1) lack of fitness, (2) incompetence, (3) neglect of duties, or (4) corruption." (Alaska Statutes 15.45.510)

Arizona

"Every recall petition must contain a general statement, in not more than 200 words, of the grounds of such demand…" (Arizona Constitution, Article VIII, Section 2)

In 1925, the Arizona Supreme Court in Abbey v. Green, 28 Ariz. 53 ruled that any ground was sufficient for a recall.

California

"Recall of a state officer is initiated by delivering to the Secretary of State a petition alleging reason for recall. Sufficiency of reason is not reviewable". (California Constitution, Article 2, Section 14(a))

Colorado

"…such petition shall contain a general statement, in not more than two hundred words, of the ground or grounds on which such recall is sought, which statement is intended for the information of the registered electors, and the registered electors shall be the sole and exclusive judges of the legality, reasonableness and sufficiency of such ground or grounds assigned for such recall, and said ground or grounds shall not be open to review." (Colorado Constitution, Article XXI, Section 1)

Georgia

"…(7) 'Grounds for recall' means:

(A) That the official has, while holding public office, conducted himself or herself in a manner which relates to and adversely affects the administration of his or her office and adversely affects the rights and interests of the public; and

(B) That the official:

(i) Has committed an act or acts of malfeasance while in office;

(ii) Has violated his or her oath of office;

(iii) Has committed an act of misconduct in office;

(iv) Is guilty of a failure to perform duties prescribed by law; or

(v) Has willfully misused, converted, or misappropriated, without authority, public property or public funds entrusted to or associated with the elective office to which the official has been elected or appointed.

Discretionary performance of a lawful act or a prescribed duty shall not constitute a ground for recall of an elected public official..." (Georgia Code, Section 21-4-7)

Idaho

"...(the recall petition shall be in substantially the following form: ...We...respectfully demand that ....., holding the office of ...., be recalled by the registered electors of this state for the following reasons, to-wit: (setting out the reasons for recall in not more than 200 words)..." (Idaho Statutes 34-1703)

Kansas

"Grounds for recall are conviction of a felony, misconduct in office, incompetence or failure to perform duties prescribed by law. No recall submitted to the voters shall be held void because of the insufficiency of the grounds..." (Kansas Statutes 25-4302)

Louisiana

"...Section 26. The legislature shall provide by general law for the recall by election of any state, district, parochial, ward, or municipal official except judges of the courts of record. The sole issue at a recall election shall be whether the official shall be recalled." (Louisiana Constitution, Article X, Section 26)

Michigan

"State clearly each reason for the recall. Each reason for the recall shall be based upon the officer's conduct during his or her current term of office..." (Michigan Election Law 168.952)

"The sufficiency of any statement of reasons (for recall) or grounds procedurally required shall be a political rather than a judicial question. (Michigan Constitution Article II, Section 8)

Minnesota

"...The grounds for recall of an officer other than a judge are serious malfeasance or nonfeasance during the term of office in the performance of the duties of the office or conviction during the term of office of a serious crime. A petition for recall must set forth the specific conduct that may warrant recall. A petition may not be issued until the supreme court has determined that the facts alleged in the petition are true and are sufficient grounds for issuing a recall petition..." (Minnesota Constitution, Article VIII, Section 6)

Montana

"...(3) Physical or mental lack of fitness, incompetence, violation of his oath of office, official misconduct, or conviction of a felony offense enumerated in Title 45 is the only basis for recall.." (Montana Code Annotated, 2-16-603)

Zimmerman, in The Recall, points out that "In 1982, the Montana Supreme Court also emphasized the legal aspects of the recall by describing it as "special, extraordinary, and unusual" and a process that involves the "harsh" remedy of removing an officer prior to the expiration of a fixed term...the court interprets statutory removal grounds narrowly in favor of the targeted officer, and any errors in recall procedures invalidate the recall effort." (at page 38)

Nevada

"...shall file their petition (for recall), in the manner herein provided, demanding his recall by the people. They shall set forth in said petition, in not exceeding two hundred (200) words, the reasons why said recall is demanded..." (Nevada Constitution, Article 2, Section 9)

In Batchelor v. District Court, 81 Nev. 629 (1965) the Nevada Supreme Court indicated that the a reason for the recall must be stated, but it would make no difference whether it is a good or bad reason.

New Jersey

"...No statement of reasons or grounds for the holding of a recall election or for the recall at such an election of an elected official shall be required in connection with the preparation or circulation of a recall petition...and to the extent that any such statement of reasons or grounds is offered by the sponsors of a recall petition or by any other person, the sufficiency of that statement shall be a political rather than a judicial question..." (New Jersey Permanent Statutes, 19:27A-4)

North Dakota

The Constitution authorizes recall. The North Dakota Century Code provides for petitions to be submitted but the only mention of grounds for a recall petition is the following in the form provided for a recall: "We, the undersigned, being qualified electors request that ____(name of the person being recalled) the _____(office of person being recalled) be recalled for the following reasons..." (North Dakota Century Code 16.1-01-09.1)

Oregon

"...(1) Every public officer in Oregon is subject, as herein provided, to recall by the electors...(3) They shall set forth in the petition the reasons for the demand (for recall)" (Oregon Constitution, Article II, Section 18)

Rhode Island

"Recall is authorized in the case of a general officer who has been indicted or informed against for a felony, convicted of a misdemeanor, or against whom a finding of probable cause of violation of the code of ethics has been made by the ethics commission..." (Rhode Island Constitution, Article IV, Section 1)

Washington

"...Every elective public officer of the state of Washington except judges of courts of record is subject to recall...whenever a petition demanding his recall, reciting that such officer has committed some act or acts of malfeasance or misfeasance while in office, or who has violated his oath of office, stating the matters complained of..." (Washington Constitution, Article I, Section 33)

"...he or they shall prepare a typewritten charge, reciting that such officer, naming him or her and giving the title of his office, has committed an actd or acts of malfeasance, or an act or acts of misfeasance while in office, or has violated his oath of office, or has been guilty of any two or more acts specified in the Constitution as grounds for recall..." (Revised Code of Washington, 29:82.010)

It appears the Washington courts will be careful in examining the grounds being provided for a recall petition based on a 1984 Supreme Court decision in that State which invalidated a recall petition because one of the charges was deemed insufficient.

Wisconsin

The Constitution (Article XIII, Section 12) authorizes the filing of a petition "demanding the recall of the incumbent..." This is repeated in the Wisconsin Statutes Annotated (9.10(1)(a) but there is no indication a reason must be given when seeking the replacement of the Governor.

Signatures

Signatures from a given number of registered voters are required at two stages in the recall process. Firstly, constitutions and statutes require a certain number of signatures on the petition for recall before an election will be held. In California that threshold is met by acquiring the signatures equivalent to 12% of the vote in the prior election for the office being contested. The second signature requirement is imposed on the candidates who wish to challenge to replace the recalled officer; in California this step also requires a cash deposit of $3500 and 65 signatures or 10,000 signatures with no cash deposit. It was the latter requirement which opened the door to a proliferation of candidates in the California recall election, and which has prompted cries for further modification of the recall procedure in that State. Apart from the candidacy of three or four well known figures, the ultimate ballot included individuals who had either no credible program to offer or who were touting views held by insignificant fringe elements in that State. The result was a ballot which described a profusion of candidates, holding an even wider spectrum of opinion, offering the voters and the general public what amounted to a side show involving serious political activities. *(See Appendix H for Samples of Candidate pamphlets).*

Basic signature requirements in other jurisdictions for a recall of statewide offices are:

Alaska: Must file signatures of qualified voters equal to 25% of those who voted in the preceding election for this office.
Arizona: 25% of qualified votes cast in preceding election for the office.
Colorado: 25% of qualified votes cast in preceding election for the office.
Georgia: 15% of the number of individuals who were registered and qualified to vote at the last preceding election.
Idaho: 20% of the number of individuals who were registered and qualified to vote at the last preceding election.
Kansas: 40% of the votes cast for the officer sought to be recalled in the last general election at which he or she was elected.
Louisiana: If over 1,000 eligible voters, then 33.3% of the votes cast in the last preceding election for the office.
Michigan: 25% of the number of persons voting in the preceding election.
Minnesota: 25% of the number of votes cast for the office at the last preceding election.
Montana: 10% of the number of persons registered to vote at the last election.
New Jersey: 25% of the registered voters in the last preceding election for the officer subject to the recall.

Nevada: 25% of the number who actually voted in the preceding election for this office.
North Dakota: 25% of the total votes cast in the last election for this office.
Oregon: 15% of the total votes cast in the last election for this office.
Rhode Island: 15% of the total number of votes cast in the last preceding general election for the office.
Washington: 25% of the total number of votes cast in the last preceding election for this office.
Wisconsin: 25% of the vote cast for the office at the last preceding election.

As is readily apparent, garnering the requisite number of signatures in Georgia or Idaho would be a far more difficult task than in Oregon or Rhode Island. With prior electoral experience showing that normally only about 30-35% of registered voters vote in a State election, one could anticipate it is relatively easier to collect a percentage of those voting than an equal or smaller percentage of all those who were registered and qualified to vote.

Time Frames – For Signatures and to Invoke Recall

In addition to requiring a set number of signatures to trigger a petition for recall, Constitutions and Statutes set a time limit for acquiring those signatures. Clearly, this "filter" varies with the number of days permitted to garner signatures. None of the eighteen States authorizing recall of state officials gives less than 60 days as called for in the Colorado Statutes:

> "(1) The petition shall be prepared and circulated pursuant to this Part 1. No signature shall be counted that was placed on a petition prior to approval of the petition by the designated election official or more than sixty days after the designated election official's approval of the petition..." (1-12-108)

Idaho, Nevada, and Wisconsin have this same requirement. From this minimum, other jurisdictions require 90 (Georgia, Kansas, Minnesota, Montana, Oregon, Rhode Island), 120 (Arizona), 160 (California), 180 (Louisiana) and from there one reaches New Jersey where the Governor can be recalled by petition with the requisite signatures obtained within 320 days.

The second area where time is an important factor for a recall petition rests in those provisions which prohibit a petition unless a certain time period has elapsed since the official was elected, or which prohibit a petition within a set period prior to the end of the official's end of term. Both limitations are seen in the Georgia Code provisions which state:

> "21-4-5. (a) No application for a recall petition may be filed during the first 180 days or during the last 180 days of the term of office of any public official subject to recall..."

Another example of these limitations is contained in the Kansas Statutes which states: "No application for the recall of a state officer may be filed during the first 120 days or the last 200 days of the term of office of such officer." (25-4305)

Both limitations compress the time within which the elected official is subject to recall. Other than in Georgia and Oregon other jurisdictions which permit the recall of state wide officers have the following requirement:

Alaska: The application to file a petition may not be filed during the first 120 days of the term of office.
Arizona: No recall petition can be circulated until the officer has held his office for six months.
Idaho: No petition can be circulated against any officer until he has actually held his office for ninety days.
Michigan: No petition can be filed until the officer has completed six months in office, and none can be

filed during the last six months in office.
Montana: No recall petition may be approved for circulation until the officer has held office for two months.
Nevada: No petition shall be circulated or filed against any officer until he has actually held his office six months.
Oregon: No petition shall be circulated against any officer until he has held the office six months.
Rhode Island: Recall shall not be instituted during the first six months or the last year in office.
Washington: No recall petition can be circulated or filed when the official has less than six months to serve in his term.
Wisconsin: The petition for recall can be filed after the official has completed one year of the term.

Choosing the Successor

There has been a great deal of debate over the manner in which the successor to an official who has been recalled should be chosen. In California, the procedure involves only one step and there are limitations on who can be placed on the ballot:

a. Candidates to succeed the recalled official are listed on the same ballot which asks whether a recall should be made. This meant that voters were given the opportunity to cast their ballot for replacing Gray Davis and to vote for the person they wished to see in office as a second element. As pointed out elsewhere, this presented voters with a complex ballot, lumping the initial critical decision on recalling Davis with the equally important decision on who should succeed him. Other jurisdiction split the decision making process by circulating a ballot on recall and then scheduling a subsequent vote for a successor in a separate election. For example, in Alaska the statutory provisions call for a "yes" or "no" vote on recall and "If a majority of the votes cast on the question of recall favor the removal of the official, the director shall so certify and the office is vacant on the day after the date of certification." (AS 15.45.690)

b. California also had a requirement (In the California Election Code Section 11382) which required a voter to cast a vote for recall and a vote for a successor or that vote would be declared invalid. The Federal Court, on July 29, 2003 ruled that provision unconstitutional thereby permitting a voter to ignore the recall and vote for a successor. Colorado also has the original California requirement in their Constitution which states:

> "On such ballots (for recall), there shall also be printed the names of those persons who have been nominated as candidates to succeed the person sought to be recalled; but no vote cast shall be counted for any candidate for such office, unless the voter also voted for or against the recall of such person sought to be recalled from said office."
> (Colorado Constitution, Article XXI, Section 3)

Nevada has a variation of this procedure. In its Statutory provisions, Nevada provides that a special election for recall must name the office holder, and the words "For Recall" and "Against Recall" if there are no other nominees to replace that person. If there are other nominees, the officeholder and those nominees are placed on the special election ballot and the words "For recall" and "Against Recall" are omitted. (Nevada Revised Statutes 306.070)

c. The procedure in California also prohibits the person being recalled from standing for election, essentially permitting the electorate to express their opinion that he or she should be recalled, and then inviting them to vote for him or her when evaluated against the other candidates standing to succeed. Given the final slate of candidates in California there are many who argue that voters would have voted for

Gray Davis had his name been on the ballot. For comparison, in Arizona the person recalled is automatically placed on the special election ballot to choose a successor without nomination (Arizona Constitution, Article 8, Part 1, Section 4.)

CHAPTER SIX

Recall Elections – Possible Improvements

Numerous changes have been proposed to amend the substance and procedures surrounding recall elections in various jurisdictions. The following suggestions are particularly well suited for state wide recall elections. Adopting some, or all of them would make such elections more efficient, less controversial, while still preserving the democratic system as we wish it to operate.

Signature and the Cash Deposit Requirements.

To participate in a recall election one is usually required to produce a given number of signatures and to submit a specific cash deposit (one or both, depending on the circumstances). In California the cash required appears to be unreasonably low, presenting the electorate (at least in the Davis recall election) with a proliferation of candidates, many of whom could never expect to garner votes, with most offering up their name in order to achieve some additional publicity, or to push some specific point of view. The amount required is $3,500, plus 65 signatures or no cash deposit if one presents 10,000 signatures.

The flood of candidates in California included, predictably, a large number of totally unqualified candidates for the post of Governor for the largest State in the Union. For example, included in the list of candidates were actors, comedians, an adult film actress (who came in tenth in the election), a sumo wrestler, a sex magazine publisher and a billboard celebrity. To the surprise of few, one of the actors actually won the election! Campaign materials distributed by a few of these candidates are included in Appendix H to illustrate the diversity of views and personalities. Having to cope with 135 candidates in a State wide election increased the complexity of the process, escalated the costs associated with the vote, and diminished the credibility of the democratic process aimed at selecting a new chief executive for California.

Though one could argue that it is contrary to our political practice to place restrictions on who can run in such elections, the results in California clearly illustrate that the negative features associated with permitting so many candidates to run outweigh the potential benefit associated with giving the maximum number of people the opportunity to run. The number of votes acquired by candidates offers one way to examine the efficacy of the current procedure. In fact, one finds that the 10th place candidate (Mary Cook, the adult film actress) garnered 10,929 votes, with the remaining candidates obtaining a far fewer with the individual in last place obtaining only 189 votes. Put another way, 85 of the candidates received less than 2000 each in votes. Compare this to the fact that Arianna Huffington, who had withdrawn from the race, came in fifth with 46,709 votes. Though Schwarzenegger received a significant number of votes, it is possible under the California system for a candidate to win the race for Governor with a relatively small plurality.

Presenting the electorate with such a slate encourages legal challenges to the system in addition to the increased the costs for managing the election. Questions such as the type of ballot, the description of the candidates, and other procedural factors become unduly complicated thereby endangering the process and the final results. And it can not be overemphasized that producing such a diverse set of candidates offered the press ample opportunity to publicize what many in the world felt was a comedy, rather than a serious and far reaching political contest.

The second "signature" requirement attaches specifically to the number required to effect a recall election – in the case of California this is only 12% of the voters in the last gubernatorial election. As pointed out earlier in this work, the percentages generally are substantially higher in those jurisdictions which permit the recall of state wide officials, but in California and one or two other jurisdictions, it is entirely too easy to meet the signature requirement. This is particularly true for those jurisdictions where elections tend to draw extremely small percentages of eligible voters – sometimes as few as 30% - meaning that a recall can be triggered with only 12% of the 30% of eligible voters in a state such as California! Making a change to the percentage in California would require an amendment to their constitution.

In setting the cash amount and signature requirements legislators should, where possible, carefully construct a system which balances ensuring access to the political process with the need to provide an election where the electorate is offered a clear and unambiguous opportunity to vote for a candidate who has some chance of getting elected.

Recommendation:

Set the cash requirement at $50,000 along with a second requirement that the nominee must present no less than 10,000 signatures to qualify for the ballot.

Amending the Grounds for Recall.

The Constitutions and Statutes covering recalls should present those managing the process and those utilizing this vehicle with a clear description of what constitutes the proper grounds for recalling a public official. Of course, such guidance would also be particularly helpful to the person actually subject to the recall! Much has been written concerning the distinction between those jurisdictions which treat recall as a political decision (justifying vague guidance on what constitutes proper grounds) and those which address the question as a legal matter.

Minnesota's recall procedure is a prime example of a jurisdiction taking the "legal" approach. The constitutional provision states:

> "...A petition for recall must set forth the specific conduct that may warrant recall. A petition may not be issued until the supreme court has determined that the facts alleged in the petition are true and are sufficient grounds for issuing a recall petition..."(Article VIII, Section 6) And that provision describes "serious malfeasance or nonfeasance...or conviction..." as the only grounds for recall. The Minnesota Statutes then define "malfeasance" and "nonfeasance" as follows:
>
> "Malfeasance" means the intentional commission of an unlawful or wrongful act by a state officer...in the performance of the officer's duties that is substantially outside the scope of the authority of the officer and that substantially infringes on the rights of any person or entity."
>
> "Nonfeasance means the intentional, repeated failure of a state officer... to perform specific acts that are required duties of the officer."

Not only must the Chief Justice of the Minnesota Supreme Court decide the petition for recall is based on acceptable grounds, his decision in that regard merely triggers a public hearing, chaired by an active or retired judge, sitting as a "Master" and this person must report within seven days after the hearing whether proponents of the recall have, among other things:

> "...shown that the facts found to be true are sufficient grounds for issuing a recall petition..."

That report goes back to the Supreme Court which must decide whether the standards have been met and, if in the affirmative, the court decides what words shall be placed on the petition for recall.

At the other end of the spectrum are provisions in the Alaska Statutes which state:

> "The grounds for recall are (1) lack of fitness, (2) incompetence, (3) neglect of duties, or (4) corruption." (AS 15.45.510)

In a subsequent provision, the Statutes list reasons by the application for a petition can be denied stating only:

> "(1) the application is not substantially in the required form..." (AS 15.45.550)

Colorado has provisions which are similarly broad with its Constitution providing that:

> "...such petition shall contain a general statement...of the ground or grounds on which such recall is sought, which statement is intended for the information of the registered electors, and the registered electors shall be the sole and exclusive judges of the legality, reasonableness and sufficiency of such ground or grounds assigned for such recall, and said ground or grounds shall not be open to review." (Article XXI, Section 1)

Such broad provisions open the door for recalls based on the flimsiest reasons as can be seen in Arizona where an individual claiming to be a citizen of the Confederate States of America is gathering signatures to recall the Governor, claiming the Governor is violating the Arizona constitution and has failed to act responsibly on several other subject. Another example of such frivolities is the recall petition against Governor Kenny Guinn of Nevada, listing as grounds that citizens have lost faith in the Governor because, among other things, he:

> "...increased the state's budget by over one billion dollars...blantantly pandering to certain special interests, and;
>
> "...sued the Legislature in the Nevada Supreme Court, which resulted in nullifying the will of the people as expressed in their amendment to the Nevada Constitution, requiring a super-majority vote of the legislature to raise taxes or impose new taxes..."

The petition goes on to claim "All of which was done by him on behalf of special interests; leaving the People of the State of Nevada no choice but to recall him from office." Petitioners filed their notice on August 27, 2003 and were required to get 128,109 signatures within 90 days. Press reports dated November 24, 2003 reported only 51,000 signatures were obtained by the deadline. The Chairman of the recall committee reportedly stated: "The recent recall of former Gov. Gray Davis 'really crucified us...That was such a circus, such a show, with a stripper, a porn star, Gary Coleman as candidates.'"

Clarify Method for Choosing Replacements

The California procedure of utilizing one ballot for both the recall question and the selection of a successor has come under some criticism. One justification for this system is cost, with advocates pointing out that by utilizing one document it is possible to, in a sense, "kill two birds with one stone". In addition, carrying out both actions with one ballot significantly shortens the time needed to make a decision and, if needed, name a replacement. In other jurisdictions, the prospect of having a virtually limitless process to find a successor does exist, most particularly in those jurisdictions which utilize a legal process for the procedure.

Where constitutions or statutes utilize the two step process it is easy for them to include a provision which permits the incumbent to run again for election. Obviously, this offers that individual (and his supporters) ample opportunity to clarify their positions, to take the initiative against the other candidates who are standing for the positions, and presents the voters with the possibility of having authorized a recall, only to elect the individual back into office. As has been pointed out elsewhere, California does NOT permit the incumbent to be carried as a candidate for the position if the recall is successful but other jurisdictions do permit this action.

Recommendation:

Retain the one step process for recall/selection utilized by California and eliminate provisions which permit the incumbent to stand for election should a recall be successful.

Voter Education

Voters should be given ample opportunity to understand the recall process and to make their decision with a firm foundation of accurate, precise, information. Some statutes require the preparation of voter information on recall and other electoral procedures (See Appendix I for a sample of the Alaska handbook). Though such materials as carried in the Appendix are useful, the procedures for recall are so complex in some jurisdictions that it is virtually impossible to expect voters to understand exactly what they are accomplishing with a recall.

Recommendation:

Provide voters with current information on recalls, utilizing both electronic information sources and printed material which can be circulated to voters before recalls are initiated.

APPENDIX A

Biographical Information on Governor Hiram Johnson

Hiram Johnson
23rd Governor, Republican
(1911-1917)

Hiram Johnson was born and raised in Sacramento, and it was there that he was indoctrinated into politics. As a young man, he accompanied his father, armed with pistols, into a "den" of dishonest politicians and watched as he fearlessly denounced them for their corruption. Although the political poles of father and son were to differ in later years, the younger Johnson was never to waiver in his campaign against corruption. Johnson initially worked in law offices as a stenographer and shorthand reporter, but eventually became a lawyer himself. He attracted the attention of politicians statewide when he successfully took over as special prosecutor in a notorious graft trial when the chief prosecutor was gunned down in the courtroom. Two years later, Johnson, politically a Progressive, was elected Governor. He had never held public office before.

Administration under Governor Hiram Johnson

- Inaugural Address - January 3, 1911
- Inaugural Address - January 5, 1915

The Life of Governor Hiram Johnson

Born: September 2, 1866, Sacramento, California
Died: August 6, 1945, Bethesda Naval Hospital, Maryland

Family

First Lady: Minnie L. McNeal
Children: 2 sons

** All Biographies excerpted from The Governors of California and their Portraits (see credits) Governors of California is a service from the California State Library to the People of California*

APPENDIX B

Inaugural Speech of Hiram Johnson on January 3, 1911

To the Senate and Assembly of the State of California:

In the political struggle from which we have just emerged the issue was so sharply defined and so thoroughly understood that it may be superfluous for me to indicate the policy which in the ensuing four years will control the executive department of the State of California. The electorate has rendered its decision, a decision conclusive upon all its representatives; but while we know the sort of government demanded and decreed by the people, it may not be amiss to suggest the means by which that kind of administration may be attained and continued. "Successful and permanent government must rest primarily on recognition of the rights of men and the absolute sovereignty of the people. Upon these principles is based the superstructure of our republic. Their maintenance and perpetuation measure the life of the republic." It was upon this theory that we undertook originally to go to the people; it was this theory that was adopted by the people; it is upon this theory, so far as your Executive is concerned, that this government shall be henceforth conducted. The problem first presented to us, therefore, is how best can the government be made responsive to the people alone? Matters of material prosperity and advancement, conservation of resources, development of that which lies within our borders, are easy of solution when once the primal question of the people's rule shall have been determined. In some form or other nearly every governmental problem that involves the health, the happiness, or the prosperity of the State has arisen, because some private interest has intervened or has sought for its own gain to exploit either the resources or the politics of the State. I take it, therefore, that the first duty that is mine to perform is to eliminate every private interest from the government, and to make the public service of the State responsive solely to the people. The State is entitled to the highest efficiency in our public service, and that efficiency I shall endeavor at all times to give. It is obvious that the requisite degree of efficiency can not be attained where any public servant divides his allegiance between the public service and a private interest. Where under our political system, therefore, there exists any appointee of the Governor who is representing a political machine or a corporation that has been devoting itself in part to our politics, that appointee will be replaced by an official who will devote himself exclusively and solely to the service of the State. In this fashion, so far as it can be accomplished by the Executive, the government of California shall be made a government for the people. If there are in existence now any appointees who represent the system of politics which has been in vogue in this State for many years and who have divided their allegiance between the State and a private interest of any sort, or if there be in existence any Commission of like character, and I can not alone deal with either, then I shall look to the Legislature to aid me in my design to eliminate special interests from the government and to require from our officials the highest efficiency and an undivided allegiance; and I shall expect such legislative action to be taken as may be necessary to accomplish the desired result.

In pursuing this policy, so long as we deal only with the ward-heeler who holds a petty official position as a reward for political service, or with the weak and vacillating small politician, we will have the support and indeed the commendation of all the people and all the press; but as we go a little higher, with firm resolve and absolute determination, we will begin to meet with opposition here and there to our plan, and various arguments, apparently put forth in good faith for the retention of this official or that, will make their appearance; and finally when we reach, if we do, some representative, not only of the former political master of this State, the Southern Pacific Company, but an apostle of "big business" as well (that business that believes all government is a mere thing for exploitation and private gain), a storm of indignation will meet us from all of those who have been parties to or partisans of the political system that has obtained in the past; and particularly that portion of the public press which is responsive to private interest and believes that private interest should control our government, will, in mock indignation and pretended horror, cry out against the desecration of the public service and the awful politics which would permit the people to rule. Much, doubtless, will be said of destructiveness, of abuse of power, of anarchistic tendencies and the like, and of the astounding and incomparable fitness of him who represents "big business" to represent us all. And in the end it may be that the very plan, simple, and direct, to which we have set ourselves in this administration will be wholly distorted and will be understood only by those who, with singleness of purpose, are working for a return of popular government in California.

It matters not how powerful the individual may be who is in the service of the State, nor how much wealth and influence there may be behind him, nor how strenuously he may be supported by "big business" and by all that has been heretofore powerful and omnipotent in our political life, if he be the representative of Southern Pacific politics, or if he be one of that class who divides his allegiance to the State with a private interest and thus impairs his efficiency, I shall attack him the more readily because of his power and his influence and the wealth behind him, and I shall strive in respect to such a one in exactly the same way as with his weaker and less powerful accomplices. I prefer, as less dangerous to society, the political thug of the water front to the smugly respectable individual in broadcloth of pretended respectability who from ambush employs and uses that thug for his selfish political gain.

In the consummation of our design at last to have the people rule, we shall go forward, without malice or hatred, not in animosity or personal hostility, but calmly, coolly, pertinaciously, unswervingly and with absolute determination, until the public service reflects only the public good and represents alone the people.

The Initiative, Referendum and Recall

When, with your assistance, California's government shall be composed only of those who recognize one sovereign and master, the people, then is presented to us the question of, How best can we arm the people to protect themselves hereafter? If we can give to the people the means by which they may accomplish such other reforms as they desire, the means as well by which they may prevent the misuse of the power temporarily centralized in the Legislature, and an admonitory and precautionary measure which will ever be present before weak officials, and the existence of which will prevent the necessity for its use, then all that lies in our power will have been done in the direction of safeguarding the future and for the perpetuation of the theory upon which we ourselves shall conduct this government. This means for accomplishing other reforms has been designated the "Initiative and the referendum," and the precautionary measure by which a recalcitrant official can be removed is designated the "Recall." And while I do not by any means believe the initiative, the referendum, and the recall are the panacea for all our political ills, yet they do give to the electorate the power of action when desired, and they do place in the hands of the people the means by which they may protect themselves. I recommend to you, therefore, and I most strongly urge, that the first step in our design to preserve and perpetuate popular government shall be the adoption of the initiative, the referendum, and the recall. I recognize that this must be accomplished, so far as the State is concerned, by constitutional amendment. But I hope that at the earliest possible date the amendments may be submitted to the people, and that you take the steps necessary for that purpose. I will not here go into detail as to the proposed measures. I have collected what I know many of your members have—the various constitutional amendments now in force in different states—and at a future time, if desired, the detail to be applied in this State may be taken up. Suffice it to say, so far as the recall is concerned, did the solution of the matter rest with me, I would apply it to every official. I commend to you the proposition that, after all, the initiative and the referendum depend on our confidence in the people and in their ability to govern. The opponents of direct legislation and the recall, however they may phrase their opposition, in reality believe the people can not be trusted. On the other hand, those of us who espouse these measures do so because of our deep-rooted belief in popular government, and not only in the right of the people to govern, but in their ability to govern; and this leads us logically to the belief that if the people have the right, the ability, and the intelligence to elect, they have as well the right, ability, and intelligence to reject or to recall; and this applies with equal force to an administrative or a judicial officer. I suggest, therefore, that if you believe in the recall, and if in your wisdom you desire its adoption by the people, you make no exception in its application. It has been suggested that by immediate legislation you can make the recall applicable to counties without the necessity of constitutional amendment. If this be so, and if you believe in the adoption of this particular measure, there is no reason why the Legislature should not at once give to the counties of the State the right which we expect to accord to the whole State by virtue of constitutional amendment.

Were we to do nothing else during our terms of office than to require and compel an undivided allegiance to the State from all its servants, and then to place in the hands of the people the means by which they could continue that allegiance, with the power to legislate for themselves when they desired, we would have thus accomplished perhaps the greatest service that could be rendered our State. With public servants whose sole thought is the good of the State the prosperity of the State is assured, exaction and extortion from the people will be at an end, in every material aspect advancement will be ours, development and progress will follow as a matter of course, and popular government will be perpetuated.

The Railroad Question

For many years in the past, shippers, and those generally dealing with the Southern Pacific Company, have been demanding protection against the rates fixed by that corporation. The demand has been answered by the corporation by the simple expedient of taking over the government of the State; and instead of regulation of the railroads, as the framers of the new Constitution fondly hoped, the railroad has regulated the State.

To Californians it is quite unnecessary to recall the motives that actuated the framers of the new Constitution when Article XII was adopted. It was thought that the Railroad Commission thereby created would be the bulwark between the people and the exactions and extortions and discriminations of the transportation companies. That the scheme then adopted has not proved effective has become only too plain. That this arose because of the individuals constituting the Railroad Commission is in the main true, but it is also apparent there has been a settled purpose on the part of the Southern Pacific Company not only to elect its own Railroad Commission, but also wherever those Commissioners made any attempt, however feeble, to act, to arrest the powers of the Commission, and to have those powers circumscribed within the narrowest limits. All of us who recall the adoption of the new Constitution will remember that we then supposed the most plenary powers were conferred upon the Commission. It has been gravely asserted of late, however, by those representing the Railroad Company, and they insist that in the decisions of our courts there is foundation for the assertion, that the Constitution does not give the Commission power to fix absolute rates. In my opinion this power is conferred upon the Commission, and in this I am upheld by the Attorney General of the State, and by the very able and eminent attorneys who represent the various traffic associations.

The people are indeed fortunate now in having a Railroad Commission of ability, integrity, energy, and courage. I suggest to you, and I recommend, that you give to the Commission the amplest power that can be conferred upon it. The president of the Railroad Commission, Mr. John M. Eshleman, in conjunction with Attorney General Webb, Senator Stetson, and others, in all of whom we have the highest confidence, has been at work preparing a bill which shall meet the requirements of the case, and I commend to your particular attention this instrument.

I would suggest that an appropriation of at least $75,000 be made for the use of the Commission that it may, by careful hearing and the taking of evidence, determine the physical value of the transportation companies in the State of California, and that the Commission may have the power and the means to determine this physical value justly and fairly, and thereafter ascertain the value of improvements, betterments and the like, and upon the values thus determined may fix the railroad rates within the State of California.

It is asserted that some ambiguity exists in that portion of the language of Section 22 of Article XII of the Constitution, which fixes the penalty when any railroad company shall fail or refuse to conform to rates established by the Commission or shall charge rates in excess thereof, and it is claimed that the use of the last phrase "or shall charge rates in excess thereof" excludes the power to punish discrimination by the railroad companies. The rational construction of the language used can lead to no such conclusion; but if you believe there is any ambiguity in the constitutional provision as it now exists, or any doubt of the power conferred by it upon the Railroad Commission, I would suggest that this matter be remedied by a constitutional amendment. In no event, however, should action in reference to needed legislation and that herein suggested be deferred. It is not unlikely that the ingenuity of those who represent the railroad companies will pretend, and find some advocates in this, that all legislative action should await the amendment of the Constitution. I trust that you will not permit this specious plea to prevail, but that you will at once accord the power to the Commission that is designed by the bill referred to.

I beg of you not to permit the bogie man of the railroad companies, "Unconstitutionality," to deter you from enacting the legislation suggested, if you believe that legislation to be necessary; and I trust that none of us will be terrified by the threat of resort to the courts that follows the instant a railroad extortion is resented or attempted to be remedied. Let us do our full duty, now that at last we have a Railroad Commission that will do its full duty, and let us give this Commission all the power and aid and resources it requires; and if thereafter legitimate work done within the law and the Constitution shall be nullified, let the consequences rest with the nullifying power.

Amendment of Direct Primary Law

California took a long step toward popular government when the direct primary law was enacted. The first experiment under the direct primary law has been made, and despite the predictions of the cynical and the critical, the law has been a success and has come to stay. It may, however, be improved in many respects, and so recent has been the discussion of the minor imperfections of the act that they are familiar to us all; and I think the desire is general to remedy those defects. When the law shall have been amended and its imperfections corrected, and when it shall have been made less difficult for one to become a candidate for public office (and this should be one of the designs of amendment, I think), the important question of dealing with the candidacy for United States Senator remains. Of course, the Constitution of the United States requires that United States Senators shall be elected by state legislatures. Notwithstanding the popular demand expressed now for a quarter of a century that United States Senators should be elected by direct vote of the people, we have been unable to amend the Federal Constitution; but the people in more than half the states are striving to effect the same result by indirection. The result is that our people, in common with those of most of the states, are seeking to have the people themselves elect United States Senators. I do not think it is extravagant to say that nine electors out of ten in California desire the electorate directly to choose United States Senators, and if they possessed the power they would remove the selection wholly from the Legislature. The present primary law in its partisan features does not attain the desired result. And the present law, in its provision relating to United States Senators, is at variance with the wishes of an overwhelming majority of our people. Some of those who desire direct election may wish a selection made by parties, while others would eliminate all partisan features in such an election; yet all wish a selection by the whole State by plurality; and the present provisions of the primary law meet with the approval of none who really wish the election of United States Senator by direct vote. I suggest to you, therefore, that the present law be amended so that there be a state-wide advisory vote upon United States Senator; and the logical result of a desire to elect United States Senators by direct vote of the people is that that election shall be of any person who may be a candidate, no matter what party he may be affiliated with. For that reason I favor the Oregon plan, as it is termed, whereby the candidate for this office as for any other office may be voted for, and by which the candidate receiving the highest number of votes may be ultimately selected. If in your wisdom you believe we should not go to the full extent expressed in my views, then, in any event, the primary law should make the vote for the United States Senator state-wide so that the vote of the whole State, irrespective of districts, shall control.

Short Ballot

The most advanced thought in our nation has reached the conclusion that we can best avoid blind voting and best obtain the discrimination of the electorate by a short ballot. A very well known editor in our State, during a recent lecture at Stanford University, challenged the faculty of that great institution to produce a single man who had cast an intelligent vote for the office of State Treasurer, and none was produced. Fortunately our State Treasurer is the highest type of citizen and official. The reason the challenge could not be met was that, in the hurry of our existence and in the engrossing importance of the contests for one or two offices, we can not or do not inform ourselves sufficiently regarding the candidates for minor offices. Again, we elect some officials whose duties are merely clerical or ministerial and whose qualifications naturally can not be well understood. Of course it is undesirable, and indeed detrimental, that we should elect officials of whom we know nothing and concerning whom the electorate can not learn and can not discriminate. It is equally undesirable that those occupying merely clerical positions should be voted for by the entire electorate of the State. The result of a long ballot is that often candidates for minor offices are elected who are unfit or unsatisfactory. This conclusion, I think, has been reached by students and the farseeing in every state in the Union. If we can remedy this condition it is our duty to do so, and it is plain that the remedy is by limiting the elective list of offices to those that are naturally conspicuous. One familiar with the subject recently said: "The little offices must either go off the ballot and be appointed, no matter how awkwardly, or they must be increased in real public importance by added powers until they rise into such eminence as to be visible to all the people. * * *

That candidates should be conspicuous is vital. The people must be able to see what they are doing; they must know the candidates, otherwise they are not in control of the situation but are only going through the motions of controlling."

The Supreme Court of the State has asked that the Clerk of the Supreme Court, now elective, shall be made appointive. It is eminently just that this should be so. It is quite absurd that the people of an entire state should be called upon to vote for a clerk of the Supreme Court. The office of State Printer is merely administrative. Presumably an expert printer is selected to fill this position, and in the selection of an expert no reason at all exists for the entire electorate selecting that particular expert. The Surveyor General likewise performs merely ministerial duties, presumably is only an expert, and his selection should be by appointment rather than election. The Superintendent of Public Instruction, an expert educator, is in the same category. The government of the United States is conducted with all of its departments with only two elective officers, the President and Vice-President. The President has surrounding him a Cabinet, the members of which perform all of the duties that are ministerial in character. The Treasurer of the State of California performs duties akin to those of the Secretary of the Treasury of the United States. He does nothing initiative in character, and his office could better be filled by appointment than election. The Secretary of State is in reality merely the head clerk of the State, and as a clerk of the Supreme Court may be better selected by the Supreme Court itself, so the Secretary of State, as chief clerk of the State, may be better selected by the head of the State. The Attorney General could in like fashion be appointed, and if appointed his office could be made the general office of all legal departments of the State. Every attorneyship of the State that now exists, of commissions, and boards, and officials, could be put under his control, and a general scheme of state legal department could thus be successfully evolved—a department economical, efficient, and permanent, and even non-partisan in its character if desired.

Were these various officials appointed by the Governor, the chief officer of the State could surround himself with a cabinet like the cabinet of the Chief Executive of the nation, and a more compact, perhaps more centralized and possibly a more efficient government, established. I would leave the Controller an elective officer because, theoretically at least, the Controller is a check upon the other officials of the State, and thus should be independent. Were these suggestions carried out, the State ballot would consist of a Governor, Lieutenant Governor, Controller, members of the judiciary, and members of the Legislature. Of course, any change we might make as herein suggested could not operate upon officials now in office or during any of our terms.

I recognize that the reform here suggested is radical and advanced, but I commend it to your careful consideration.

Other Ballot Reform

All of the parties in the State of California are committed to the policy of restoring the Australian ballot to its original form; and, therefore, I merely call to your attention that restoration as one of the duties that devolves upon us because of party pledges.

Non-Partisan Judiciary

And the return of the Australian ballot to the form which first we adopted in this State provides an easy mode for the redemption of the promises that have been made in respect to non-partisan judiciary. With the party circle eliminated, and with the names of the candidates for office printed immediately under the designation of the office, when upon the ballot the title of the judiciary is reached, the names of all the candidates may be printed without any party designation following those names; and in this fashion all of the candidates for judicial position will be presented to the people with nothing to indicate the political parties with which they have been affiliated.

County Home Rule

One of the most vexatious subjects with which legislatures have to deal is respecting classification, salaries, etc., of the various counties. The astonishing amount of time occupied by our Legislature in county government bills can only be understood by those who have been familiar with legislative work. I quote from a report by Controller Nye upon the subject:

"The first Legislature after the adoption of the Constitution commenced by making ten classes of counties, which number soon increased to more than forty, and at the present time there are fifty-eight classes, exactly equaling the number of counties. "If there were no other evidence of the folly of trying to legislate on county salaries by general laws, this would be conclusive. But the change of these general laws to meet the supposed needs of different counties has been incessant. In the legislative session of 1905 there were forty-five amendments to the salary schedules of as many counties; in 1907 there were fifty-seven such amendments, one for every county then existing, and in 1909 there were fifty. "So great are the evils of this form of legislation that we deem the only permanent remedy for them to be the submission and adoption of an amendment which will permit each county, proceeding along the same general lines as those prescribed for cities, to draft its own county government act, subject to ratification by the Legislature. The amendment should enumerate the subjects which may be embraced in these county government acts, or county charters, so framed, and they should include the number and compensation of officers, the granting or withholding of fees, the determination whether the county board of supervisors shall be elected by districts or at large, also the determination whether other county officers shall be elected or appointed, and such other similar matters of local concern as will not interfere with the operation of the general plan of State Government."

I quite agree with the views expressed by our Controller, and adopt his recommendation. It is but just and proper that counties should rule themselves just as cities do, and if this be accomplished we will have succeeded in taking from the Legislature perhaps a most vexatious subject, and one with which of necessity it oftentimes can not deal with intelligence, and we will have saved to the Legislature and the State the immense amount of time that is now expended by the Legislature upon the subject. Of course, care must be exercised in any change that practical uniformity is preserved.

Civil Service and the Merit System

In the first subject with which I have dealt, I defined clearly my attitude in regard to public service. Too often it has occurred that appointments to the public service have been made solely because of political affiliations or as a reward for political service. It is a design of the present administration to put in force the merit system, and it is our hope to continue that system by virtue of a civil service enactment. The committee recently appointed by the Republican State

Central Committee presented an act, covering the subject, which I commend to you.

Conservation

In the abstract all agree upon the policy of conservation. It is only when we deal with conservation in the concrete that we find opposition to the enforcement of the doctrine enunciated originally by Gifford Pinchot and Theodore Roosevelt. Conservation means development, but development and preservation; and it would seem that no argument should be required on the question of preserving, so far as we may, for all of the people, those things which naturally belong to all. The great natural wealth of water in this State has been permitted, under our existing laws and lack of system, to be misappropriated and to be held to the great disadvantage of its economical development. The present laws in this respect should be amended. If it can be demonstrated that claims are wrongfully or illegally held, those claims should revert to the State. A rational and equitable code and method of procedure for water conservation and development should be adopted.

Reformatory For First Offenders

Humanity requires that we should provide a reformatory for first offenders. All of us are agreed upon this matter, and your wisdom will determine the best mode of its consummation.

Employer's Liability Law

Upon the righteousness of an Employers' Liability Law, no more apt _expression can be found than that of ex-President Roosevelt on last Labor Day. He said:

"In what is called 'Employers' Liability' legislation other industrial countries have accepted the principle that the industry must bear the monetary burden of its human sacrifices, and that the employee who is injured shall have a fixed and definite sum. The United States still proceeds on an outworn and curiously improper principle, in accordance with which it has too often been held by the courts that the frightful burden of the accident shall be borne in its entirety by the very person least able to bear it. Fortunately, in a number of states—in Wisconsin and in New York, for instance—these defects in our industrial life are either being remedied or else are being made a subject of intelligent study, with a view to their remedy."

In this State all parties stand committed to a just and adequate law whereby the risk of the employment shall be placed not upon the employee alone, but upon the employment itself. Some new legal questions will be required to be solved in this connection, and the fellow servant rule now in vogue in this State will probably be abrogated and the doctrine of contributory negligence abridged. It is hoped that those in our State who have given most study to this subject will soon present to you a comprehensive bill, and when this shall have been done the matter will again be made a subject of communication by me.

I have purposely refrained to-day from indulging in panegyrics upon the beauty, grandeur, wealth, and prosperity of our State; or from solemnly declaring that we will foster industries, and aid in all that is material. It goes without saying that, whatever political or other differences may exist among our citizens, all are proud of California, its unbounded resources, its unsurpassed scenic grandeur, its climatic conditions that compel the wandering admiration of the world; and all will devotedly lend their aid to the proper development of the State, to the protection and preservation of that which our citizens have acquired, and that which industrially is in our midst. Ours of course is a glorious destiny, to the promotion and consummation of which we look forward with pride and affection, and to which we pledge our highest endeavor. Hand in hand with that prosperity and material development that we foster, and that will be ours practically in any event, goes political development. The hope of governmental accomplishment for progress and purity politically is with us in this new era. This hope and wish for accomplishment for the supremacy of the right and its maintenance, I believe to be with every member of the Legislature. It is in no partisan spirit that I have addressed you; it is in no partisan spirit that I appeal to you for aid. Democrats and Republicans alike are citizens, and equal patriotism is in each. Your aid, your comfort, your highest resolve and endeavor, I bespeak, not as Republicans or Democrats, but as representatives of all the people of all classes and political affiliations, as patriots indeed, for the advancement and progress and righteousness and uplift of California.

And may God in his mercy grant us the strength and the courage to do the right!

APPENDIX C

"California Energy Crisis" from wikipedia.org

Overview

The California electricity crisis of 2000 and 2001 followed the partial deregulation of the electricity market in the state. The deregulation was signed into law by Governor Gray Davis's predecessor, Pete Wilson. Part of the process of increasing competition involved the partial divestiture of electricity generation stations by the incumbent utilities, who were still responsible for electricity distribution and were competing with independents in the retail market.

Wholesale prices were deregulated, but retail prices were regulated for the incumbents as part of a deal with the regulator allowing the incumbents to recover the cost of assets that would be stranded as a result of greater competition. Things went well for the incumbents for several years due to the fact that excess generating capacity kept wholesale electricity prices lower than the capped retail rates.

However, rapid growth in demand for electricity soon ate into the excess capacity and in the summer of 2000 two events compounded the situation. These were a drought in the North West states and a large increase in the price of natural gas. California depends on the supply of hydroelectricity from the north and gas fired generation within the state.

When electricity wholesale prices exceeded retail prices, end user demand was unaffected, but the incumbent utility companies still had to purchase power, albeit at a loss. This allowed independent producers to manipulate prices in the electricity market by withholding electricity generation at some plant, arbitraging the price between internal generation and imported (interstate) power and causing artificial transmission constraints. In economic terms, the incumbents who were still subject to retail price caps were faced with inelastic demand. They were unable to pass the higher prices on to consumers without approval from the public utilities commission. The affected incumbents were Southern California Edison (SoCalEd) and Pacific Gas & Electric (PG&E). Pro-privatization advocates insist the cause of the problem was that the Regulator still held too much control over the market, and true market processes were stymied.

Prior to deregulation, the electricity market in California was largely in private hands. The main players were PG&E, SoCalEd, and San Diego Gas and Electric. The problems arose from an inefficient deregulation of the market. Ownership of certain power stations was transferred in order to increase competition in the wholesale market. In return for divesting some of their power stations the major utilities negotiated a deal to protect them from their assets being stranded. Part of this deal involved price caps for retail customers and a prohibition on the utilities from entering into hedging arrangements. The consequence was the PG&E and SoCalEd were forced to buy from a spot market at very high prices but were unable to raise retail rates. They lost billions and were reneging on power purchase deals and limiting supply. San Diego had worked through the stranded asset provision and was in a position to increase prices to reflect the spot market. Small businesses were badly affected.

Customers of some municipal utility districts (namely the Los Angeles Department of Water and Power, Glendale, Burbank, and Imperial County) were not affected by rolling blackouts.

Crisis timeline

- January 17, 2001 - Governor Davis declares a state of emergency. Rolling blackouts in northern and central California.

- January 18, 2001 - Rolling blackouts in northern and central California.
- March 19, 2001 - Rolling blackouts statewide.
- March 20, 2001 - Rolling blackouts statewide.
- November 13, 2003 - Governor Davis ends the state of emergency declared on January 17, 2001.

Handling of the Crisis

Perhaps the heaviest point of controversy is the question of blame for the California electricity crisis. Governor Davis's critics often charge that he did not respond properly to the crisis, while his defenders attribute the crisis solely to the corporate accounting scandals and say that Davis did all he could.

Signs of trouble first cropped up in the spring of 2000 when electricity bills skyrocketed for customers in San Diego, the first area of the state to deregulate. Experts warned of an impending energy crisis, but Governor Davis did little to respond until the crisis became statewide that summer. Davis would issue a state of emergency on January 17, 2001, when wholesale electricity prices hit new highs and the state began issuing rolling blackouts.

The crisis, and the subsequent government intervention and bailout of the utilities, have had political ramifications, and is regarded as one of the major contributing factors to the 2003 recall election of Governor Davis.

On November 13, 2003, shortly before leaving office, Davis officially brought the energy crisis to an end by issuing a proclamation ending the state of emergency he declared on January 17, 2001. The state of emergency allowed the state to buy electricity for the financially strapped utility companies. The emergency authority allowed Davis to order the California Energy Commission to streamline the application process for new power plants. During that time, California issued licenses to 38 new power plants, amounting to 14,365 megawatts of electricity production when completed.

Retrieved from
"http://en.wikipedia.org/wiki/California_electricity_crisis"

APPENDIX D

Campaign Statement for Candidate Joe Guzzardi

"Many Californians have asked me why I am a candidate for governor in the Recall Election. Since I have never held elective office, the question is reasonable and my answer is simple.

I am running because Californians need to hear the truth about what has happened to our once golden state. And Californians must elect a governor who is not afraid to make the bold decisions to put our state back on its way to greatness.

Enlightened Californians know exactly what's wrong. Every day we see evidence of how illegal immigration has changed California. But you would never know about it if you counted on Governor Gray Davis to tell you.

I pledge that when I am the Governor of California, you – the people – will hear only the truth. Californians deserve a Governor they can trust. Sadly, since 1999, you have been subjected to deceit and duplicity. Governor Davis has refused to listen to your voice.

I will work to remove every magnet that the government of California now provides to entice illegal aliens to enter California. A government, like a doctor, should first do no harm. The Gray Davis government not only doesn't have solutions for California problems, but its present policies are the primary cause of most of the critical problems like water and energy shortages, traffic congestion, sprawl, environmental degradation, school overcrowding, financial crises in the health, education and the penal system and wage depression among the state's workers.

On the issues section of this website, you can read my position on the major challenges that California faces. But because unchecked immigration is California's most pressing social issue, I will address several aspects of that topic here.

As Abraham Lincoln said, "Let the people know the facts, and the country will be safe."

Davis has mocked those of us who argue that the U.S. immigration laws should be obeyed. Instead Davis, a graduate of the Columbia University Law School, has worked tirelessly to promote illegal immigration. Davis has joined with fifth column lobbying groups who want to push an illegal alien agenda that is destructive to all of California.

Examine these two statements Davis made about Proposition 187 during his very first months as Governor:

April 15, 1999, "I'm a governor, not a judge. I've taken an oath to uphold all the laws of the state, no matter how much I may disagree with those laws."

April 16, 1999. "If this (Proposition 187) were a piece of legislation, I would veto it, but it's not. It's an initiative, passed by nearly 60 percent of the voters through a process specifically designed to go over the heads of the Legislature and the governor. If officials choose to selectively enforce only the laws they like, our system of justice will not long endure."

Sadly, Davis was not telling the truth. Despite his sanctimonious pledges of fidelity to democracy. Governor Davis had already entered into mediation agreements with most of the major opponents of Proposition 187, and none of its supporters. Davis' objective was to keep it from reaching the Supreme Court. He was successful with this deceit.

Davis' capitulation on Proposition 187 marked the beginning of five long years of abandoning decent, hard-working Californians who object to having their voice stifled. Instead of responding to financial and social consequences of the illegal alien invasion, Davis feeds it.

Unfortunately, Davis' failure to defend Proposition 187 has the predictable consequences for our K-12 school system. Shortly after being elected for his first term, Davis promised to make education his "first, second and third priority". Now, on the eve of his recall, the high school exit exam – touted as the barometer of California's projected new education standards – has been postponed until 2006.

As a teacher, I will tell you that there are only two types of exams possible. For students to pass, the test would have to be watered down to junior high school level. If the test were meaningful, the percentage of failures would be so high that shock waves would reverberate all over California.

Why do kids fail? Chief among many reasons is that teachers are so absorbed dealing with the 1.5 million non-English speaking students in the California K-12 system that they cannot focus on their main task – teaching. Take it from me as an education insider; the reason your public school kids don't know anything is because learning isn't number one on the K-12 agenda. Academics are subordinate to English language development, ethnic awareness and diversity.

Here's a side note on education: the cost to school those 1.5 million English Language Learners (to slip momentarily into education jargon) who don't speak English is about $10 billion. To be sure, because of our nonsensical immigration laws, some of those non-English speakers are U.S. citizens. Some are legal immigrants and the rest are illegal aliens. But whether they are legal, illegal or U.S. citizens. The $10 billion you spend to educate them is directly related to immigration.

Unconstrained immigration to California has also brought the health care system to its knees. The California Medical Association white paper titled California's Emergency

Services – A System in Crisis revealed that 80 percent of the hospital emergency rooms lost money in fiscal 1999. More than 9 million patients were treated that year in emergency rooms at an average loss of $46 per visit. Hospitals statewide lost $317 million in their emergency departments. Emergency physicians provided an additional $100 million in uncompensated care. Since this report was issued, conditions have gotten worse.

Add to this millions of dollars in payments for child delivery services and Temporary Assistance for Needy Families for women illegally in California and you begin to understand why the state is sinking in red ink.

As your Governor, I will use the powerful influence of my office to do the following:

- If possible, return Proposition 187 to the courts for review and encourage Proposition 187-type legislation to end subsidies to illegal aliens for all but emergency medical care. This was the original and true intention of the 1994 voter initiative. And enforce the section of Proposition 187 which Judge Pfaelzer said was within the purview of the State of California which calls for stronger state penalties on manufacture, sale and use of fraudulent identification.

- Tolerate no further delays in the high school exit exam.

- Immediately send the National Guard to patrol the border.

- I will demand a hearing on the constitutionality of SB 60, the bill to grant driver's licenses to illegal aliens.

- Mount an immediate legal challenge to revoke AB 540 that gives in-state university tuition to illegal aliens.

- Take immediate steps to invalidate the acceptance of the so-called Matricula Consular card currently accepted at government and business offices throughout the state. All such cards issued by any government would no longer be permitted in the State of California.

- Promote a photo voter identification card to eliminate the growing problem of voter fraud taking place in California. I will initiate legislation that requires mandatory purging of voter rolls every four years. Purging is the most effective way of making sure only registered voters cast ballots.

- Demand that the Government of Mexico extradite violent felons who have committed capital crimes on California soil. Until those criminals are returned to the proper law enforcement authorities, no Mexican government officials will be welcome at the Governor's Mansion."

(From: http://www.guzzardiforgov.com/jg/jg_statement.html)

APPENDIX E

Article on Immigration from The Mercury News, online dated October 1, 2003

IN THEIR OWN WORDS
IMMIGRATION: IMPACT REACHES ACROSS SPECTRUM OF POLITICS IN GOLDEN STATE

Author: JESSIE MANGALIMAN, Mercury News

In a state without a racial or ethnic majority, immigration is a hot-button election topic that is inextricably linked with many other issues confronting Californians.

A recent Field Poll found that immigration ranked as one of the top issues important to California voters in the recall election, along with the economy, education and health care, among others.

Both advocates and critics of immigration agree it's impossible forcandidates to speak about issues such as public schools or health care without mentioning immigration.

That's particularly true for a state where 27 percent of the population is foreign-born, said Marielena Hincapie, a staff attorney with the National Immigration Law Center, a non-profit advocacy group in Oakland.

"Given the demographics of the state, clearly we need to make sure the recall candidates or the next governor has a realistic understanding of the impact of immigrants on the economy and the contributions of immigrants to the state," Hincapie said.

It's little surprise, then, that the state's most divisive immigration initiative, Proposition 187, has had an enduring impact on California politics. Early in the recall campaign, candidates had to address how they voted on the 1994 initiative that sought to deny public benefits to illegal immigrants.

The latest flash point over immigration in the Oct. 7 bid to oust Gov. Gray Davis came as the governor signed the controversial legislation that allows illegal immigrants to apply for driver's licenses. The bill allows Californians to use a tax-identification number instead of a Social Security card when applying.

Supporters, including leading Democratic candidates, believe that licensing all California drivers is an issue of safety. Republicans, who have vowed to repeal the legislation, say it's a system that will be vulnerable to fraud and abuse.

Sharing the Oct. 7 ballot with the recall candidates will be the equally controversial initiative Proposition 54, which would ban the collection of racial and ethnic data by state government agencies.

Ward Connerly, a University of California regent who wrote the initiative, said it's the next step to banning racial preferences, which Connerly successfully campaigned for in 1996 with Proposition 209. That law banned race as a criterion in state hiring, awarding of contracts and university admissions.

Opponents of Proposition 54 say racial and ethnic data is central to documenting discrimination.

Yeh Ling-Ling, executive director of Diversity Alliance for a Sustainable America, an Oakland group that advocates a moratorium on immigration, said that despite debates over Propositions 54 and 187, there is little discussion in the recall campaign about the impact of immigration on California.

"You can think of any issue -- education, transportation,"

Yeh said. "Each of these is tied to excessive levels of . . . immigration."

The indelible mark of immigrants on Golden State politics is also on the candidate roster. Immigrants, notably actor Arnold Schwarzenegger, are among 135 candidates vying for the chance to run the world's fifth-largest economy.

Voters "are very smart," Hincapie said. "They're looking not just at people who have similar experiences . . . but people who will be passing laws that will improve the lives of all Californians."

What was your position on Proposition 187, the 1994 initiative that proposed to cut public benefits to illegal immigrants? Did you vote for it or against it?

Davis: I voted against Proposition 187, and actively fought against it. Proposition 187 would have gone so far as to deny medical treatment to children. Proposition 187 was unconscionable.

Bustamante: I opposed Proposition 187.
Camejo: I voted "No" on Prop. 187. It was wrong, and it also endangered the public by increasing the likelihood of gang violence and of major public-health problems. Fortunately, the courts overturned most of the worst provisions.

McClintock: I campaigned and voted for Proposition 187, as did a large percentage of Latino Americans. There are millions of Latino families who have obeyed our immigration laws and come to our nation legally to become Americans and to see their children prosper as Americans. Illegal immigration is a process of cutting in line in front of the people obeying our immigration laws. It is unfair to all of those from around the world who have stood in line to obey our laws to grant preference to those who have cut in line in front of them.

Schwarzenegger: I am pro-immigration and pro-immigrant. I voted in favor of Proposition 187 because of simple fairness. Californians should not have to bear costs that are the result of the federal government's failure to enforce immigration laws and to implement a fair and effective immigration policy.

Do you support allowing undocumented immigrants to get California driver's licenses?

Davis: Yes. Legislation I recently signed extended access to driver's licenses to California immigrants, who work hard, pay taxes, and are already on the road. This legislation will allow immigrants to get car insurance and be tested on the rules of the road, lowering costs, reducing the number of uninsured drivers and improving roadway safety. Furthermore, we will add to the DMV database of driver's names, addresses and fingerprints to help law enforcement do their jobs. This is good legislation, which is why it is supported by law enforcement officials like Los Angeles Police Chief William Bratton and elected officials like Insurance Commissioner John Garamendi. In addition, city councils in several municipalities, including the city of San Jose, have passed resolutions supporting the bill.

Bustamante: Yes.

Camejo: Yes, people who are living here and paying taxes cannot be denied a normal status for driving. It is also a public-safety issue. Everyone who is driving on California's roads needs to pass the standard tests. -- we We must not increase the dangers to drivers by ignoring the reality that exists.

McClintock: No. I led the opposition to S.B. 60 and now support the effort to have a referendum on the March ballot before this dangerous law can take affecteffect.

Schwarzenegger: I oppose providing driver's licenses to

undocumented immigrants. as provided by Senate Bill 60. I am listening to the voices of law enforcement, and this bill does not provide for a system of background checks and creates national-security concerns. Gov. Davis, who vetoed similar legislation in the past because of concerns over national security and fraud, has now put his personal political interests above the interests of California. I am pro-immigrant. That is why I oppose second-class identification for undocumented immigrants but support a properly regulated temporary worker-visa program.

Should undocumented immigrants be allowed to pay in-state tuition in the state's public university system?

Davis: Yes. I signed legislation to allow immigrants to pay in-state tuition. Children who grew up and graduated from high school here (and were brought here by their parents) should not be priced out of a good future.

Bustamante: Yes.

Camejo: Yes -- if they have been educated in California and meet our standard residency requirements, then they should be allowed to pay the same amount of tuition that other in-state students pay.

McClintock: I oppose making illegal aliens eligible for in-state tuition. It is wrong, especially when citizens of California are being turned away and American citizens from other states must pay the higher out-of-state tuitions.

Schwarzenegger: I support the provision in the "Development, Relief, and Education for Alien Minors Act" (DREAM Act), sponsored by Sen. Orrin Hatch, which gives states the authority to determine this important question. I support in-state tuition for undocumented immigrants who have graduated from a California high school or who have been in California for more than five years.

What was your position on Proposition 209, the 1996 state initiative that banned affirmative action in higher education? Did you vote for it or against it?

Davis: I am opposed to wedge issue politics, and I opposed Proposition 209. As governor, I have worked to maintain a strong commitment to diversity in higher education. In my first term, I put into place an initiative called the Four-Percent Admissions Program. This program ensures admission at a UC school for the top 4 percent of students from every high school in California. It has helped increase freshman admissions among African-American students by 30 percent and Latino students by 37 percent. In addition, my merit-based scholarship programs have provided more than 300,000 awards to the top 10 percent of every high school in grades 9-11, and we have guaranteed financial aid for the cost of tuition for every eligible student attending public universities in California.

Bustamante: I opposed Proposition 209.

Camejo: I opposed and voted against Proposition 209. This misguided initiative has curtailed programs designed to expand equal opportunity and prevent race and gender discrimination, and higher education in California is now suffering because of it. Now that the U.S. Supreme Court has ruled that affirmative action can be used in college admissions, I will work to overturn Prop. 209.

McClintock: I voted for and support Proposition 209 to move us toward a colorblind society.

Schwarzenegger: I believe that everyone should be treated equally and that all Californians deserve a shot at the American Dream. I embrace the diversity of California and deplore discrimination in all its manifestations. I support race-neutral measures to advance historically underrepresented groups in education, employment and public contracting. I support and advance current efforts to identify and advance students from underrepresented communities into higher education.

What is your position on Proposition 54, the initiative on the recall ballot that would ban local and state governments from collecting racial and ethnic data?

Davis: I am 100 percent against Proposition 54, a measure that would eliminate important medical data and information about student achievement, test scores, graduation rates, dropout rates and truancy rates. This information is vital to the school-accountability program California established in 1999, which is designed to help every child succeed. This information ban would jeopardize our ability to collect data on diseases -- data we need to protect public health. In addition, the initiative would prohibit the collection of data on the victims of hate crimes, and it would ban the collection (even the voluntary collection) of data on racial profiling. I believe this proposition is divisive and represents a return to wedge issue politics. The Information Ban would be bad policy and bad for all Californians.

Bustamante: I oppose Proposition 54.

Camejo: We must strongly oppose Proposition 54. This initiative is a radical measure that would damage our ability to address disparities by race or ethnicity in health care and disease patterns, educational resources and academic achievement, and hate crime and discrimination. Everyone should vote "No" on Prop. 54.

Huffington: I'm campaigning against Proposition 54 all around the state. It is bad for health care, bad for education, bad for public policy. It is nothing more than racial discrimination without a paper trail.

McClintock: I strongly endorse and support it. I do not

believe that a person's skin color should determine how they are treated by their government.

Schwarzenegger: I oppose Proposition 54 because while I share Dr. King's dream for a colorblind society, I recognize discrimination persists and only by acknowledging this fact can we seek to overcome it. My position on this issue is informed by my years visiting inner-city schools and neighborhoods and seeing the lingering effects of racial discrimination.

Republished with permission from San Jose Mercury News, October 1, 2003. Distributed by Knight Ridder Digital.

APPENDIX F

Provisions on recall in the California Elections Code

ELECTIONS CODE
SECTION 11000-11007

11000. This division governs the recall of elective officers of the State of California and of all counties, cities, school districts, county boards of education, community college districts, special districts, and judges of courts of appeal and trial courts. It does not supersede the provisions of a city charter or county charter, or of ordinances adopted pursuant to a city charter or county charter, relating to recall.

11001. For the purposes of this division, judges of courts of appeal shall be considered state officers, and judges of trial courts shall be considered county officers.

11002. For the purposes of this division, "elections official" means one of the following:

(a) A county elections official in the case of the recall of elective officers of a county, school district, county board of education, community college district, or resident voting district, and of judges of trial courts.

(b) A city elections official, including, but not necessarily limited to, a city clerk, in the case of the recall of elective officers of a city.

(c) The secretary of the governing board in the case of the recall of elective officers of a landowner voting district or any district in which, at a regular election, candidate's nomination papers ar efiled with the secretary of the governing board.

11003. For the purposes of this division, "governing board" means a city council, the board of supervisors of a county, the board of trustees of a school district or community college district, or the legislative body of a special district, as the context requires. In the case of the recall of a trial court judge, "governing board" means the board of supervisors.

11004. For the purposes of this division, a "local officer" is an elective officer of a city, county, school district, community college district, or special district, or a judge of a trial court.

11005. The proponents of a recall must be registered voters of the electoral jurisdiction of the officer they seek to recall.

11006. Proceedings may be commenced for the recall of any elective officer, including any officer appointed in lieu of election or to fill a vacancy, by the service, filing and publication or posting of a notice of intention to circulate a recall petition pursuant to this chapter.

11007. Except when a person has been appointed to office pursuant to Section 10229 because no person had been nominated to office, proceedings may not be commenced against an officer of a city, county, special district, school district, community college district, or county board of education in the event of one or more of any of the following:

(a) He or she has not held office during his current term for more than 90 days.
(b) A recall election has been determined in his or her favor within the last six months.
(c) His or her term of office ends within six months or less.

ELECTIONS CODE
SECTION 11020-11024

11020. The notice of intention shall contain all of the following:

(a) The name and title of the officer sought to be recalled.
(b) A statement, not exceeding 200 words in length, of the

reasons for the proposed recall.
(c) The printed name, signature, and residence address of each of the proponents of the recall. If a proponent cannot receive mail at the residence address, he or she must provide an alternative mailing address. The minimum number of proponents is 10, or equal to the number of signatures required to have been filed on the nomination paper of the officer sought to be recalled, whichever is higher.
(d) The provisions of Section 11023.

11021. A copy of the notice of intention shall be served by personal delivery, or by certified mail, on the officer sought to be recalled. Within seven days of serving the notice of intention, the original thereof shall be filed, along with an affidavit of the time and manner of service, with the elections official or, in the case of the recall of a state officer, the Secretary of State. A separate notice of intention shall be filed for each officer sought to be recalled.

11022. A copy of the notice, except the provisions required by subdivision (d) of Section 11020, shall be published at the proponents' expense pursuant to Section 6061 of the Government Code. Publication shall be required unless there is no newspaper of general circulation able to provide timely publication in the jurisdiction of the officer sought to be recalled. If this publication is not possible, the notice, except the provisions required by subdivision (d) of Section 11020, shall be posted in at least three public places within the jurisdiction of the officer to be recalled.

11023. (a) Within seven days after the filing of the notice of intention, the officer sought to be recalled may file with the elections official, or in the case of a state officer, the Secretary of State, an answer, in not more than 200 words, to the statement of the proponents.
(b) If an answer is filed, the officer shall, within seven days after the filing of the notice of intention, also serve a copy

of it, by personal delivery or by certified mail, on one of the proponents named in the notice of intention.
(c) The answer shall be signed and shall be accompanied by the printed name and business or residence address of the officer sought to be recalled.

11024. The statement and answer are intended solely for the information of the voters. No insufficiency in form or substance thereof shall affect the validity of the election proceedings.

ELECTIONS CODE SECTION 11040-11047

11040. (a) The petition may consist of any number of separate sections, which shall be duplicates except as to signatures and matters required to be affixed by signers and circulators. The number of signatures attached to each section shall be at the pleasure of the person soliciting the signatures.
(b) Each section of the petition may consist of any number of separate pages. A page shall consist of each side of a sheet of paper on which any signatures appear.

11041. (a) The proponents shall use the recall petition format provided by the Secretary of State and available from the county elections official or the Secretary of State. Before any signature may be affixed to a recall petition, each page of each section must bear all of the following in no less than 8-point type:

(1) A request that an election be called to elect a successor to the officer. However, if the officer is a justice of the Supreme Court or of a court of appeal, as specified in sub division (a) of Section 16 of Article VI of the California Constitution, the request shall be that the Governor appoint a successor to the officer.

(2) A copy of the notice of intention, including the statement of grounds for recall. For purposes of this paragraph, the copy of the notice of intention shall contain the names of at least 10 recall proponents that

appear on the notice of intention and that are selected by the proponents. The elections official shall not require the names of more than 10 proponents to be included as part of the language of the notice of intention. The provisions of Section 11023 do not need to be included as part of the language of the notice of intention.
(3) The answer of the officer sought to be recalled, if any. If the officer sought to be recalled has not answered, the petition shall so state.
(b) All petition sections shall be printed in uniform size and darkness with uniform spacing.

11042. (a) Within 10 days after filing of the answer to the notice of intention, or, if no answer is filed, within 10 days after the expiration of the seven-day period specified in Section 11023, the proponents shall file two blank copies of the petition with the elections official in his or her office during normal office hours as posted or, in the case of a recall of a state officer, with the Secretary of State, in his or her office during normal office hours as posted, who shall ascertain if the proposed form and wording of the petition meets the requirements of this chapter.
(b) At the time of the filing of the two blank copies of the petition, the proponents shall also file proof of publication of the notice of intention, if the notice of intention was published, or an affidavit of posting of the notice of intention, if the notice of intention was posted. The elections official or, in the case of a recall of a state officer, the Secretary of State, shall, within 10 days of receiving the blank copies of the petition, notify the proponents in writing of his or her finding.
(c) If the elections official finds that the requirements of this chapter are not met, the elections official shall include in his or her findings a statement as to what alterations in the petition are necessary. The proponents shall, within 10 days after receiving the notification, file two blank copies of the corrected petition with the elections official in his or her office during normal office hours as posted. The 10-day correction notification period and the 10-day filing period for

corrected petitions shall be repeated until the elections official or the Secretary of State finds no alterations are required.
(d) No signature may be affixed to a recall petition until the elections official or, in the case of the recall of a state officer, the Secretary of State, has notified the proponents that the form and wording of the proposed petition meet the requirements of this chapter.

11043. (a) The petition sections shall be designed so that each signer shall personally affix all of the following:
(1) His or her signature.
(2) His or her printed name.
(3) His or her residence address, giving street and number, or if no street or number exists, adequate designation of residence so that the location may be readily ascertained.
(4) The name of the incorporated city or unincorporated community in which he or she resides.

(b) A margin, at least one inch wide, shall be left blank across the top of each page of the petition. A margin, at least one-half inch wide, shall be left blank along the bottom of each page of the petition.

(c) A space, at least one inch wide, shall be left blank after each name for the use of the elections official in verifying the petition.

11043.5. (a) The Secretary of State shall provide to county elections officials a recall petition format for distribution to proponents of a recall. The recall petition format shall be made available upon request by the county elections official and by the Secretary of State.
(b) The recall petition format made available pursuant to this section shall be utilized by proponents of a recall election.

11044. Separate petitions are necessary to propose the recall of each officer.

11045. Only registered voters of the electoral jurisdiction of the officer sought to be recalled are qualified to circulate or sign a recall petition for that officer.

11046. To each section of a petition shall be attached a declaration, signed by the circulator thereof, that complies with Section 104. The declaration shall include a statement that the circulator is a registered voter in the jurisdiction of the officer sought to be recalled.

11047. When a petition is circulated in more than one county for the recall of an officer, each section of the petition shall bear the name of the county in which it is circulated, and only registered voters of that county may sign that section.

ELECTIONS CODE
SECTION 11100-11110

11100. (a) This chapter applies only to the recall of state officers.
(b) In addition to this chapter, Sections 13 to 18, inclusive, of Article 11 of the California Constitution and the applicable provisions of Chapter 1 (commencing with Section 11000) and Chapter 4 (commencing with Section 11300) shall govern the recall of state officers.

11101. Unless and until it is otherwise proven upon official investigation, it shall be presumed that the petition presented contains the signatures of the requisite number of registered voters.

11102. Each section of a recall petition shall be filed with the elections official of the county in which it was circulated.

11103. Each section of the petition shall be filed by the proponents or by any person or persons authorized, in writing, by a proponent. Each time an authorized person or persons files a section or sections of a petition, a copy of the written authorization shall be submitted to the elections official.

11104. (a) The elections official, 30 days after a recall has been initiated and every 30 days thereafter, or more frequently at the discretion of the elections official, shall report to the Secretary of State all of the following:
(1) The number of signatures submitted on the recall petition sections for the period ending five days previously, excluding Saturdays, Sundays, and holidays.
(2) The cumulative total of all signatures received since the time the recall was initiated and through the period ending five days previously, excluding Saturdays, Sundays, and holidays.
(3) The number of valid signatures, verified pursuant to subdivision (b), submitted during the previous reporting period, and of valid signatures verified during the current reporting period.
(4) The cumulative total of all valid signatures received since the time the recall was initiated and ending five days previously, excluding Saturdays, Sundays, and holidays.

(b) Signatures shall be verified in the same manner set forth in subdivisions (b), (c), (d), (e), (f), and (g) of Section 9030, and in Section 9031.

(c) The elections official, at the end of each 30-day period, shall attach to the petition a form provided by the Secretary of State, properly dated, that includes the information required by subdivision (a), and submit a copy of the petition, except as to the signatures appended thereto, to the Secretary of State and file a copy of the form in his or her office.

(d) Notwithstanding subdivisions (a) and (b), and Section 11106, the elections official shall not be required to verify signatures on a recall petition until the signatures submitted equal at least 10 percent of the total signatures required to qualify the recall for the ballot, as determined by the Secretary of State.

11105. Upon each submission, if less than 500 signatures are submitted to the elections official, he or she shall count the number of signatures and submit those results to the

Secretary of State. If 500 of more signatures are submitted, the elections official may verify, using a random sampling technique, either 3 percent of the signatures submitted, or 500, whichever is less. The random sample of signatures to be verified shall be drawn in such a manner that every signature filed with the elections official shall be given an equal opportunity to be included in the sample. Upon completion of the signature verification, the elections official shall report the results to the Secretary of State pursuant to Section 11104.

11106. Immediately after the deadline for submission of all signatures, the elections official shall verify any remaining signatures in the same manner set forth in subdivisions (b), (c), (d), (e), (f), and (g) of Section 9030, and in Section 9031. This verification shall apply to all signatures submitted to each county elections official.

11107. The elections official, upon the completion of each examination, shall forthwith attach to the petition a certificate, properly dated, showing the result of the examination, and submit a copy of the petition, except as to the signatures appended thereto, to the Secretary of State and file a copy of the certificate in his or her office.

11108. When the Secretary of State has received from one or more county elections officials a petition certified to have been signed by the stated number of registered voters, he or she shall, within 10 days, transmit to each county elections official a certificate showing that fact, and showing the total number of signatures collected by the proponents. The county elections official shall file the certificate in his or her office.

11109. When the Secretary of State determines that the proponents have collected sufficient signatures, he or she shall certify that fact to the Governor.

11110. Upon receiving certification of the sufficiency of the recall petitions from the Secretary of State, the Governor shall make or cause to be made publication of notice for the holding of the election. Officers charged by law with duties concerning elections shall make all arrangements for the election. The election shall be conducted, returned, and the results declared, in all respects as are other state elections.

11300. No insufficiency in a petition against any officer shall bar the later filing of a new petition against that officer.

11301. If a petition is found insufficient by the elections official or, in the case of the recall of a state officer, the Secretary of State, the petition signatures may be examined in accordance with Section 6253.5 of the Government Code.

11302. If a vacancy occurs in an office after a recall petition is filed against the vacating officer, the recall election shall nevertheless proceed. The vacancy shall be filled as provided by law, but any person appointed to fill the vacancy shall hold office only until a successor is selected in accordance with Article 4 (commencing with Section 11360) or Article 5 (commencing with Section 11380), and the successor qualifies for that office.

11303. Any voter who has signed a recall petition shall have his or her signature withdrawn from the petition upon filing a written request therefor with the elections official prior to the day the petition section bearing the voter's signature is filed.

ELECTIONS CODE
SECTION 11320-11327

11320. The following shall appear on the ballots at every recall election, except in the case of a landowner voting district, with respect to each officer sought to be recalled:

(a) The question "Shall (name of officer sought to be recalled) be recalled (removed) from the office of (title of office)?"

(b) To the right of the foregoing question, the words

"Yes" and "No" on separate lines with an enclosed voting space to the right of each.

11322. In addition to the material contained in Section 11320, the following shall appear on ballots at all recall elections, except at a landowner voting district recall election:

(a) The names of the candidates nominated to succeed the officer sought to be recalled shall appear under each recall question.

(b) Following each list of candidates, the ballot shall provide one blank line with a voting space to the right of it for the voter to write in a name not printed on the ballot.

11323. A voter shall indicate, by using the stamp or other marking device to place a mark in the voting space opposite either "Yes" or "No", his vote for or against the recall proposal, respectively.

11324. The official responsible for preparing the ballot shall, at least 10 days prior to the recall election, mail a sample ballot to each registered voter of the electoral jurisdiction of the officer sought to be recalled.

11325. (a) With the sample ballot there shall be mailed for each officer whose recall is sought, a printed copy of the following:
(1) The statement of reasons for recall that appeared on the notice of intent to recall that was filed by the proponents of the recall with the elections official, or in the case of a state officer, with the Secretary of State.
(2) The answer to the statement of reasons for recall that was filed by the officer whose recall is sought with the elections official or, in the case of a state officer, with the Secretary of State, if any answer was filed.

(b) The printed copies of the statement and the answer to that statement shall be mailed with the sample ballot either in a document separate from the sample ballot or in the same document in which the sample ballot appears.

Both the statement and answer shall be printed on the same page, or on facing pages of the document, and shall be of equal prominence.

(c) If the recall of more than one officer is sought, the statement and answer for each officer shall be printed together and shall be clearly distinguished from those of any other officer.

11327. An officer whose recall is being sought may file a statement with the elections official in accordance with Section 13307, to be sent to each voter, together with the sample ballot.

ELECTIONS CODE
SECTION 11328-11329

11328. A recall election shall be conducted, canvassed, and the results declared in substantially the manner provided by law for a regular election for the office.

11329. One election is sufficient for the recall of several officers.

ELECTIONS CODE
SECTION 11381-11386

11381. Nominations of candidates to succeed the recalled officer shall be made in the manner prescribed for nominating a candidate to that office in a regular election insofar as that procedure is consistent with this article. The following exceptions shall be made to that procedure:

(a) For recalls of state officers, the nomination papers and the declaration of candidacy shall, in each case, be filed no less than 59 days prior to the date of the election and not before the day the order of the election is issued. The Secretary of State shall certify the names of the candidates to be placed on the ballot by the 55th day prior to the election.

(b) For recalls of local officers, the nomination papers and the declaration of candidacy shall, in each case, be filed not less than 75 days prior to the date of the election and not before the day the order of the election is issued. If the elections official is required to certify to the governing board the names of the candidates to be placed on the bal lot, that shall be done by the 71st day prior to the election.
(c) No person whose recall is being sought may be a candidate to succeed himself or herself at a recall election nor to succeed any other member of the same governing board whose recall is being sought at the same election.

11382. No vote cast in the recall election shall be counted for any candidate unless the voter also voted for or against the recall of the officer sought to be recalled.

11383. If one-half or more of the votes at a recall election are "No", the officer sought to be recalled shall continue in office.

11384. If a majority of the votes on a recall proposal are "Yes", the officer sought to be recalled shall be removed from office upon the qualification of his successor.

11385. If at a recall election an officer is recalled, the candidate receiving the highest number of votes for the office shall be declared elected for the unexpired term of the recalled officer.

11386. If the candidate who received the highest number of votes fails to qualify within 10 days after receiving his or her certificate of election, the office to which he or she was elected shall be vacant, and shall be filled according to law.

APPENDIX G

Petition to recall Governor Gray Davis

DAVISRECALL.com

A Special Project of People's Advocate

Petition Instructions

Part 1 One to five registered voters may complete a box by **printing** their name and address and **signing** in the space provided.
All signers on a petition must be a **registered voter** in the county designated on the petition.

Part 2 In the box "DECLARATION OF PERSON CIRCULATING SECTION OF RECALL PETITION" you must fill in all shaded areas in your own handwriting. Follow the instructions carefully to avoid rejection of the petition.

-Only **registered** voters of **California** may sign and circulate petitions.

-You may circulate as many petitions as you wish, however, you can only sign the petition for recall **once**.

-You can circulate petitions in more than one County, but all signers of each petition must be from the **same** county. Start a new petition for each County

-A petition is valid even with **one** signature.

-Return petitions **immediately** to 3407 Arden Way, Sacramento, CA 95825.

-To receive additional petitions: download petitions from our website; "DavisRecall.com', or call (916) 482-6175, (800) 501-8222.

Example Petition

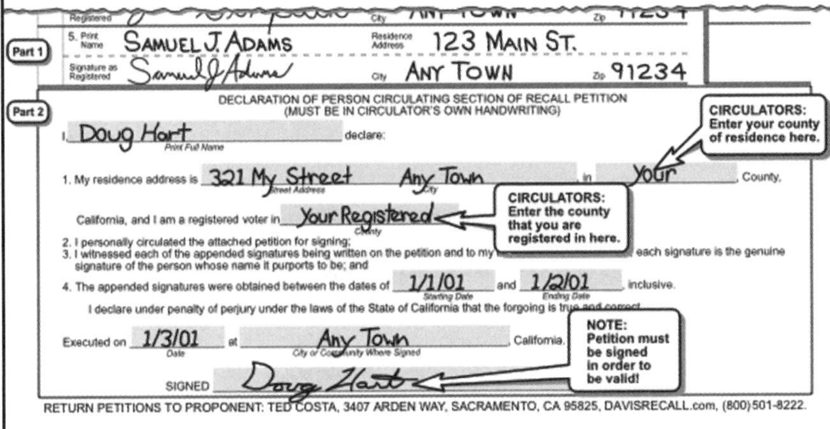

Part 1

5. Print Name SAMUEL J. ADAMS Residence Address 123 MAIN ST.
Signature as Registered Samuel J Adams City ANY TOWN Zip 91234

Part 2

DECLARATION OF PERSON CIRCULATING SECTION OF RECALL PETITION
(MUST BE IN CIRCULATOR'S OWN HANDWRITING)

I, Doug Hart (Print Full Name) declare:

1. My residence address is 321 My Street (Street Address) Any Town (City) in Your County, California, and I am a registered voter in Your Registered (County)
2. I personally circulated the attached petition for signing;
3. I witnessed each of the appended signatures being written on the petition and to my [obscured] each signature is the genuine signature of the person whose name it purports to be; and
4. The appended signatures were obtained between the dates of 1/1/01 (Starting Date) and 1/2/01 (Ending Date), inclusive.

I declare under penalty of perjury under the laws of the State of California that the forgoing is true and correct.

Executed on 1/3/01 (Date) at Any Town (City or Community Where Signed), California.

SIGNED Doug Hart

RETURN PETITIONS TO PROPONENT: TED COSTA, 3407 ARDEN WAY, SACRAMENTO, CA 95825, DAVISRECALL.com, (800)501-8222.

PETITION FOR RECALL

TO THE HONORABLE California Secretary of State.

Pursuant to the California Constitution and California election laws, we the undersigned registered and qualified electors of the State of California, respectfully state that we seek the recall and removal of Gray Davis holding the office of Governor, in California.

We demand an election of a successor to that office. Governor of California.

The following Notice of Intention to Circulate Recall Petition was served on 2/5/2003 to Gray Davis:

NOTICE OF INTENTION TO CIRCULATE RECALL PETITION. TO THE HONORABLE GRAY DAVIS:

Pursuant to Section 11020, California Election Code, the undersigned registered qualified voters of the State of California, hereby give notice that we are the proponents of a recall petition and that we intend to seek your recall and removal from the office of Governor of the State of California, and to demand election of a successor in that office. The grounds for the recall are as follows: Gross mismanagement of California Finances by overspending taxpayers' money, threatening public safety by cutting funds to local governments, failing to account for the exorbitant cost of the energy fiasco, and failing in general to deal with the state's major problems until they get to the crisis stage. California should not have to be known as the state with poor schools, traffic jams, outrageous utility bills, and huge debts....all caused by gross mismanagement.

The printed names, signatures, and business or residence addresses of the proponents are as follows: Edward J Costa; J. Wayne Scherffius; John B. Carney; Stephanie L Brown; Donald M. Nelson Sr.; William A. Stenson, Jr.; John A. Burtscher; Destyn R. Vetter; Loren Oliver Todd; Mark A. Hazen; Thomas H. Wells; Adam M Mrotek; Diane M Schachterle; Mary A. Jensen; Charles T. Jensen; Kenneth J. Payne.

To contact proponents: Ted Costa at People's Advocate: (916)482-6175.

The answer of the officer sought to be recalled is as follows: IF YOU SIGN THIS PETITION, IT MAY LEAD TO A SPECIAL ELECTION THIS SUMMER COSTING US TAXPAYERS AN ADDITIONAL $20-40 MILLION. Last November, almost 8,000,000 Californians went to the polls. They voted to elect Governor Davis to another term. Just days after the Governor's inauguration in January, however, a handful of rightwing politicians are attempting to overturn the voters' decision. They couldn't beat him fair and square, so now they're trying another trick to remove him from office. This effort is being led by the former Chairman of the State Republican Party, who was censured by his own party. We should not waste scarce taxpayers' dollars on sour grapes. The time for partisanship and campaigning is past. It's time for both parties to work together on our State's problems. Moreover, the allegations leveled against the Governor are false. As Governor, Davis has vetoed almost $9 BILLION in spending. California, along with 37 other states, is facing a budget deficit due to the bad national economy. The Bush Administration has announced the federal deficit this year will be the biggest in history, $304 BILLION. In these difficult and dangerous times, LET'S WORK TOGETHER, not be diverted by partisan mischief. /s/ Gray Davis Governor Gray Davis 9911 W. Pico Boulevard, Suite 980 Los Angeles, CA 90035

Each of the undersigned states for himself/herself that he or she is a registered and qualified elector of the County of ______________, California.

			This column for official use only
1. Print Name	Residence Address		
Signature as Registered	City	Zip	
2. Print Name	Residence Address		
Signature as Registered	City	Zip	
3. Print Name	Residence Address		
Signature as Registered	City	Zip	
4. Print Name	Residence Address		
Signature as Registered	City	Zip	
5. Print Name	Residence Address		
Signature as Registered	City	Zip	

DECLARATION OF PERSON CIRCULATING SECTION OF RECALL PETITION (MUST BE IN CIRCULATOR'S OWN HANDWRITING)

I, ______________ declare:
Print Full Name

1. My residence address is ______________ (*Street Address*, *City*), in ______________, County, California, and I am a registered voter in ______________ (*County*);
2. I personally circulated the attached petition for signing;
3. I witnessed each of the appended signatures being written on the petition and to my best information and belief, each signature is the genuine signature of the person whose name it purports to be; and
4. The appended signatures were obtained between the dates of ______________ (*Starting Date*) and ______________ (*Ending Date*), inclusive.

I declare under penalty of perjury under the laws of the State of California that the forgoing is true and correct.

Executed on ______________ (*Date*) at ______________ (*City or Community Where Signed*), California.

SIGNED ______________

RETURN PETITIONS TO PROPONENT: TED COSTA, 3407 ARDEN WAY, SACRAMENTO, CA 95825, DAVISRECALL.com, (800)501-8222.

APPENDIX H

Candidate pamphlets from California recall election

Mary Carey

My Gubernatorial Platform

The most important issue facing California right now is our $38 billion deficit and 6.7% unemployment rate. California needs a governor who will get our finances in order! As a "political outsider," I have fresh, original ideas for helping the state generate revenue and reduce its deficit. Here are just some of them:

1. Legalize gay marriage in California. This will generate a tremendous amount of revenue for the state as a honeymoon destination.

2. Tax breast implants. From Beverly Hills alone, we should bring in millions in tax revenue. (Note: I am all-natural and I personally discourage the use of implants!)

3. Make lap dances a tax deductible business expense. This will help grease the wheels of business in California and stimulate our economy.

4. If I'm elected Governor, I will wire the Governor's Mansion with live web cams in every room. We will create a pay site, and all money collected will go toward reducing the deficit. Californians will get to see their government in action - literally! (Also, we will have people from around the globe helping to pay off our debt, so it doesn't all fall on the shoulders of Californians.)

5. I will create a "Porn for Pistols" program to take handguns off the streets. Dealing with the violence and injuries associated with handguns is a huge drain on our state's resources.

6. As Governor, I will recruit fellow performers from the adult video industry as ambassadors of good will. These ambassadors will be a great help to California when it comes to such things as negotiating rates for buying electricity from neighboring states.

7. I will coordinate the state's unemployment and jury systems, so that anyone who applies for unemployment will instantly be called for jury duty. This will save California state and local governments millions of dollars, because we won't have to pay for jury duty. It will also relieve those with jobs from the stress of serving on lengthy juries.

8. I will fight the federal government's attempts to harass the adult video industry. Adult video is an $11 billion industry that creates more than $23 million in taxes each year for the state of California. We can't afford to lose this tax base!

9. If elected, I will support legislation to allow bars throughout the state of California to remain open until 4am. It will generate extra revenue, give additional hours of employment to the working class, and have a positive chain reaction throughout our economy.

10. I will address the HIV/AIDS epidemic that is costing our state millions of dollars and an incalculable toll in human lives.

New position highlights include:

- Ms. Carey is against government-provided universal health coverage
- She supports physician-assisted suicide
- She is pro-choice
- She supports legalizing ferrets

Angelyne

Think rational! The Pink Party.

Angelyne's Platform: Honesty

Angelyne urges every citizen to take a stand for your rights with your tax money, and say no to crooked politicians.

1. The number one cardinal matter to implement is:
   - All the tax money will be used to pay off the bills.
   - No bribes, no misappropriating the funds, and not allowing the money to be confiscated.
   - I have had it researched that by May of 2005, all of the California debt will be paid and we will be back to 0 balance with a surplus of money for the following year.
2. A law will be implemented where every tax payer will be able to check online how the government is spending the taxpayer's money.
3. Car Registration will be lowered back to what it originally was and be even 10% cheaper.
4. To raise money for the immediate now:
A room will be decorated in the Capitol building, for anyone who wishes to spend the night and get a personal tour of the building hosted by Angelyne for the amount of $10,000.00.
5. The School system will be appropriately upgraded.
6. The roadwork will be reassessed and only the necessary roadwork will be done and be done right.

7. Police activity will be highly scrutinized and any reports against the police will be taken very seriously. The 3 strikes law will be evaluated and redesigned to a more logistic fashion.
8. The court system shall be cleaned up. No frivolous law suits, and no abusing the system.
9. Corporate companies will not be allowed to take advantage of the taxpayer. They will have to deal fairly with all citizens of California.
10. State of the Art medical assistance will be implemented and available to those without health insurance.
11. Every Taxpayer will have a chance to be personally heard by the Lieutenant Governor or appointed official by appointment, and everything will be taken into consideration.
12. The capitol building will be painted hot pink.
13. Steps will be taken to save our natural resources with alternative natural resources.
14. There will be no more homeless people in California.

Cheryl Bly-Chester

Pro-Business
Pro-Education
Pro-Environment

"California needs a timeout from politics to take care of business. I'm a pro-business, pro-environment, fiscally responsible small business owner of Rosewood Environmental Engineering who owes no political favors. Throughout my 27-year engineering career in the transportation, energy and environmental fields, I've learned to hang tough and will not yield to political leveraging."

California Contributor's Program:
"I have a proposal to tap into our abundance and generosity that will resolve many issues plaguing Californians and help close the budget gap."

Organization Proposal: "As governor, I will exercise extensive financial control with my broad powers of appointment, and authority over the entire organization and administration of the executive branch."

"As an environmental expert, I can keep businesses in California by eliminating regulatory overlap without risking human health or resources." Reducing Obstructions for Better business: "Some regulatory bodies within the State do not operate within the check and balance structure prescribed in the California Constitution."

Pro-business, pro-environment, fiscal conservative and small business owner (Rosewood Environmental Engineering), Cheryl has over twenty-seven years engineering experience in transportation, energy and environmental fields.

On Energy Production: "If there are truly concerns about risks to human health or the environment with the building of power plants in the State of California, then they must be addressed."

Alternative Energy: "I will require that all new roofs with sufficient square footage and appropriate solar exposure, be built to sustain the load of a solar energy system."

Cheryl is involved in public education. CBEST qualified, She is a single mother of three wonderful children and classroom volunteer. "I will restore teaching as the primary school function, protecting educational funding and separating social and health services from educational responsibilities." Education: "Not enough of our public school educational funding is going to the intended recipient, the classroom, to benefit the students. When the educational system is also required to provide meals, security, transportation, public health programs, social services, language training, physical fitness, etc., the classroom suffers."

Waste, Fraud and Abuse:
"I will institute a three-month amnesty program for the reporting of suspected misuse of state funds, fraud perpetrated upon or under cover of the State of California and abuse of State governmental authority."

APPENDIX I

Recall handbook from Alaska

INTRODUCTION

DEFINITIONS

The initiative is the procedure by which the people instead of the legislature introduce and enact a law. A specified number of voters propose the law they wish to be placed on a ballot to have it be voted on by the people. [Ref. AS 15.45.010-245]

The referendum is the procedure by which the people approve or reject a law already passed by the legislature. The referendum petition must be filed within 90 days after the adjournment of the legislative session at which the law was passed, in order for it to appear on a ballot to be voted on by the people. [Ref. AS 15.45.250-465]

The recall is the procedure by which the people may remove the governor, lieutenant governor, or members of the state legislature from office. The recall question appears on a ballot to be voted on by the people. [Ref. AS 15.45.470-720]

STEPS IN THE PROCESS

The three petition processes follow the same basic steps:

- PREPARATION OF LANGUAGE by a petition committee for the application
- COLLECTION OF SIGNATURES of qualified voters who agree to act as sponsors for petition circulation purposes
- APPLICATION for a petition presented to the Lt. Governor
- REVIEW by the Lt. Governor, Department of Law and Division of Elections

- PETITION BOOKLETS PRINTED by the Division of Elections for the petition committee
- COLLECTION OF SIGNATURES of qualified voters who support the petition
- FILING OF THE PETITION with the Division of Elections
- REVIEW of signatures by the Division of Elections
- NOTIFICATION by the Lt. Governor if the petition was or was not sufficient (i.e., there were enough signatures) to appear on the ballot
- NOTIFICATION TO THE LEGISLATURE that the petition was successful
- PREPARATION of ballot language

RESTRICTIONS

Initiative
No initiative may be proposed to:

1. dedicate revenues;
2. make or repeal appropriations;
3. create courts;
4. define the jurisdiction of courts or prescribe their rules; or
5. enact local or special legislation.

[Ref. AS 15.45.010]

Referendum
No referendum may be applied to:

1. dedication of revenues;
2. appropriations;
3. local or special legislation; or
4. laws necessary for the immediate preservation of the public peace, health, or safety.

[Ref. AS 15.45.250]

Recall

1. The application for a recall petition may not be filed during the first 120 days of the term of office of any state public official subject to recall.

2. The recall petition may not be filed if the public official has fewer than 180 days remaining to serve in that office. [Ref. AS 14.45.490 and AS 15.45.610]

INITIATIVE

HOW TO FILE AN APPLICATION

An initiative is proposed by filing an application with the Lieutenant Governor. A form is available at the Division of Elections Offices and on the Division's web site. A deposit of $100 must accompany the application. The money will be refunded if the petition is properly filed, and retained if the petition is improperly filed. (A petition is considered properly filed if the Lieutenant Governor certifies the petition for the ballot.) [Ref. AS 15.45.020]

In addition to the deposit, the application must include:

1. the designation and signatures of 3 prime sponsors with a statement saying they are the initiative committee representing all sponsors of the initiative. They must be properly registered voters.
2. the signatures and addresses of no fewer than 100 properly registered voters who will serve as sponsors. Their names must be attached to the application statement. The 3 initiative committee sponsors must also sign as a qualified registered voter on the signature page. (Note: Each page of signatures must include a statement saying that the sponsors are qualified voters who signed the application with the proposed bill attached.)
3. the proposed bill (i.e., proposed law) to be initiated, attached to the application form
[Ref. AS 15.45.030]

The proposed bill must conform to the following specifications:
1. it must be confined to one subject;
2. the subject of the bill must be expressed in the title;
3. the enacting clause of the bill must state, "Be it enacted by the People of the State of Alaska;" and
4. the bill must not include a restricted subject.
[Ref. AS 15.45.040]

REVIEW OF APPLICATION

After the Department of Law submits an opinion on the content of the proposed bill, the Lieutenant Governor either certifies the application or denies certification. In either case, the initiative committee is advised of the Lieutenant Governor's action. [Ref. AS 15.45.070]
The Lieutenant Governor denies certification if:

1. the proposed bill to be initiated is not in the required form;
2. the application is not substantially in the required form; or
3. there is an insufficient number of qualified sponsors.
[Ref. AS 15.45.080]

PREPARING THE INITIATIVE PETITION

The Division of Elections is responsible for printing 500 petition booklets and the initial distribution of the booklets to the prime sponsors. The prime sponsors distribute petition booklets to each of the other qualified sponsors or circulators who will circulate the petition and gather the required signatures of registered voters. (This number is 10 percent of those voting in the previous general election and residing in at least two-thirds of the house districts in the state.)
Petition booklets include:

1. a copy of the proposed bill (if 500 words or less);
2. an impartial summary of the subject matter of the bill;
(Note: If the petition is properly filed, the impartial summary

will appear on the ballot. [Ref. AS 15.45.180])
3. a statement of warning as prescribed in AS 15.45.100;
4. sufficient space for signatures and addresses;
5. sufficient space at the bottom of each page for payment information required by AS 15.45.130(8); and
6. other specifications prescribed by the Lieutenant Governor.
[Ref. AS 15.45.090 and 6 AAC 25.240]

DESIGNATING CIRCULATORS

Qualified voters who sign the application are designated as sponsors, who may or may not circulate the petition. The initiative committe may designate additional circulators by giving their names and addresses in written notice to the Lieutenant Governor. [Ref. AS 15.45.060] If circulators designated by the initiative committee are not registered voters, they must sign a certificate of Alaska residency available from the Division of Elections.

PAYING PETITION CIRCULATORS

Petition circulators may not receive payment greater than $1 a signature, and a person or organization may not pay an amount greater than $1 a signature for collecting signatures on a petition. Additionally, a person or organization may not pay someone to sign or refrain from signing a petition. Anyone who violates this section of the law is guilty of a class B misdemeanor. [Ref. AS 15.45.110]

FILING THE PETITION

Before an initiative petition is filed, each petition book must be certified by an affidavit from the person who circulated the petition. This affidavit states:

1. the person signing the affidavit is a citizen, 18 years old or older, who has been a resident of Alaska for 30 days;

2. the person is the only circulator of the petition booklet;
3. the signatures were made in the circulator's presence;
4. the signatures, to the best of the circulator's knowledge, are those of the persons whose names are signed;
5. the signatures are of persons who were qualified voters on the date of signature;
6. the circulator has not entered into an agreement in violation of AS 15.45.110(c);
7. the circulator has not violated AS 15.45.110(d), and
8. the circulator prominently placed his or her name and payment arrangements on the petition.
[Ref. AS 15.45.130 and 6 AAC 25.240(g) and (h)]
Sponsors must file the petition within 365 days from the time they received notice from the Lieutenant Governor that the petition booklets were ready for delivery to them. If the petition is not filed within one year, the petition has no force or effect. [Ref. AS 15.45.140 and 6 AAC 25.240(c), (d), and (e)]
The petition must be signed by qualified voters:

1. equal in number to 10% of those who voted in the preceding General Election; and
2. who reside in at least two-thirds of the house districts of the state. (There are 40 house districts in Alaska.)
[Ref. AS 15.45.140]

REVIEWING THE PETITION

The Lieutenant Governor must review an initiative within 60 days from the date the petition was filed. The Lieutenant Governor then notifies the committee whether the petition was properly or improperly filed and also at which election the proposition will appear on the ballot. [Ref. AS 15.45.150] If an initiative petition is properly filed, the $100 deposit is refunded. [Ref. AS 15.45.020]

IMPROPER FILING

An initiative is improperly filed if:

1. there is an insufficient number of qualified signers; or
2. the voters did not reside in at least two-thirds of the house districts of the state.
[Ref. AS 15.45.160 and 6 AAC 25.240(f)]

FILING A SUPPLEMENTARY PETITION

There is no time allowed to gather or submit supplementary signatures for an initiative petition.

PLACING THE INITIATIVE ON THE BALLOT

The proposition will be placed on the election ballot of the first statewide general, special or primary election that is held after:

1. the petition has been filed;
2. a legislative session has convened and adjourned; and
3. a period of 120 days has expired since the adjournment of the legislative session.

[Ref. AS 15.45.190]
Note: If the Lieutenant Governor, with the concurrence of the Attorney General, determines that an act of the legislature, substantially the same as the proposed law, was enacted after the petition had been filed and before the date of the election, the petition is void, and the Lieutenant Governor so notifies the committee.)

WHEN DOES A PROPOSED INITIATIVE BECOME LAW?

If a majority of the voters vote in favor of the initiative, the measure passes. The law becomes effective 90 days following certification of the election results.

REFERENDUM

HOW TO FILE AN APPLICATION

A referendum is proposed by filing an application with the Lieutenant Governor in the same manner as an initiative is

proposed. A form is available at the Division of Elections offices and on the Division's web site. A deposit of $100 must accompany the application. The money will be refunded if the petition is properly filed and retained if the petition is improperly filed. (A referendum petition is considered properly filed if the Lieutenant Governor certifies the petition for the ballot.) [Ref. AS 15.45.260]
In addition to the deposit, the application must include:

1. the designation and signatures of 3 prime sponsors with a statement saying they are the referendum committee representing all sponsors of the referendum. They must be properly registered voters.
2. the signatures and addresses of no fewer than 100 properly registered voters who will serve as sponsors.
(Note: Each page of signatures must include a statement saying that the sponsors are qualified voters who signed the application with the proposed bill attached.)
3. the act (i.e., law) to be referred, attached to the application form
[Ref. AS 15.45.270]

REVIEW OF APPLICATION

The Lieutenant Governor must review the application within seven calendar days after ithas been received. After the Department of Law issues an opinion on content, the Lieutenant Governor either certifies the application or denies certification. In either case, the referendum committee is advised of the decision. [Ref. AS 15.45.300]
The Lieutenant Governor denies certification if:

1. the application is not substantially in the required form;
2. there is an insufficient number of qualified sponsors; or
3. more than 90 days have expired since the adjournment of the legislative session at which the referred act was passed.
[Ref. AS 15.45.310]

PREPARING THE REFERENDUM PETITION

If the application is certified, the petition booklets will be prepared within seven calendar days. The Division of Elections is responsible for printing 500 booklets and the initial distribution of the booklets to the prime sponsors. The prime sponsors distribute petition booklets to persons who will circulate the petition and gather the required signatures of registered voters. The booklets will contain:

1. a copy of the Act to be referred (if 500 words or less);
2. an impartial summary of the subject matter of the act; (Note: If the petition is properly filed, the impartial summary will appear on the ballot. [Ref. AS 15.45.410]
3. a statement of warning as prescribed in AS 15.45.330;
4. sufficient space for signatures and addresses; and
5. other specifications prescribed by the Lieutenant Governor.

[Ref. AS 15.45.320]

FILING THE PETITION

Before a referendum petition is filed, each petition bookLET must be certified by an affidavit from the sponsor who circulated the petition. This affidavit states:

1. the person signing the affidavit is a citizen, 18 years old or older who has been a resident of Alaska for 30 days;
2. the person is the only circulator of the petition booklet;
3. the signatures were made in the circulator's presence; and
4. the signatures, to the best of the circulator's knowledge, are those of the persons whose names are signed.

[Ref. AS 15.45.360]
The sponsors must file the petition within 90 days after the adjournment of the legislative session at which the Act was passed. [Ref. AS 15.45.370]

The petition must be signed by qualified voters:

1. equal in number to 10% of those who voted in the preceding General Election; and
2. who reside in at least two-thirds of the house districts of the state.

REVIEWING THE PETITION

The Lieutenant Governor must review a referendum within 60 days from the date the petition was filed. The Lieutenant Governor then notifies the committee whether the petition was properly or improperly filed and also at which election the proposition will appear on the ballot. [Ref. AS 15.45.380] If a referendum petition is properly filed, the $100 deposit is refunded. [Ref. AS 15.45.260]

IMPROPER FILING

A referendum is improperly filed if:
1. there is an insufficient number of signatures of qualified signers;
2. the signers did not reside in at least two-thirds of the house districts of the state; or
3. the petition was not filed within 90 days after the adjournment of the legislative session at which the Act was passed. [Ref. AS 15.45.390]

FILING A SUPPLEMENTARY PETITION

If a referendum is improperly filed, the referendum committee may amend and correct the petition by circulating and filing a supplementary petition within 10 days of the date that notice was given by the Lieutenant Governor. However, 90 days must not have expired since the adjournment of the legislative session at which the Act was passed. [Ref. AS 15.45.400]

PLACING THE REFERENDUM ON THE BALLOT

The proposition will be placed on the ballot for the first

statewide general, special or primary election that is held more than 180 days after adjournment of the legislative session at which the Act was passed. [Ref. AS 15.45.420]

REJECTION OF THE ACT

If a majority of the votes cast on the referendum favor the rejection of the Act referred, the Act is rejected, and the Lieutenant Governor shall so certify. The Act rejected by referendum is void 30 days after certification. [Ref. AS 15.45.440]

RECALL

HOW TO FILE AN APPLICATION

A recall is proposed by filing an application with the Director of the Division of Elections. A deposit of $100 must accompany the application. The money will be refunded if the petition is properly filed, and retained if the petition is improperly filed. (A recall petition is considered properly filed if the Lieutenant Governor certifies the petition for the ballot.) [Ref. AS 15.45.480]
In addition to the deposit, the application must include:

1. the name and office of the person to be recalled;
2. the grounds for recall described in particular in a statement of not more than 200 words;
3. the designation and signatures of 3 prime sponsors with a statement that they are the recall committee representing all sponsors and petition signers in matters relating to the recall. They must be properly registered voters.
4. the signatures of at least 100 properly registered voters who will serve as sponsors. Their names must be attached to the application statement of recall. (Note: Each page of signatures must include a statement saying that the sponsors are qualified voters who signed the application with the ground for recall attached.)

5. the signatures and addresses of qualified voters equal in number to 10% of those who voted in the preceding general election in the state or in the senate or house district of the official sought to be recalled. [Ref. AS 15.45.500]

REVIEW OF APPLICATION

After the Department of Law submits an opinion on content, the Director of the Division of Elections either certifies the application or denies certification. In either case, the recall committee is notified of the decision. [Ref. AS 15.45.540]
The Director denies certification if:

1. the application is not substantially in the required form;
2. the application was filed during the first 120 days of the term of office of the official subject to recall or within fewer than 180 days of the termination of the term of office of any official subject to recall;
3. the person named in the application is not subject to recall; or
4. there is an insufficient number of qualified subscribers.

[Ref. AS 15.45.550]

PREPARING THE RECALL PETITION

For the recall, the Division of Elections is responsible for printing petition booklets in a number reasonably calculated to allow full circulation throughout the state or throughout the senate or house district of the official sought to be recalled. [Ref. AS 15.45.560]
Petition booklets include:

1. the name and office of the person to be recalled;
2. the statement of the grounds for recall included in the application;
3. the statement of warning as required in AS 15.45.570;
4. sufficient space for signatures and addresses; and

5. other specifications prescribed by the Director of Elections. [Ref. AS 15.45.560]

FILING THE PETITION

Before a recall petition is filed, each petition booklet must be certified by an affidavit from the sponsor who circulated the petition. The affidavit states:

1. the person signing the affidavit is a citizen, 18 years old or older, who has been a resident of Alaska for 30 days;
2. the person is the only circulator of the petition booklet;
3. the signatures were made in the circulator's presence; and
4. the signatures, to the best of the circulator's knowledge, are those of the persons whose names are signed. [Ref. AS 15.45.600]

The petition may not be filed if the public official subject to recall has fewer than 180 days left in his or her term of office. [Ref. AS 15.45.610]

The recall petition must be signed by qualified voters equal in number to 25% of those who voted in the preceding general election in the state or in the senate or house district of the official sought to be recalled. [Ref. AS 15.45.610]

REVIEWING THE PETITION

For a recall petition, the Director of the Division of Elections shall review it within 30 days of the date of filing, and shall notify the recall committee and the person subject to recall whether the petition was properly or improperly filed. [Ref. AS 15.45.620]

IMPROPER FILING

A recall petition is improperly filed if:
1. there is an insufficient number of qualified signers; or
2. the petition was filed within fewer than 180 days of the

termination of the term of office of the official subject to recall. [Ref. AS 15.45.630]

FILING A SUPPLEMENTARY PETITION

If a recall petition is improperly filed, the committee may amend and correct the petition by circulating and filing a supplementary petition within 20 days of the date that notice was given, if filed within fewer than 180 days of the termination of the term of office of the person subject to recall. [AS 15.45.640]

SPECIAL ELECTION CALLED

If the petition is properly filed, and if the office is not vacant, the director shall prepare the ballot and shall call a special election to be held no fewer than 60 nor more than 90 days after the date that notification is given that the petition was properly filed. If a primary or general election is to be held no fewer than 60 nor more than 90 days after the date that notification is given that the petition was properly filed, the special election shall be held on the date of the primary or general election. [Ref. AS 15.45.650]

SPECIAL ELECTION CONDUCTED

All provisions regarding the conduct of a general election govern the conduct of a special election for the recall of a state public official. [Ref. AS 15.45.670]

DISPLAY OF STATEMENTS FOR AND AGAINST RECALL

The Director of Elections will provide each election board in the state or in the senate or house district of the person subject to recall copies of the statement of the grounds for recall included in the recall petition. The director also provides each election board with copies of a statement, no longer than 200 words, made by the official subject to recall in justification of the official's conduct in office. Copies are posted in the polling place. [Ref. AS 15.45.680]

CERTIFICATION OF ELECTION RESULTS

If a majority of the votes cast on the question of recall favor the removal of the official, the Director of Elections so certifies and the office is vacant on the day after the date of certification. [Ref. AS 15.45.690]

RULES FOR FILLING VACANCY

A vacancy caused by a recall is filled as a vacancy caused by any other means is filled. [Ref. AS 15.45.700]

APPENDIX J

Constitutions and Statutes on recall in 17 States

NOTE: PROVISIONS OF THE CONSTITUTIONS AND STATUTES COVERING RECALL ARE REPRODUCED ONLY FOR THE GENERAL INFORMATION OF THE READER WHO SHOULD REFER TO THE ORIGINAL DOCUMENTS IN ORDER TO GET THE LEGALLY ACCEPTABLE VERSIONS OF THESE DOCUMENTS.

THE ALASKA CONSTITUTION
Article XI. Initiative, Referendum, and Recall

Section 8. Recall

All elected public officials in the State, except judicial officers, are subject to recall by the voters of the State or political subdivision from which elected. Procedures and grounds for recall shall be prescribed by the legislature.

THE ALASKA STATUTES (AS 15.45.470 et sec)
beginning with Provision and Scope for Use of Recall

AS 15.45.470
AS 15.45.480
AS 15.45.490
AS 15.45.500
AS 15.45.510
AS 15.45.520
AS 15.45.530
AS 15.45.540
AS 15.45.550
AS 15.45.560
AS 15.45.570
AS 15.45.580
AS 15.45.590

AS 15.45.600
AS 15.45.610
AS 15.45.620
AS 15.45.630
AS 15.45.640
AS 15.45.650
AS 15.45.660
AS 15.45.670
AS 15.45.680
AS 15.45.690
AS 15.45.700
AS 15.45.710
AS 15.45.720

AS 15.45.470. Provision and Scope For Use of Recall.

The governor, the lieutenant governor, and members of the state legislature are subject to recall by the voters of the state or the political subdivision from which elected.

AS 15.45.480. Filing Application.

The recall of the governor, lieutenant governor, or a member of the state legislature is proposed by filing an application with the director. A deposit of $100 must accompany the application. This deposit shall be retained if a petition is not properly filed. If a petition is properly filed the deposit shall be refunded.

AS 15.45.490. Time of Filing Application.

An application may not be filed during the first 120 days of the term of office of any state public official subject to recall.

AS 15.45.500. Form of Application.

The application must include

(1) the name and office of the person to be recalled;

(2) the grounds for recall described in particular in not more than 200 words;

(3) a statement that the sponsors are qualified voters who signed the application with the statement of grounds for recall attached;

(4) the designation of a recall committee of three sponsors who shall represent all sponsors and subscribers in matters relating to the recall;

(5) the signatures of at least 100 qualified voters who subscribe to the application as sponsors for purposes of circulation; and

(6) the signatures and addresses of qualified voters equal in number to 10 percent of those who voted in the preceding general election in the state or in the senate or house district of the official sought to be recalled.

AS 15.45.510. Grounds For Recall.

The grounds for recall are (1) lack of fitness, (2) incompetence, (3) neglect of duties, or (4) corruption.

AS 15.45.520. Manner of Notice.

Notice on all matters pertaining to the application and petition may be served on any member of the recall committee in person or by mail addressed to a committee member as indicated on the application.

AS 15.45.530. Notice of the Number of Voters.

The director, upon request, shall notify the recall committee of the official number of persons who voted in the preceding general election in the state or in the senate or house district of the official to be recalled.

AS 15.45.540. Review of Application.

The director shall review the application and shall either certify it or notify the recall committee of the grounds of refusal.

AS 15.45.550. Bases of Denial of Certification.

The director shall deny certification upon determining that

(1) the application is not substantially in the required form;

(2) the application was filed during the first 120 days of the term of office of the official subject to recall or within less than 180 days of the termination of the term of office of any official subject to recall;

(3) the person named in the application is not subject to recall; or

(4) there is an insufficient number of qualified subscribers.

AS 15.45.560. Preparation of Petition.

Upon certifying the application, the director shall prescribe the form of, and prepare, a petition containing (1) the name and office of the person to be recalled, (2) the statement of the grounds for recall included in the application, (3) the statement of warning required in AS 15.45.570 , (4) sufficient space for signatures and addresses, and (5) other specifications prescribed by the director to assure proper handling and control. Petitions, for purposes of circulation, shall be prepared by the director in a number reasonably calculated to allow full circulation throughout the state or throughout the senate or house district of the official sought to be recalled. The director shall number each petition and shall keep a record of the petitions delivered to each sponsor.

AS 15.45.570. Statement of Warning.

Each petition and duplicate copy shall include a statement of warning that a person who signs a name other than the person's own to the petition, or who knowingly signs more than once for the same proposition at one election, or who signs the petition while knowingly not a qualified voter, is guilty of a class B misdemeanor.

AS 15.45.580. Circulation.

The petitions may be circulated only in person throughout the state or senate or house district represented by the official sought to be recalled.

AS 15.45.590. Manner of Signing and Withdrawing Name From Petition.

Any qualified voter may subscribe to the petition by signing the voter's name and address. A person who has signed the petition may withdraw the person's name only by giving written notice to the director before the date the petition is filed.

AS 15.45.600. Certification of Circulator.

Before being filed, each petition shall be certified by an affidavit by the person who personally circulated the petition. The affidavit shall state in substance that (1) the person signing the affidavit meets the residency, age, and citizenship qualifications of AS 15.05.010 , (2) the person is the only circulator of that petition or copy, (3) the signatures were made in the circulator's actual presence, and (4) to the best of the circulator's knowledge, the signatures are those of the persons whose names they purport to be. In determining the sufficiency of the petition, the director may not count subscriptions on petitions not properly certified.

AS 15.45.610. Filing of Petition.

A petition may not be filed within less than 180 days of the termination of the term of office of a state public official subject to recall. The sponsor may file the petition only if signed by qualified voters equal in number to 25 percent of those who voted in the preceding general election in the state or in the senate or house district of the official sought to be recalled.

AS 15.45.620. Review of Petition.

Within 30 days of the date of filing, the director shall review the petition and shall notify the recall committee and the person subject to recall whether the petition was properly or improperly filed.

AS 15.45.630. Bases For Determining the Petition Was Improperly Filed.

The director shall notify the committee that the petition was improperly filed upon determining that

(1) there is an insufficient number of qualified subscribers; or

(2) the petition was filed within less than 180 days of the termination of the term of office of the official subject to recall.

AS 15.45.640. Submission of Supplementary Petition.

Upon receipt of notice that the filing of the petition was improper, the committee may amend and correct the petition by circulating and filing a supplementary petition within 20 days of the date that notice was given, if filed within less than 180 days of the termination of the term of office of the person subject to recall.

AS 15.45.650. Calling Special Election.

If the director determines the petition is properly filed and if the office is not vacant, the director shall prepare the ballot and shall call a special election to be held on a date not less than 60, nor more than 90, days after the date that notification is given that the petition was properly filed. If a primary or general election is to be held not less than 60, nor more than 90, days after the date that notification is given that the petition was properly filed, the special election shall be held on the date of the primary or general election.

AS 15.45.660. Preparation of Ballot.

The ballot shall be designed with the question of whether the public official shall be recalled, placed on the ballot in the following manner: "Shall (name of official) be recalled from the office of . . . . . .?". Provision shall be made for marking the question "Yes" or "No."

AS 15.45.670. Conduct of Special Election.

Unless specifically provided otherwise, all provisions regarding the conduct of a general election shall govern the conduct of a special election for the recall of the state public official, including but not limited to, provisions concerning voter qualification; provisions regarding duties, powers, rights and obligations of the director, of other election officials, and of municipalities; provision for notification of the election; provision for the payment of election expenses; provisions regarding employees being allowed time from work to vote; provisions for counting, reviewing, and certification of returns; provision for the determination of votes and of recount contests and court appeal; and provisions for absentee voting.

AS 15.45.680. Display of Bases For and Against Recall.

The director shall provide each election board in the state or in the senate or house district of the person subject to recall with 10 copies of the statement of the grounds for recall included in the application and 10 copies of the statement of not more than 200 words made by the official subject to recall in justification of the official's conduct in office. The person subject to recall may provide the director with the statement within 10 days after the date the director gave notification that the petition was properly filed. The election board shall post three copies of the statements for and against recall in three conspicuous places in the polling place.

AS 15.45.690. Certification of Election Results.

If a majority of the votes cast on the question of recall favor the removal of the official, the director shall so certify and the office is vacant on the day after the date of certification.

AS 15.45.700. Filling Vacancy.

A vacancy caused by a recall is filled as a vacancy caused by any other means is filled.

AS 15.45.710. Insufficiency of Grounds, Application, or Petition.

A recall submitted to the voters may not be held void because of the insufficiency of the grounds, application, or petition by which the submission was procured.

AS 15.45.720. Judicial Review.

Any person aggrieved by a determination made by the director under AS 15.45.470 - 15.45.710 may bring an action in the superior court to have the determination reviewed within 30 days of the date on which notice of determination was given.

ARIZONA CONSTITUTION
Part I, Section 1 et sec. Beginning with Officers Subject to recall; petitioners.

1. Officers subject to recall; petitioners
Section 1. Every public officer in the state of Arizona, holding an elective office, either by election or appointment, is subject to recall from such office by the qualified electors of the electoral district from which candidates are elected to such office. Such electoral district may include the whole state. Such number of said electors as shall equal twenty-five per centum of the number of votes cast at the last preceding general election for all of the candidates for the office held by such officer, may by petition, which shall be known as a recall petition, demand his recall.

2. Recall petitions; contents; filing; signatures; oath
Section 2. Every recall petition must contain a general statement, in not more than two hundred words, of the grounds of such demand, and must be filed in the office in which petitions for nominations to the office held by the incumbent are required to be filed. The signatures to such recall petition need not all be on one sheet of paper, but each signer must add to his signature the date of his signing said petition, and his place of residence, giving his street and number, if any, should he reside in a town or city. One of the signers of each sheet of such petition, or the person circulating such sheet, must make and subscribe an oath on said sheet, that the signatures thereon are genuine.

3. Resignation of officer; special election
Section 3. If such officer shall offer his resignation it shall be accepted, and the vacancy shall be filled as may be provided by law. If he shall not resign within five days after a recall petition is filed as provided by law, a special election shall be

ordered to be held as provided by law, to determine whether such officer shall be recalled. On the ballots at such election shall be printed the reasons as set forth in the petition for demanding his recall, and, in not more than two hundred words, the officer's justification of his course in office. He shall continue to perform the duties of his office until the result of such election shall have been officially declared.

4. Special election; candidates; results; qualification of successor
Section 4. Unless the incumbent otherwise requests, in writing, the incumbent's name shall be placed as a candidate on the official ballot without nomination. Other candidates for the office may be nominated to be voted for at said election. The candidate who receives the highest number of votes shall be declared elected for the remainder of the term. Unless the incumbent receives the highest number of votes, the incumbent shall be deemed to be removed from office, upon qualification of the successor. In the event that the successor shall not qualify within five days after the result of said election shall have been declared, the said office shall be vacant, and may be filled as provided by law.

5. Recall petitions; restrictions and conditions
Section 5. No recall petition shall be circulated against any officer until he shall have held his office for a period of six months, except that it may be filed against a member of the legislature at any time after five days from the beginning of the first session after his election. After one recall petition and election, no further recall petition shall be filed against the same officer during the term for which he was elected, unless petitioners signing such petition shall first pay into the public treasury which has paid such election expenses, all expenses of the preceding election.

6. Application of general election laws; implementary legislation
Section 6. The general election laws shall apply to recall elections in so far as applicable. Laws necessary to facilitate the

operation of the provisions of this article shall be enacted, including provision for payment by the public treasury of the reasonable special election campaign expenses of such officer.

ARIZONA REVISED STATUTES
Section 19-201 et sec. Beginning with Officers subject to recall; number of petitioners.

Ariz. Rev. Statutes Section 19-201
Ariz. Rev. Statutes Section 19-202
Ariz. Rev. Statutes Section 19-202.01
Ariz. Rev. Statutes Section 19-203
Ariz. Rev. Statutes Section 19-204
Ariz. Rev. Statutes Section 19-205
Ariz. Rev. Statutes Section 19-205.02
Ariz. Rev. Statutes Section 19-205.03
Ariz. Rev. Statutes Section 19-206
Ariz. Rev. Statutes Section 19-207
Ariz. Rev. Statutes Section 19-208
Ariz. Rev. Statutes Section 19-208.01
Ariz. Rev. Statutes Section 19-208.02
Ariz. Rev. Statutes Section 19-208.03
Ariz. Rev. Statutes Section 19-208.04
Ariz. Rev. Statutes Section 19-208.05
Ariz. Rev. Statutes Section 19-209
Ariz. Rev. Statutes Section 19-210
Ariz. Rev. Statutes Section 19-212
Ariz. Rev. Statutes Section 19-213
Ariz. Rev. Statutes Section 19-214
Ariz. Rev. Statutes Section 19-215
Ariz. Rev. Statutes Section 19-216
Ariz. Rev. Statutes Section 19-217

19-201. Officers subject to recall; number of petitioners

A. Every public officer holding an elective office, either by election, appointment or retention, is subject to recall from such office by the qualified electors of the electoral district from which candidates are elected to that office. Such electoral district may include the whole state. A number of qualified electors equaling twenty-five per cent of the number of votes cast at the last preceding general election for all the candidates for the office held by the officer, even if the officer was not elected at that election, divided by the number of offices that were being filled at that election may, by recall petition, demand his recall.

B. In the case of a public officer holding office in a newly created division or district of an elective office, either by election or appointment, a number of qualified electors equaling twenty-five per cent of the number of votes cast at the last preceding general election for all those who were candidates for other divisions or districts of the same office held by the officer in that county or city divided by the number of offices that were being filled at that election may, by recall petition, demand his recall.

19-202. Recall petition; limitations; subsequent petition

A. A recall petition shall not be circulated against any officer until he has held office for six months, except that a petition may be filed against a member of the legislature at any time after five days from the beginning of the first session after his election. The commencement of a subsequent term in the same office does not renew the six month period delaying the circulation of a recall petition.

B. After one recall petition and election, no further recall petition shall be filed against the same officer during the term for which he was elected unless the petitioners signing the petition first, at the time of application for the subsequent recall petition, pay into the public treasury from which such election expenses were paid all expenses of the preceding election.

C. Signatures obtained on recall petitions by a committee or any of its officers, agents, employees or members before the filing of the committee's statement of organization are void and shall not be counted in determining the legal sufficiency of the petition.

19-202.01. Application for recall petition

A. A person or organization intending to file a recall petition shall, before causing the petition to be printed and circulated, submit an application setting forth his name or, if an organization, its name and the names and titles of its officers, address, his intention to circulate and submit such petition, the text of the general statement required by section 19-203 and a request for issuance of an official number to be printed on the signature sheets of the petition. Such application shall be submitted to the office of secretary of state if for recall of a state officer, including a member of the state legislature, or a member of Congress, and with the county officer in charge of elections if for a county or district officer or superior court judge, with the city or town clerk if for a city or town officer and with the county school superintendent if for a governing board member of a school district.

B. On receipt of the application, the receiving officer shall forthwith assign a number to the petition, which number shall appear in the lower right-hand corner on each side of each signature sheet, and issue that number to the applicant. A record shall be maintained by the receiving officer of each application received, of the date of its receipt and of the number assigned and issued to the applicant.

19-203. Recall petition; contents; submission for verification; nonacceptance

A. A recall petition shall contain a general statement of not more than two hundred words stating the grounds of the demand for the recall. The petition shall be submitted for verification of signatures to the office of the secretary of state if for a state officer, including a member of the legislature or a member of Congress, with the county officer in charge of elections if for a county or district officer or superior court judge, with the city or town clerk if for a city or town officer and with the county school superintendent if for a governing board member of a school district. No recall petition is considered filed for purposes of this chapter until the verification process is complete and the petition is filed pursuant to section 19-208.03, subsection A, paragraph 1.

B. A recall petition shall not be accepted for such verification if more than one hundred twenty days have passed since the date of submission of the application for recall petition, as prescribed by section 19-202.01.

19-204. Form of petition

A. The caption and body of a recall petition shall be substantially as follows:

Recall Petition

We, the qualified electors of the electoral district from which ____ _ (name and title of office) was elected, demand his recall.

The grounds of this demand for recall are as follows:

(State in two hundred words or less the grounds of the demand)

B. The remaining portion of the petition shall be as prescribed for initiative and referendum except that a designation for paid or volunteer circulators is not required on the petition and signatures are valid without regard to whether they were collected by a paid or volunteer circulator.

19-205. Signatures and verification

A. Every qualified elector signing a petition for a recall election shall do so in the presence of the person who is circulating the petition and who is to execute the affidavit of verification on the reverse side of the signature sheet. At the time of signing, the qualified elector shall sign and print his first and last name and the elector so signing shall write, in the appropriate spaces following the signature, his residence address, giving street and number or, if the elector has no street address, a description of his residence location, and the date on which he signed the petition.

B. The person before whom the signatures were written on the signature sheet shall in an affidavit subscribed and sworn to by him before a notary public verify that each of the names on the sheet was signed in his presence on the date indicated, and that in his belief each signer was a qualified elector of the election district on the date indicated in which such recall election will be conducted. All signatures of petitioners on a signature sheet shall be those of qualified electors who are registered to vote in the same county. However, if signatures from more than one county appear on the same signature sheet, only the valid signatures from the same county which are most numerous on the signature sheet shall be counted. In the absence of a legible signature, the name as it is printed shall be the name used to determine the validity of the signature.

C. The affidavit shall be in the form prescribed for initiative and referendum. In addition it shall also require a statement by the circulator that the circulator believes that the circulator is qualified to register to vote and all signers thereof are qualified to vote in the recall election.

19-205.02. Prohibition on circulating of petitions by certain persons

No county recorder or justice of the peace and no person other than a person who is qualified to register to vote pursuant to section 16-101 may circulate a recall petition, and all signatures verified by any such unqualified person are void and shall not be counted in determining the legal sufficiency of the petition.

19-205.03. Prohibition on signing petition for profit; classification

Any person who knowingly gives or receives money or any other thing of value for signing a recall petition, excluding payments made to a person for circulating such petition, is guilty of a class 1 misdemeanor.

19-206. Coercion or other unlawful acts; classification

A. A person who knowingly induces or compels any other person, either directly or indirectly or by menace or threat that he will or may be injured in his business, or discharged from employment, or that he will not be employed, to sign or subscribe, or to refrain from signing or subscribing, his name to a recall petition, or, after signing or subscribing his name, to have his name taken therefrom, is guilty of a class 1 misdemeanor.

B. A person knowingly signing any name other than his own to a petition, except in a circumstance where he signs for a person, in the presence of and at the specific request of such person, who is incapable of signing his own name, because of physical infirmity or knowingly signing his name more than once for the same recall issue, at one election, or who knowingly is not at the time of signing a qualified elector of this state is guilty of a class 1 misdemeanor.

19-207. Notice to officer; statement of defense

Upon filing the petition as prescribed by section 19-208.03, subsection A, paragraph 1, the officer with whom it is filed shall within forty-eight hours, excluding Saturdays, Sundays or other legal holidays, give written notice to the person against whom it is filed. The notice shall state that a recall petition has been filed, shall set forth the grounds thereof, and shall notify the person to whom it is addressed that the person has the right to prepare and have printed on the ballot a statement containing not more than two hundred words defending the person's official conduct. If the person fails to deliver the defensive statement to the officer giving notice within ten days thereafter, the right to have a statement printed on the ballot shall be considered waived.

19-208. Resignation of person

If a person against whom a recall petition is filed desires to resign, the person may do so by filing a written tender thereof with the officer with whom the petition demanding the person's recall is filed within five days, excluding Saturdays, Sundays and other legal holidays, after the filing of the petition as prescribed by section 19-208.03. In such event the person's resignation shall be accepted and the vacancy shall be filled as provided by law.

19-208.01. Certification of number of signatures

A. Within ten days after submission of a recall petition for verification of signatures pursuant to section 19-203, the receiving officer shall perform the steps prescribed in section 19-121.01, subsection A. If the total number of signatures eligible for verification equals or exceeds the minimum number required by the Arizona Constitution the receiving officer shall reproduce a facsimile of the front of each signature sheet on which any signature eligible for verification appears. The receiving officer shall transmit promptly to each county recorder facsimile sheets on which a signature of any individual claiming to be a qualified elector of that county appears. The receiving officer shall also certify the number of sheets and signatures on the sheets that are being transmitted and retain a record of such certification in his office. Such receiving officer shall obtain a dated, signed receipt from the county recorder for copies of the original signature sheets transmitted under this section.

B. If the number of signatures on the sheets submitted to the receiving officer does not equal the minimum number required by the constitution, he shall so notify the person or organization submitting them and shall return the sheets to the persons or organization.

19-208.02. Certification by county recorder

A. Within sixty days after receipt of the signature sheets from the receiving officer, the county recorder shall determine the number of signatures or affidavits of individuals whose names were transmitted that must be disqualified for any of the reasons set forth in section 19-121.02, subsection A, and the county recorder shall certify such number to the receiving officer in the form prescribed by the secretary of state.

B. At the time of such certification, the county recorder shall:

1. Return the original signature sheets to the receiving officer, obtaining a dated, signed receipt therefor.

2. Send notice of the results of certification by mail to the person or organization that submitted the recall petitions and to the secretary of state.

19-208.03. Disposition of petition; date of filing

A. Within five days, excluding Saturday, Sunday and legal holidays, after the county recorders have certified the number of qualified signatures to a petition, or sooner if a sufficient number of signatures have been certified to qualify for placement of the recall on the ballot, the receiving officer shall total the number of signatures certified, and:

1. If the number equals or exceeds the minimum number required by the Constitution, he shall forthwith officially file the petition, notify the governor and each county recorder affected, stating that no more signatures need be checked, and the recall shall be placed on the ballot in the manner provided by law.

2. If the number is insufficient to qualify for calling a recall election the receiving officer shall follow the procedure prescribed by section 19-208.01, subsection B.

B. The date of filing the petition as provided for in subsection A, paragraph 1, of this section is the date of filing referred to in sections 19-207, 19-208 and 19-209.

19-208.04. Judicial review of actions by county recorder

A. If the county recorder fails to comply with the provisions of section 19-208.02, any elector may apply, within ten calendar days after such refusal, to the superior court for a writ of mandamus to compel him to do so. If the court finds that the county recorder has not complied with the provisions of section 19-208.02, the court shall issue an order for the county recorder to comply.

B. If an elector wishes to challenge the number of signatures certified by the county recorder under the provisions of section 19-208.02, he shall, within ten calendar days after the receiving officer has notified the governor and the county recorders of the number of certified signatures received by him, commence an action in the superior court for a determination thereon. The action shall be advanced on the calendar and heard and decided by the court as soon as possible. Either party may appeal to the supreme court within ten calendar days after judgment.

C. An action filed in the superior court under the provisions of this section against a county recorder shall be filed in the county of such county recorder, except that when any such action involves more than one county recorder such action shall be filed in Maricopa county.

19-208.05. Special fund for reimbursement of county recorders

A. Receiving officers shall establish a separate fund from which county recorders shall be reimbursed for actual expenses incurred by county recorders for performance of duties under section 19-208.02, but not to exceed the rate of fifty cents per signature.

B. A county recorder who claims to be entitled to reimbursement under the provisions of this section shall submit a claim to the receiving officer.

C. The special fund established pursuant to this section shall be exempt from the provisions of section 35-190, relating to lapsing of appropriations.

19-209. Order for special recall election

A. If the officer against whom a petition is filed does not resign within five days, excluding Saturdays, Sundays and other legal holidays, after the filing as determined pursuant to section 19-208.03, the order calling a special recall election shall be issued within fifteen days and shall be ordered to be held on the next following consolidated election date pursuant to section 16-204 that is ninety days or more after the order calling the election.

B. A recall election shall be called:

1. If for a state office, including a member of the legislature, by the governor.

2. If for a county officer, or judge or other officer of the superior

court in a county, by the board of supervisors of that county.

3. If for a city or town officer, by the legislative body of the city or town.

4. If for a member of a school district governing board, by the county school superintendent of the county in which the school district is located.

C. If a recall petition is against an officer who is directed by this section to call the election it shall be called:

1. If for a state office, by the secretary of state.

2. If for a county office, by the clerk of the superior court.

3. If for a city or town office, by the city or town clerk.

19-210. Reimbursement for county expenses in conducting special recall election

The political subdivision or district in which a public officer subject to recall serves shall reimburse the county for all expenses incurred in conducting the special recall election.

19-212. Nomination petition; form; filing

A. Unless the officer otherwise requests in writing, the name of the officer against whom a recall petition is filed shall be placed as a candidate on the official ballot without nomination. Other candidates for the office may be nominated to be voted upon at the election and shall be placed upon the official recall ballot after filing a nomination petition that is signed by a number of qualified electors that is equal to at least two per cent of the total votes cast for all candidates for that office at the last election for that office. Nomination petition signers shall be qualified electors of the electoral district of the officer against whom the recall petition is filed.

B. The title and body of the nomination petition shall be substantially in the following form:

Nomination Petition--Recall Election

We, the undersigned electors, qualified to vote in the recall election mentioned herein, residents of the precinct indicated by the residence addresses given, and residents of the county of ______, state of Arizona, hereby nominate ______, who resides at ____, in the county of ______ to be a candidate in the recall election for the office of ______ to be held on ________________________________, and we further declare that

(date)

we have not signed and will not sign any nomination paper for any other person for such office.

The remainder of the petition shall be substantially in the form prescribed in section 16-315.

C. If recall petitions have been filed against more than one member of a multimember public body whose members serve at large, the nomination petition and paper of the other candidates shall state which member they oppose.

D. To each nomination petition shall be appended a certificate by a person who is qualified to register to vote pursuant to section 16-101 stating that to the best of his knowledge and belief all the signers of the nomination petition are qualified electors of the precinct which they give as their residence. E. Such nomination petition shall be filed not more than ninety days nor less than sixty days prior to the date of the recall election.

19-213. Form and contents of ballot

On the ballots for the election shall be printed the reasons as set forth in the petition for demanding the officer's recall, and, in not more than two hundred words, the officer's justification of his conduct in office. There shall be no party designation upon the recall ballot. The form of the ballot shall conform as nearly as practicable to the ballot prescribed for general elections.

19-214. Recall election board; consolidation of precincts

A. A recall election board shall consist of one inspector and two judges who, together with two clerks, shall be appointed for each precinct if for a state or county election and shall be paid in the same manner as election boards.

B. If for a city or town election, the recall election board shall be appointed by the clerk of the city or town and shall be paid in the same manner as city or town election boards.

C. If for a trustee of a school district, the recall election board shall be appointed by the county school superintendent, and shall be paid from school district funds in the same manner as election boards for state or county elections.

D. Two or more precincts may be consolidated for purposes of voting if determined practicable and reasonable by the appointing authority.

19-215. General election laws applicable

The powers and duties conferred or imposed by law upon boards of election, registration officers, canvassing boards and other public officials who conduct general elections, are conferred and imposed upon similar officers conducting recall elections under the provisions of this article together with the penalties prescribed for the breach thereof.

19-216. Election results

A. The candidate receiving the largest number of votes shall be declared elected for the remainder of the term and shall begin serving the remainder of the term on his qualification for the office and on completion of the canvass. Unless the incumbent receives the largest number of votes he shall be deemed removed from office upon qualification of his successor. If the incumbent's successor does not qualify within five days after the results of the election have been declared, the office shall be vacant, and may be filled as provided by law.

B. The incumbent shall continue to perform the duties of his office until the completion of the canvass of the election returns.

19-217. Recall petition; changes; applicability

Notwithstanding any other law, any change in the law or procedure adopted by a governing body with respect to circulation or filing of recall petitions after a recall petition application is submitted pursuant to section 19-202.01 for a state officer, a member of Congress, a county or district officer, a superior court judge, a city or town officer or a member of a school district governing board does not apply to the recall petition.

CALIFORNIA STATUTES

(See Appendix F)

COLORADO CONSTITUTION

Article XXI, Section 1 et sec. Beginning with State Officers May be Recalled.

Section 1
Section 2
Section 3
Section 4

Article XXI
Recall from Office

Section 1. State officers may be recalled. Every elective public officer of the state of Colorado may be recalled from office at any time by the registered electors entitled to vote for a successor of such incumbent through the procedure and in the manner herein provided for, which procedure shall be known as the recall, and shall be in addition to and without excluding any other method of removal provided by law.

The procedure hereunder to effect the recall of an elective public officer shall be as follows:

A petition signed by registered electors entitled to vote for a successor of the incumbent sought to be recalled, equal in number to twentyˇfive percent of the entire vote cast at the last preceding election for all candidates for the position which the incumbent sought to be recalled occupies, demanding an election of the successor to the officer named in said petition, shall be filed in the office in which petitions for nominations to office held by the incumbent sought to be recalled are required to be filed; provided, if more than one person is required by law to be elected to fill the office of which the person sought to be recalled is an incumbent, then the said petition shall be signed by registered electors entitled to vote for a successor to the incumbent sought to be recalled equal in number to twentyˇfive percent of the entire vote cast at the last preceding general election for all candidates for the office, to which the incumbent sought to be recalled was elected as one of the officers thereof, said entire vote being divided by the number of all officers elected to such office, at the last preceding general election; and such petition shall contain a general statement, in not more than two hundred words, of the ground or grounds on which such recall is sought, which statement is intended for the information of the registered electors, and the registered electors shall be the sole and exclusive judges of the legality, reasonableness and sufficiency of such ground or grounds assigned for such recall, and said ground or grounds shall not be open to review.

Section 2. Form of recall petition. Any recall petition may be circulated and signed in sections, provided each section shall contain a full and accurate copy of the title and text of the petition; and such recall petition shall be filed in the office in which petitions for nominations to office held by the incumbent sought to be recalled are required to be filed.

The signatures to such recall petition need not all be on one sheet of paper, but each signer must add to his signature the date of his signing said petition, and his place of residence, giving his street number, if any, should he reside in a town or city. The person circulating such sheet must make and subscribe an oath on said sheet that the signatures thereon are genuine, and a false oath, willfully so made and subscribed by such person, shall be perjury and be punished as such. All petitions shall be deemed and held to be sufficient if they appear to be signed by the requisite number of signers, and such signers shall be deemed and held to be registered electors, unless a protest in writing under oath shall be filed in the office in which such petition has been filed, by some registered elector, within fifteen days after such petition is filed, setting forth specifically the grounds of such protest, whereupon the officer with whom such petition is filed shall forthwith mail a copy of such protest to the person or persons named in such petition as representing the signers thereof, together with a notice fixing a time for hearing such protest not less than five nor more than ten days after such notice is mailed. All hearings shall be before the officer with whom such protest is filed, and all testimony shall be under oath. Such hearings shall be summary and not subject to delay, and must be concluded within thirty days after such petition is filed, and the result thereof shall be forthwith certified to the person or persons representing the signers of such petition. In case the petition is not sufficient it may be withdrawn by the person or a majority of the persons representing the signers of such petition, and may, within fifteen days thereafter, be amended and refiled as an original petition. The finding as to the sufficiency of any petition may be reviewed by any state court of general jurisdiction in the county in which such petition is filed, upon application of the person or a majority of the persons representing the signers of such petition, but such review shall be had and determined forthwith. The sufficiency, or the determination of the sufficiency, of the petition referred to in this section shall not be held, or construed, to refer to the ground or grounds assigned in such petition for the recall of the incumbent sought to be recalled from office thereby.

When such petition is sufficient, the officer with whom such recall petition was filed, shall forthwith submit said petition, together with a certificate of its sufficiency to the governor, who shall thereupon order and fix the date for holding the election not less than thirty days nor more than sixty days from the date of submission of said petition; provided, if a general election is to be held within ninety days after the date of submission of said petition, the recall election shall be held as part of said general election.

Section 3. Resignation ˇ filling vacancy. If such officer shall offer his resignation, it shall be accepted, and the vacancy caused by such resignation, or from any other cause, shall be filled as provided by law; but the person appointed to fill such vacancy shall hold his office only until the person elected at the recall election shall qualify. If such officer shall not resign within five days after the sufficiency of the recall petition shall have been sustained, the governor shall make or cause to be made publication of notice for the holding of such election, and officers charged by law with duties concerning elections shall make all arrangements for such election, and the same shall be conducted, returned and the result thereof declared in all respects as in the case of general elections.

On the official ballot at such elections shall be printed in not more than 200 words, the reasons set forth in the petition for demanding his recall, and in not more than three hundred words there shall also be printed, if desired by him, the officer's justification of his course in office. If such officer shall resign at any time subsequent to the filing thereof, the recall election shall be called notwithstanding such resignation.

There shall be printed on the official ballot, as to every officer whose recall is to be voted on, the words, "Shall (name of person against whom the recall petition is filed) be recalled from the office of (title of the office)?" Following such question shall be the words, "Yes" and "No", on separate lines, with a blank space at the right of each, in which the voter shall indicate, by marking a cross (X), his vote for or against such recall.

On such ballots, under each question, there shall also be printed the names of those persons who have been nominated as candidates to succeed the person sought to be recalled; but no vote cast shall be counted for any candidate for such office, unless the voter also voted for or against the recall of such person sought to be recalled from said office. The name of the person against whom the petition is filed shall not appear on the ballot as a candidate for the office.

If a majority of those voting on said question of the recall of any incumbent from office shall vote "no", said incumbent shall continue in said office; if a majority shall vote "yes", such incumbent shall thereupon be deemed removed from such office upon the qualification of his successor.

If the vote had in such recall elections shall recall the officer then the candidate who has received the highest number of votes for the office thereby vacated shall be declared elected for the remainder of the term, and a certificate of election shall be forthwith issued to him by the canvassing board. In case the person who received the highest number of votes shall fail to qualify within fifteen days after the issuance of a certificate of election, the office shall be deemed vacant, and shall be filled according to law.

Candidates for the office may be nominated by petition, as now provided by law, which petition shall be filed in the office in which petitions for nomination to office are required by law to be filed not less than fifteen days before such recall election.

Section 4. Limitation ˇ municipal corporations may adopt, when. No recall petition shall be circulated or filed against any officer until he has actually held his office for at least six months, save and except it may be filed against any member of the state legislature at any time after five days from the convening and organizing of the legislature after his election.

After one recall petition and election, no further petition shall be filed against the same officer during the term for which he was elected, unless the petitioners signing said petition shall equal fifty percent of the votes cast at the last preceding general election for all of the candidates for the office held by such officer as herein above defined.

In any recall election of a state elective officer, if the incumbent whose recall is sought is not recalled, he shall be repaid from the state treasury for the expenses of such election in the manner provided by law. The general assembly may establish procedures for the reimbursement by a local governmental entity of expenses incurred by an incumbent elective officer of such governmental entity whose recall is sought but who is not recalled.

If the governor is sought to be recalled under the provisions of this article, the duties herein imposed upon him shall be performed by the lieutenantˇgovernor; and if the secretary of state is sought to be recalled, the duties herein imposed upon him, shall be performed by the state auditor.

The recall may also be exercised by the registered electors of each county, city and county, city and town of the state, with reference to the elective officers thereof, under such procedure as shall be provided by law.

Until otherwise provided by law, the legislative body of any such county, city and county, city and town may provide for the manner of exercising such recall powers in such counties, cities and counties, cities and towns, but shall not require any such recall to be signed by registered electors more in number than twenty-five percent of the entire vote cast at the last preceding election, as in section 1 hereof more particularly set forth, for all the candidates for office which the incumbent sought to be recalled occupies, as herein above defined.

Every person having authority to exercise or exercising any public or governmental duty, power or function, shall be an elective officer, or one appointed, drawn or designated in accordance with law by an elective officer or officers, or by some board, commission, person or persons legally appointed by an elective officer or officers, each of which said elective officers shall be subject to the recall provision of this constitution; provided, that, subject to regulation by law, any person may, without compensation therefor, file petitions, or complaints in courts concerning crimes, or do police duty only in cases of immediate danger to person or property.

Nothing herein contained shall be construed as affecting or limiting the present or future powers of cities and counties or cities having charters adopted under the authority given by the constitution, except as in the last three preceding paragraphs expressed.

In the submission to the electors of any petition proposed under this article, all officers shall be guided by the general laws of the state, except as otherwise herein provided.

This article is self-executing, but legislation may be enacted to facilitate its operations, but in no way limiting or restricting the provisions of this article, or the powers herein reserved.

COLORADO REVISED STATUTES
Section 1-12-101 et sec. Beginning with Elected Officers Subject to Recall.

Colo. Rev. Statutes, Section 1-12-101
Colo. Rev. Statutes, Section 1-12-102
Colo. Rev. Statutes, Section 1-12-103
Colo. Rev. Statutes, Section 1-12-104
Colo. Rev. Statutes, Section 1-12-105
Colo. Rev. Statutes, Section 1-12-106
Colo. Rev. Statutes, Section 1-12-107
Colo. Rev. Statutes, Section 1-12-108
Colo. Rev. Statutes, Section 1-12-109
Colo. Rev. Statutes, Section 1-12-110
Colo. Rev. Statutes, Section 1-12-111
Colo. Rev. Statutes, Section 1-12-112
Colo. Rev. Statutes, Section 1-12-113
Colo. Rev. Statutes, Section 1-12-114
Colo. Rev. Statutes, Section 1-12-115
Colo. Rev. Statutes, Section 1-12-116
Colo. Rev. Statutes, Section 1-12-117
Colo. Rev. Statutes, Section 1-12-118
Colo. Rev. Statutes, Section 1-12-119
Colo. Rev. Statutes, Section 1-12-120
Colo. Rev. Statutes, Section 1-12-121
Colo. Rev. Statutes, Section 1-12-122
Colo. Rev. Statutes, Section 1-12-123

1-12-101. Elected officers subject to recall

Every elected officer of this state or any political subdivision thereof is subject to recall from office at any time by the eligible electors entitled to vote for a successor to the incumbent.

The recall of any state officer shall be governed by the recall of state officers procedure set forth in this article.

1-12-102. Limitations

(1) No recall petition shall be circulated or filed against any elected officer until the officer has actually held office for at least six months following the last election; except that a recall petition may be filed against any member of the general assembly at any time after the fifth day following the convening and organizing of the general assembly after the election.

(2) After one recall petition and election, no further petition may be filed against the same state or county officer during the term for which the officer was elected, unless the petitioners signing the petition equal fifty percent of the votes cast at the last preceding general election for all of the candidates for the office held by the officer.

(3) After one recall petition and election, no further petition shall be filed against the same nonpartisan officer during the term for which the officer was elected, unless the petitioners signing the petition equal one and one-half times the number of signatures required on the first petition filed against the same officer, until one year has elapsed from the date of the previous recall election.

(4) No recall petition shall be circulated or filed against any elected officer whose term of office will expire within six months.

1-12-103. Petition for recall

Eligible electors of a political subdivision may initiate the recall of an elected official by signing a petition which demands the election of a successor to the officer named in the petition. The petition shall contain a general statement, consisting of two hundred words or less, stating the ground or grounds on which the recall is sought. The statement is for the information of the electors who shall be the sole and exclusive judges of the legality, reasonableness, and sufficiency of the ground or grounds assigned for the recall. The ground or grounds shall not be open to review.

1-12-104. Signatures required for state and county officers

(1) A petition to recall a state or county officer shall be signed by eligible electors equal in number to twenty-five percent of the entire vote cast at the last preceding general election for all candidates for the office which the incumbent sought to be recalled occupies.

(2) If more than one person is required by law to be elected to fill the office to which the person sought to be recalled is an incumbent, then the petition shall be signed by eligible electors entitled to vote for a successor to the incumbent sought to be recalled equal in number to twenty-five percent of the entire vote cast at the last preceding general election for all candidates for the office to which the incumbent sought to be recalled was elected, the entire vote being divided by the number of all officers elected to the office at the last preceding general election.

1-12-105. Signatures required for school district officers

A petition to recall a school district officer shall be signed by eligible electors of the school district equal in number to at least forty percent of those electors who voted in such district in the last preceding election at which the director to be recalled was elected as indicated by the pollbook or abstract for such election. If no such election was held, such petition shall be signed by eligible electors of the school district equal in number to at least ten percent of those electors residing within the school district on the date that the form of the petition is approved under section 1-12-108(4). In no case shall the number required for recall be less than ten percent of eligible electors qualified to vote in the most recent biennial school election; except that no more than fifteen thousand signatures shall be required.

1-12-106. Signatures required for nonpartisan officers

A petition to recall any other nonpartisan officer shall be signed by three hundred eligible electors of the political subdivision who are entitled to vote for a successor to the incumbent sought to be recalled or forty percent of the eligible electors of the political subdivision at the time the form of the petition is approved under section 1-12-108(4), whichever number is less.

1-12-107. Designated election officials

(1) For state recall elections, the petition shall be filed with the secretary of state who shall certify the sufficiency of the petition to the governor who shall set the date for the election. The election shall be conducted by the appropriate county clerk and recorder in the manner provided in this article for state elections.

(2) For county recall elections, the petition shall be filed with the county clerk and recorder who shall certify the sufficiency of the petition and call and conduct the election.

(3) For school board recall elections, the petition shall be filed with the county clerk and recorder in which the school district's administrative offices are located. The clerk and recorder of the county shall certify the sufficiency of the petition and call and conduct the election.

(4) For all other nonpartisan elections, the petition shall be filed with the district court in the county in which the political subdivision was organized. The court shall then appoint a designated election official to certify the sufficiency of the petition and call and conduct the election.

1-12-108. Petition requirements

(1) The petition shall be prepared and circulated pursuant to this part 1. No signature shall be counted that was placed on a petition prior to approval of the petition by the designated election official or more than sixty days after the designated election official's approval of the petition.

(2)(a) The petition for the recall of an elected official may consist of one or more sheets, to be fastened together in the form of one petition section, but each sheet shall contain the same heading and each petition section shall contain one sworn affidavit of the circulator. No petition shall contain the name of more than one person proposed to be recalled from office.

(b) The petition for recall may be circulated and signed in sections, and each section shall contain a full and accurate copy of the title and text of the petition. Each petition shall designate, by name and address, three persons, referred to in this section as the "committee", that shall represent the signers in all matters affecting the petition.

(3)(a) The signatures to a recall petition need not all be appended to one paper, but no petition shall be legal that does not contain the requisite number of names of eligible electors whose names do not appear on any other petition previously filed for the recall of the same person under the provisions of this section.

(b) At the top of each page shall be printed, in bold-faced type, the following:

WARNING:
IT IS AGAINST THE LAW:

For anyone to sign this petition with any name other than one's own or to knowingly sign one's name more than once for the same measure or to knowingly sign the petition when not a registered elector.

Do not sign this petition unless you are an eligible elector. To be an eligible elector you must be registered to vote and eligible to vote in (name of political subdivision) elections.

Do not sign this petition unless you have read or have had read to you the proposed recall measure in its entirety and understand its meaning.

(c) Directly following the warning in paragraph (b) of this subsection (3) shall be printed in bold-faced type the following:

Petition to recall (name of person sought to be recalled) from the office of (title of office).

(4) No petition shall be circulated until it has been approved as meeting the requirements of this subsection (4) as to form. The official with whom the petitions are to be filed pursuant to section 1-12-107 shall approve or disapprove a petition as to form by the close of the second business day following submission of the proposed petition. The official shall mail written notice of the action taken to the person who submitted the petition and to the officer whom the petition seeks to recall on the day the action is taken.

(5)(a) Every petition shall be signed only by eligible electors.

(b) Unless physically unable, all electors shall sign their own signature and shall print their names, respective residence addresses, including the street number and name, the city or town, the county, and the date of signature. Each signature on a petition shall be made, to the extent possible, in black ink.

(c) Any person, except a circulator, may assist an elector who is physically unable to sign the petition in completing the information on the petition as required by law. On the petition immediately following the name of the disabled elector, the person providing assistance shall both sign and state that the assistance was given to the disabled elector.

(6)(a) Only an eligible elector may circulate a recall petition.

(b) To each petition section shall be attached a signed, notarized, and dated affidavit executed by the eligible elector who circulated the petition section, which shall include: The affiant's printed name, the address at which the affiant resides, including the street name and number, the city or town, the county, and the date of signature; a statement that the affiant was an eligible elector at the time the section of the petition was circulated and signed by the listed electors; a statement that the affiant circulated the section of the petition; a statement that each signature on the petition section is the signature of the person whose name it purports to be; a statement that to the best of the affiant's knowledge and belief each of the persons signing the petition section was, at the time of signing, an eligible elector; and a statement that the affiant has not paid or will not in the future pay and that the affiant believes that no other person has paid or will pay, directly or indirectly, any money or other thing of value to any signer for the purpose of inducing or causing the signer to sign the petition.

(c) The designated election official shall not accept for filing any section of a petition that does not have attached to it the notarized affidavit required by this section. Any signature added to a section of a petition after the affidavit has been executed is invalid.

(7) Deleted by Laws 1997, S.B.97-31, ß 5, eff. May 27, 1997.

(7.5) The petition may be filed at any time during the sixty-day period after the designated election official's approval of the petition form as specified in subsection (1) of this section.

The committee shall file all sections of a petition simultaneously, and any section of a petition submitted after the petition is filed shall be invalid and of no force and effect.

(8)(a) Upon filing, the designated election official for the political subdivision shall review all petition information and verify the information against the registration records, and, where applicable, the county assessor's records. The secretary of state shall establish guidelines for verifying petition entries.

(b) Any disassembly of a section of the petition prior to filing that has the effect of separating the affidavits from the signatures shall render that section of the petition invalid and of no force and effect.

(c) After review, and no later than ten working days after the initial filing of the petition, the designated election official shall notify the committee and the incumbent of the number of valid signatures and whether the petition appears to be sufficient or insufficient. Upon determining that the petition is sufficient and after the time for protest has passed, the designated election official shall certify the recall question to the ballot and, if the election is a coordinated election, notify the coordinated election official.

(9)(a) A recall petition that has been verified by the designated election official shall be held to be sufficient unless a protest in writing under oath is filed in the office of the designated election official by an eligible elector within fifteen days after the designated election official has determined the sufficiency or insufficiency of the petition under paragraph (c) of subsection (8) of this section. The petition shall set forth specific grounds for the protest. Grounds include but are not limited to failure of any portion of a petition or circulator affidavit to meet the requirements of this article or any conduct on the part of petition circulators that substantially misleads persons signing the petition. The designated election official shall forthwith mail a copy of the protest to the committee named in the petition as representing the signers, together with a notice fixing a time for hearing the protest not less than five nor more than ten days after the notice is mailed. Every hearing shall be before the designated election official with whom the protest is filed or before a district judge sitting in that county if the designated election official is the subject of the recall. The testimony in every hearing shall be under oath. The hearing shall be summary and not subject to delay and shall be concluded within thirty days after the petition is filed, and the result shall be forthwith certified to the committee.

(b) The party filing a protest has the burden of sustaining the protest by a preponderance of the evidence. The decision upon matters of substance is open to review, if prompt application is made, as provided in section 1-1-113. The remedy in all cases shall be summary, and the decision of any court having jurisdiction shall be final and not subject to review by any other court; except that the supreme court, in the exercise of its discretion, may review any judicial proceeding in a summary way.

(c) A petition for recall may be amended once at any time within sixty days from the date the petition form was approved by the designated election official under subsection (4) of this section.

(d)(I) Any signer may request that his or her name be stricken from the petition at any time within the sixty-day period prior to the date the petition is deemed sufficient and the time for protest has passed by filing a written request that his or her signature be stricken with the designated election official and delivering a copy of such request to at least one member of the committee. If such request is delivered to the member of the committee or the election official through the United States mails, it shall be deemed delivered to the committee or the election official on the date shown by the cancellation mark on the envelope containing the request received by the member or the election official. If the request is delivered to the member of the committee or the election official in any other manner, it shall be deemed delivered to the committee or the election official on the date of delivery and stamped receipt by the election official.

(II) If the designated election official receives a written request filed in accordance with this paragraph (d) after the petition is filed but before the petition is deemed sufficient and the time for protest has passed, the election official shall strike the signature of the signer who filed the request. If the election official receives such a written request before the petition is filed, the election official shall strike the signature of the signer who filed the request promptly upon the filing of the petition.

(10) Any person who willfully destroys, defaces, mutilates, or suppresses a petition, or who willfully neglects to file or delays delivery of a petition, or who conceals or removes a petition from the possession of the person authorized by law to have custody of it, or who aids, counsels, procures, or assists any person in doing any of the above acts is guilty of a misdemeanor and, upon conviction thereof, shall be punished as provided in section 1-13- 111.

1-12-109. Resignation

If an officer whose recall is sought offers a resignation it shall be accepted and the vacancy caused by the resignation shall be filled as provided by law. The person appointed to fill the vacancy caused by the resignation shall hold the office only until the person elected at the recall election is qualified.

1-12-110. Call for election

(1) If the officer whose recall is sought does not resign within five days after the sufficiency of the recall petition has been

sustained, the designated election official shall make notice by publication for the holding of a recall election, and the officers charged by law with election duties shall make necessary arrangements for the conduct of the election. The election shall be conducted pursuant to the provisions of this title.

(2) If the officer whose recall is sought resigns at any time after the filing of the certification of election question for the ballot, the recall election shall be called and held notwithstanding the resignation.

1-12-111. Date of election

If the recall petition is held to be sufficient under section 1-12-108(8)(c) and after the time for protest has passed, the officer with whom the recall petition was filed, without delay, shall submit the petition, together with a certificate of its sufficiency, to the appropriate governing body. The governing body shall set a date for the recall election not less than forty- five nor more than seventy-five days from the date of determination of sufficiency; however, if a general election is to be held within ninety days after the determination of sufficiency, the recall election shall be held as a part of the general election.

1-12-112. Ballots

(1) In addition to all other requirements of law, the official ballot shall contain a statement consisting of two hundred words or less stating the reasons set forth in the petition for demanding the officer's recall. The officer sought to be recalled may submit a statement of justification of the officer's course in conduct in three hundred words or less to the designated election official. The officer shall submit any such statement no later than ten working days after the date of issuance of the certificate of sufficiency by the designated election official. The official ballot shall contain such statement of justification if submitted pursuant to this subsection (1).

(2) Ballots for the election of a successor to the officer sought to be recalled shall contain the candidates' names which shall be placed on the ballot by lot, regardless of the method of nomination.

1-12-113. Conduct of election

The recall election and election of a successor shall be conducted according to the provisions of articles 1 to 13 of this title.

1-12-114. Absentee ballots

Applications for absentee ballots shall be made available by the appropriate designated election officials no later than twenty-four hours after the date for the recall election is set. Absentee ballots shall be available no later than thirty days before the recall election. All other provisions of article 8 of this title shall apply to the absentee ballot process.

1-12-115. Write-in candidates

No write-in vote for any office shall be counted unless an affidavit of intent has been filed indicating that the person desires the office and is legally qualified to assume the duties of the office if elected. The affidavit of intent shall be filed with the designated election official not later than the date required for filing nominating petitions pursuant to section 1-12-117.

1-12-116. Sufficiency of the recall

If a majority of those voting on the question of the recall of any incumbent from office vote "no", the incumbent shall continue in office; if a majority vote "yes", the incumbent shall be removed from office upon the qualification of the successor.

1-12-117. Nomination of successor

A candidate to succeed the officer sought to be recalled shall meet the qualifications of a party candidate or an unaffiliated candidate as provided in part 8 of article 4 of this title and shall be nominated by a political party petition or an unaffiliated petition as provided in part 9 of article 4 of this title. Nomination petitions and affidavits of intent to run as a write-in candidate shall be filed no later than fifteen days after the date on which the appropriate governing body convenes and sets the election date. Every petition shall be signed by the number of eligible electors required for the office in part 8 of article 4 of this title or as otherwise provided by law. The name of the officer who was sought to be recalled shall not be eligible as a candidate in the election to fill any vacancy resulting from the recall election.

1-12-118. Election of successor

(1) The election of a successor shall be held at the same time as the recall election. The names of those persons nominated as candidates to succeed the person sought to be recalled shall appear on the ballot; but, no vote cast shall be counted for any candidate for the office unless the voter also voted for or against the recall of the person sought to be recalled. The name of the person against whom the petition is filed shall not appear on the ballot as a candidate for office.

(2) Deleted by Laws 1995, H.B.95-1241, ß 77, eff. July 1, 1995.

1-12-119. Canvass of votes

(1) For the recall of a partisan officer, the canvass board shall be composed of one representative from each major political party and the county clerk and recorder. For the recall of a nonpartisan officer, the canvass board shall be composed of the designated election official, one member of the governing body, and one eligible elector of the political subdivision.

(2) The canvass board shall complete an abstract of votes cast no later than the day following the recall election. For

state elections, the canvass board shall contact the secretary of state on election night with the unofficial count. For county and all other elections, the canvass board shall provide the governing body with the unofficial count at the opening of business hours on the day following the recall election.

(3) The certified abstract of votes cast shall be sent by certified mail or hand delivered to the secretary of state for state elections and to the governing body for county and all other elections no later than the close of business on the fifth day after the recall election.

(4) If the majority of those voting on the recall question voted "yes", upon receipt of the certified abstract of votes cast, the designated election official shall issue a certificate of election to the successor candidate who received the highest number of votes. A copy of the certificate shall be transmitted by the secretary of state to the appropriate house of the general assembly for recall elections concerning the general assembly and to the governor for the recall of all other elections of state officers. For all other recall elections, a copy of the certificate shall be transmitted to the governing body of the political subdivision.

1-12-120. Cost of recall election

(1) If at any recall election for a state office the incumbent whose recall is sought is not recalled, the incumbent shall be repaid from the state treasury any money authorized by this article which the incumbent actually expended as an expense of the recall election. In no event shall the sum repaid be greater than an amount equal to ten cents per voter. The general assembly shall provide an appropriation for state recall elections.

(2) If at any recall election for a county or local government office the incumbent whose recall is sought is not recalled, the governing body shall authorize a resolution for repayment

from the general fund of the political subdivision any money authorized to be repaid to the incumbent by this article which the incumbent actually expended as an expense of the election. In no event shall the sum repaid exceed forty cents per eligible elector as defined in section 1-1-104(16), subject to a maximum repayment of ten thousand dollars.

(3) Authorized expenses shall include, but are not limited to, moneys spent in challenging the sufficiency of the recall petition and in presenting to the electors the official position of the incumbent, including campaign literature, advertising, and maintaining campaign headquarters.

(4) Unauthorized expenses shall include, but are not limited to: Moneys spent on challenges and court actions not pertaining to the sufficiency of the recall petition; personal expenses for meals; lodging and mileage for the incumbent; costs of maintaining a campaign staff and associated expenses; reimbursement for expenses incurred by a campaign committee which has solicited contributions; reimbursement of any kind for employees in the incumbent's office; and all expenses incurred prior to the filing of the recall petition.

(5) The incumbent shall file a complete and detailed request for reimbursement within sixty days after the date of the recall election with the governing body of the political subdivision holding the recall election, who shall then review the reimbursement request for appropriateness under subsection (2) of this section and shall refer the request, with recommendations, to the general assembly at its next general session for state recall elections or to the treasurer of the governing body for all other elections within thirty days after receipt of the request for reimbursement.

1-12-121. Special provisions
(1) If the governor is sought to be recalled under the provisions of this article by recall petition filed in the office of the secretary of state, the duties imposed upon the governor by

this article and article XXI of the state constitution as to that recall petition shall be performed by the lieutenant governor. If the secretary of state is sought to be recalled under the provisions of this article by recall petition filed in the office of the secretary of state, the duties imposed upon the secretary of state by this article and article XXI of the state constitution as to that recall petition shall be performed by the state auditor.

(2) If the recall of any other elected or appointed officer is sought who is charged with responsibilities under this article, the governing body shall appoint another officer to perform such duties.

1-12-122. Recalls subject to "Fair Campaign Practices Act"

Recall elections are subject to the appropriate sections of article 45 of this title.

1-12-123. Constitutional requirements for recall of state officers

To the extent that the provisions of this part 1 concerning the recall of state officers conflict with the provisions of article XXI of the state constitution, the provisions of article XXI of the state constitution shall control.

GEORGIA CONSTITUTION
Article II, Section II, Paragraph IV.

Paragraph IV. Recall of public officials holding elective office.

The General Assembly is hereby authorized to provide by general law for the recall of public officials who hold elective office. The procedures, grounds, and all other matters relative to such recall shall be provided for in such law.

GEORGIA CODE

Chapter 21, Section 4-1 et sec.

Beginning with This Chapter shall be known and may be cited as the 'Recall Act of 1989'.

21-4-1.
This chapter shall be known and may be cited as the 'Recall Act of 1989.

21-4-2.
The General Assembly finds that the electorate of the state overwhelmingly ratified an amendment to the Constitution of Georgia at the general election in November, 1978, authorizing the General Assembly to provide by general law for uniform and exclusive procedures to recall public officials

who hold elective office and to repeal all local recall laws and prohibit the future enactment of any local recall laws. In furtherance of the mandate of the electorate, by this general law the General Assembly establishes uniform and exclusive procedures relating to the recall of all state and local officials who hold elective office.

21-4-3.
As used in this chapter, the term:
(1) 'Elected county school board members' and 'elected county school superintendents' shall be considered county officers.
(2) 'Elected education board members' and 'elected school superintendents' of any independent school system shall be considered municipal officers.
(3) 'Election superintendent' means:
(A) In the case of any elected state officers, the Secretary of State;
(B) In the case of any elected county officers, the county board of elections, if a county has such, or the judge of the probate court, provided that, if such judge of the probate court is the officer sought to be recalled, then the election superintendent shall be the clerk of the superior court; and
(C) In the case of any elected municipal officers, the municipal clerk or municipal board of elections or municipal election superintendent, if the municipality has such a board or election officer.
(4) 'Elector' means any person who possesses all of the qualifications for voting now or hereafter prescribed by the laws of this state and who has registered in accordance with Chapter 2 of this title.
(5) 'Electoral district' means the area in which the electors reside who are qualified to vote for any of the candidates offering for a particular office.
(6) 'Failure to perform duties prescribed by law' means the willful neglect or failure by an official to perform a duty imposed by statute.
(7) 'Grounds for recall' means:

(A) That the official has, while holding public office, conducted himself or herself in a manner which relates to and adversely affects the administration of his or her office and adversely affects the rights and interests of the public; and
(B) That the official:
(i) Has committed an act or acts of malfeasance while in office;
(ii) Has violated his or her oath of office;
(iii) Has committed an act of misconduct in office;
(iv) Is guilty of a failure to perform duties prescribed by law; or
(v) Has willfully misused, converted, or misappropriated, without authority, public property or public funds entrusted to or associated with the elective office to which the official has been elected or appointed.
Discretionary performance of a lawful act or a prescribed duty shall not constitute a ground for recall of an elected public official.
(7.1) 'Legal sufficiency' means, solely as applied to the duties or functions of the election superintendent, a determination of the completeness of an application for a recall petition or a recall petition and a determination that an application for a recall petition or a recall petition contains a sufficient number of valid signatures. Such determinations shall not include any review of the sufficiency of the ground or grounds for the recall and the fact or facts upon which such ground or grounds are based.
(8) 'Misconduct in office' means an unlawful act committed willfully by an elected public official or a willful violation of the code of ethics for government service contained in Code Section 45-10-1.
(9) 'Official sponsors' or 'sponsors' means the electors who circulate or file an application for a recall petition who were registered and eligible to vote in the last general or special election for the office held by the officer sought to be recalled and who reside in the electoral district of the officer sought to be recalled.
(10) 'Elective office' means an office filled by the exercise of

the franchise of vote by electors as defined in paragraph (4) of this Code section in a general or special election as defined under the laws of this state.

21-4-4.
(a) Every public official who holds elective office, either by election or by appointment, is subject to recall from office by electors who are registered and qualified to vote in the recall election and who reside in the electoral district from which candidates are elected to that office:
(1) In the case of a state officer whose electoral district encompasses the entire state, the number of electors necessary to petition the recall of the officer shall be equal to at least 15 percent of the number of electors who were registered and qualified to vote at the last preceding election for any candidate offering for the office held by the officer. At least one-fifteenth of the number of electors necessary to petition the recall of the officer must reside in each of the United States congressional districts in the state as said congressional districts may now or hereafter exist; or
(2) In the case of a state officer whose electoral district encompasses only a part of the state or in the case of a local officer, the number of electors necessary to petition the recall of the officer shall be equal to at least 30 percent of the number of electors registered and qualified to vote at the last preceding election for any candidate offering for the office held by the officer.
(b) No recall petition shall demand the recall of more than one public official.
(c) Every public official who holds elective office, either by election or by appointment, is subject to recall on the grounds that such public official has, while holding any public office, conducted himself or herself in a manner which relates to and adversely affects the administration of his or her current office and adversely affects the rights and interests of the public if one or more additional grounds for recall exist as set forth in subparagraph (B) of paragraph (7) of Code Section 21-4-3.

21-4-5.

(a) No application for a recall petition may be filed during the first 180 days or during the last 180 days of the term of office of any public official subject to recall. No person shall be authorized to circulate, sponsor, or sign such application unless such person is an elector or sponsor as defined in Code Section 21-4-3.

(b)(1) The application shall include:

(A) The name and office of the person sought to be recalled;

(B) The printed names and signatures of the official sponsors, the date signed, residence addresses, and the name of the county of residence;

(C) The designation of one of the sponsors as the petition chairperson who shall represent the sponsors on all matters pertaining to the recall application and petition;

(D) A statement that: ____________________ (name and office) has, while holding public office, conducted himself or herself in a manner which relates to and adversely affects the administration of his or her office and adversely affects the rights and interests of the public and stating the appropriate ground or grounds for recall as set forth in subparagraph (B) of paragraph (7) of Code Section 21-4-3 with a brief statement of the fact or facts upon which the ground or grounds are based. Such statement shall be typed, printed, or reproduced by the election superintendent on the face of each application issued; and

(E)(i) An affidavit by the petition chairperson and the person circulating such recall application that each person sponsoring or signing such recall application is an elector of the electoral district of the officer sought to be recalled and that the fact or facts upon which the ground or grounds for recall are based are true.

(ii) The affidavit required by division (i) of this subparagraph shall be in the following form:

AFFIDAVIT OF CIRCULATOR
AND PETITION CHAIRPERSON

State of Georgia

County of ________

Under the penalty of a violation of Code Section 16-10-71 of the Official Code of Georgia Annotated, relating to false swearing, punishable by a fine not to exceed $1,000.00 or by imprisonment of not less than one nor more than five years, or both, we the undersigned do depose and say that each person sponsoring or signing the recall application of ____________________ is an elector of the electoral district of the officer sought to be recalled and further depose and say that the fact or facts upon which the ground or grounds for recall are based are true.

____

(Signature of circulator)

____

(Residence address)
(Number and street or route)

____

(City)

____

(Signature of petition chairperson)

____

(Residence address)
(Number and street or route)

____

(City)

Subscribed and sworn to
before me this _____
day of ____________, ___.

____

Notary public

________, Georgia

My commission expires on the _____ day of ____________, ___.

No notary public may sign the application as an elector or serve as a circulator of any application which he or she notarized. Any and all sheets of an application for a recall petition that have the circulator´s affidavit notarized by a notary public who also served as a circulator of one or more sheets of the application for a recall petition or who signed one of the sheets of the petition as an elector shall be disqualified and rejected.

(2) Applications shall be issued by the election superintendent who shall assign a number to each application. Such number shall appear on the face of each application. The election superintendent shall keep records of applications issued, including the date of issuance and number assigned. The election superintendent shall immediately notify in writing the public officer named for recall in the application that an application for a recall petition has been officially issued for circulation.

(3) The official application forms shall be printed by the office of the Secretary of State in substantially the form prescribed in this subsection and distributed to election superintendents.

(c) The number of official sponsors necessary to file an application for a recall petition must be equal in number to at least 100 electors or equal in number to at least 10 percent of the number of electors who were registered to vote at the last preceding election for any of the candidates offering for the office held by the public official sought to be recalled, whichever is smaller.

(d) Sponsors of a recall petition, before causing the petition to be circulated, shall submit the application for the petition to the election superintendent designated in Code Section 21-4-3 and request official recall petition forms.

(e) At any time prior to the date the election superintendent receives the application for a recall petition, an elector who has signed the application as an official sponsor may request withdrawal of his or her signature from the application by executing and filing an affidavit signed and sworn to before a notary public which affirms the elector´s intention to withdraw his or her signature from the application. The official affidavit of signature withdrawal shall be printed by the office of the Secretary of State and distributed to election superintendents. The form of the affidavit shall be substantially as prescribed in Code Section 21-4-9.

(f)(1) No application for a recall petition shall be accepted for verification if more than 15 days have elapsed since the application forms were issued to the sponsors. If an application for a recall petition contains more than one sheet, such application, when offered for filing, shall be bound together and each sheet shall be numbered consecutively at the foot of each page beginning with page one.

(2) On receipt of the application, the election superintendent shall file the application and proceed to determine the legal sufficiency of the application and determine if the signers are qualified electors eligible to sign the application. The election superintendent is granted unrestricted authority to examine the registration records maintained by the board of registrars, to receive evidence and testimony, and to require the personal appearance of any person signing such application for the purpose of making such determination. If the election superintendent finds that any signer is not a qualified elector eligible to sign the application, such signature shall not be counted in determining whether the application contains a sufficient number of signatures as required by law. The nullification of a signature on an application shall not affect the validity of other signatures contained in such application. The election superintendent shall certify the legal sufficiency or insufficiency of the application for a recall petition within five days after receiving the application, excluding Saturdays, Sundays, and legal holidays; provided, however, that the judge of the superior court may, upon proper application and good cause shown, grant an additional period of time not to exceed 15 days for the election superintendent to verify the application.

(3) The election superintendent shall immediately notify in writing the public officer named for recall in the application that a completed application for a recall petition has been filed with the election superintendent for verification.

(g) No application for a recall petition shall be amended, supplemented, or returned after it has been filed with the election superintendent for verification.

(h) Upon certifying the legal sufficiency of the application, the election superintendent shall immediately officially file the certification of the application, issue official recall petition forms, assign a number to the recall petition, which number shall appear on the face of each petition form, and issue that number to the sponsors. A record of each application, including the date of its receipt and the number assigned and issued to the sponsors, shall be maintained by the election superintendent.

(i) The election superintendent shall immediately notify in writing the public officer named for recall in the application that a recall petition has been officially issued for circulation.

(j) The official recall petition forms shall be printed by the office of the Secretary of State and distributed to election superintendents. The form of the petition shall be as provided in Code Section 21-4-7.

21-4-6.

(a) Within four days after the date of submission of the application for a recall petition for verification, excluding Saturdays, Sundays, and legal holidays, the officer sought to be recalled may file a petition in the superior court of the county in which such officer is domiciled applying for a review of the sufficiency of the ground or grounds for the recall and the fact or facts upon which such ground or grounds are based as set forth in such recall application.

(b) The superior court having jurisdiction of a case governed by this chapter shall be presided over by a superior court judge or senior judge. The superior court judge or senior judge who presides over the case shall be selected as set out in subsection (c) of this Code section.

(c) Upon the filing of a sufficiency review petition under this Code section, the clerk of superior court having jurisdiction shall immediately notify the administrative judge for the judicial administrative district in which that county lies, or the district court administrator, who shall immediately notify the administrative judge of the institution of proceedings under this chapter. If the county in which the proceedings were instituted is not in the circuit of the administrative judge, the administrative judge shall select a superior court judge from within the district, but not from the circuit in which the proceeding was instituted, or a senior judge who is not a resident of the circuit in which the proceeding was instituted, to preside over the contest.

(d) If the administrative judge is a member of the circuit in which the proceeding was filed, or if the other judges of the district are unable or are unwilling to preside over the proceeding, or if the other judges of the district are judges of the circuit in which the proceeding was filed, then the administrative judge shall select an administrative judge of an adjoining district to select a superior court judge from that district, or a superior court judge from the district in which the proceeding was filed, but not the circuit in which the proceeding was filed, or a senior judge who is not a resident of the circuit wherein the proceeding was filed.

(e) After a judge has agreed to preside over the case, the administrative judge who selected the judge to hear the matter shall enter an order in the superior court of the county where the proceeding was filed appointing such judge, and such judge shall promptly begin presiding over such proceedings in such court and shall determine same as soon as practicable. Such judge shall be reimbursed for his actual expenses for food and lodging and shall receive the same mileage as any other state officials and employees. Senior judges shall be entitled to compensation and reimbursement as the law provides for senior judge service.

(f) Such review shall be limited solely to a review of the legal sufficiency of the recall ground or grounds and the legal sufficiency of the alleged fact or facts upon which such ground or grounds are based as set forth in such recall application. The review of such alleged fact or facts shall include a determination of whether probable cause exists to believe that such alleged fact or facts are true. The burden shall be on the petition chairperson to prove that such probable cause exists. The judge shall consider such review petitions on an expedited basis. Discovery shall be permitted but shall not delay the consideration of the review petition by the judge. The judge may enter such orders as the judge deems necessary and appropriate to expedite any discovery and the consideration of the review petition.

(g) During the pendency of the review by the superior court, all other recall proceedings shall be suspended. If a ruling of sufficiency is rendered by such judge, then recall proceedings shall continue in the manner provided for in this chapter. The time for circulating a recall petition after the review of the sufficiency petition shall begin from the date of the order of the superior court or the issuance of recall petition forms, whichever is later, notwithstanding the fact that recall petition forms were issued before the filing of the petition for review of the sufficiency of the recall application. Valid signatures obtained on a recall petition prior to the filing of a petition for review of the sufficiency of a recall application shall be counted. The officer sought to be recalled may file a discretionary appeal in the Supreme Court of Georgia within ten days after the date of an order finding a recall application sufficient, excluding Saturdays, Sundays, and legal holidays, and such court shall consider such appeal on an expedited basis. The filing of such appeal shall not operate to stay the recall proceedings. If a ruling of insufficiency is rendered by such judge, then a discretionary appeal may be filed in the Supreme Court of Georgia within ten days after the date of such ruling, excluding Saturdays, Sundays, and legal holidays, and such court shall consider such appeal on an expedited basis.

21-4-7.

(a) The form of the recall petition shall be substantially as follows:

RECALL PETITION

____

(Official application no.)

____

(County or city)

To ______________________________
Name of election superintendent)

____

(Address)

____

(City, state, ZIP Code)
We, the electors registered to vote in the recall election herein petitioned, demand the recall of ____________________ (Name and office) on the grounds that said official has, while holding public office, conducted himself or herself in a manner which relates to and adversely affects the administration of his or her office and adversely affects the rights and interest of the public and that said official ____________ (State the appropriate ground or grounds for recall as set forth in subparagraph (B) of paragraph (7) of Code Section 21-4-3 and a brief statement, not to exceed five lines, of the fact or facts upon which such ground or grounds are based.).

Name
Date of
Signing
Residence
Address
County of
Residence

____

____

(Signature) (Number and street or route)

____

____

(Printed name of elector) (City)
(Ten lines for signatures and printed names)
(b) The following statements shall be written or printed on each petition and each signer must read, or be read, the following statements:
'(1) Any person who gives or receives money or any other thing of value for signing a recall petition or for signing an affidavit of signature withdrawal shall be guilty of a misdemeanor;

(2) If (insert appropriate number) electors sign this petition, there will be an election at which a majority of the electors voting therein will determine whether the above-named official will be removed from office.'
(c) Each recall petition shall contain a statement specifically designating the name and office of the official sought to be recalled, a statement that the named official has, while holding public office, conducted himself or herself in a manner which relates to and adversely affects the administration of his or her office and adversely affects the rights and interests of the public, a statement containing the appropriate ground or grounds for recall as set forth in subparagraph (B) of paragraph (7) of Code Section 21-4-3, and a brief statement of the fact or facts upon which such ground or grounds are based. Such statements shall be written or printed on each petition and each signer must read, or be read, such statements.

21-4-8.
(a) All signers of a single recall petition shall be electors who are registered and eligible to vote in the recall election and who reside in the electoral district of the officer sought to be recalled. When a petition for the recall of a public official is circulated in more than one county, each sheet of the petition shall bear the name of the county in which it is circulated, and only electors of the designated county may sign such sheet. No recall petition shall be circulated or signed by any person in any location where alcoholic beverages are sold or served.
(b) Every elector signing a recall petition shall do so in the presence of the person circulating the petition, who is to execute the affidavit of verification on the reverse side of the petition form. At the time of signing, the elector shall sign his name, and such elector or the person circulating the petition shall print the name of the elector below the elector's signature and shall print or write in the appropriate spaces following the signature the elector's residence address, giving number and street or route and city, the name of the county, and the date on which the elector signed the petition. No notary

public may sign the petition as an elector or serve as a circulator of any petition which he or she notarized. Any and all sheets of a recall petition that have the circulator´s affidavit notarized by a notary public who also served as a circulator of one or more sheets of the recall petition or who signed one of the sheets of the petition as an elector shall be disqualified and rejected.

(c) If an elector is incapable of signing his or her own name, he or she may specifically request the circulator of the petition to sign and print his or her name and complete the information required on the petition sheet to accompany the signature; provided, however, that the circulator shall also sign his or her full name beside the printed name of such elector.

(d) The person before whom the electors signed the recall petition shall verify, in an affidavit subscribed and sworn to by him or her before a notary public, that each of the names on the petition form was signed in his or her presence on the date indicated and that in his or her belief each signer was an elector of the electoral district of the officer sought to be recalled.

(e) The affidavit printed on the reverse side of each recall petition form shall be in the following form:

AFFIDAVIT OF CIRCULATOR

State of Georgia
County of __________

Under the penalty of a violation of Code Section 16-10-71 of the Official Code of Georgia Annotated, relating to false swearing, punishable by a fine not to exceed $1,000.00 or by imprisonment of not less than one nor more than five years, or both, I do depose and say that I am an elector registered to vote in the recall election herein petitioned for and that each petitioner signed or caused to be signed the foregoing petition in my presence on the date indicated; and I believe that each signer´s name and residence address are correctly stated, and that each signer is an elector of the electoral district in which such recall election will be conducted, and that each signer has read, or was read, the required statements which are also set out on each petition.

(Signature of affiant) ______________________
(Residence address) ______________________
(Number and street or route) ____________
(City)
Subscribed and sworn to
before me this _______
day of ____________, ___.

____
Notary public
_________, Georgia
My commission expires on the _____ day of ____________, ___.

(f) An elector may change the way his or her signature and residence address appear on the recall petition at any time prior to the filing of the petition for verification by striking through his or her name and initialing the strike-through and re-signing the petition with his or her printed name corrected accordingly.

21-4-9.

(a) At any time prior to the date an application for recall petition or a recall petition is filed for verification, an elector who has signed the application or the recall petition form may request withdrawal of his or her signature from the application or recall petition by executing and filing an affidavit, in the form prescribed by this Code section, with the election superintendent. Any signature so withdrawn shall not be counted in determining the legal sufficiency of the application or recall petition. The affidavit shall:

(1) Be signed and sworn to before a notary public;

(2) State the elector´s residence address, giving number and street or route and city, the name of the county of residence, and, in the case of a recall application or petition, the number of the recall application or petition which he or she signed; and

(3) Affirm the elector´s intention to withdraw his or her

signature from the application or recall petition.
(b) The affidavit shall be substantially in the following form:
AFFIDAVIT OF SIGNATURE WITHDRAWAL

State of Georgia
County of ____________
I, ______________________, (Name as it appears on the application or recall petition), being first duly sworn, say that I am an elector of the ____________ (electoral district) in which the recall election will be conducted.
That my residence address is

____

____

____

(Number and street or route) (City)
That I signed or caused to be signed the application or the petition for the recall of ____________________ (Name and office of person sought to be recalled) and that the recall application or petition has been assigned number ____________.
That it is my intention by the signing and filing of this affidavit to withdraw my signature therefrom.

____

Signature of elector
Subscribed and sworn to
before me this _____
day of ____________, ___.

____

Notary public
_________, Georgia
My commission expires on the _____ day of ____________, ___.
21-4-10.
No registration officer or other person authorized by law to register electors and no person other than an elector of the electoral district of the officer sought to be recalled shall

circulate a recall application or petition. No employee of the state shall circulate a recall application or petition. All signatures obtained by any such unqualified person shall be void and shall not be counted in determining the legal sufficiency of the petition.

21-4-11.

(a) The election superintendent shall be responsible for determining the legal sufficiency of the recall petition within 30 days after it has been filed with him or her; provided, however, that in cases where more than one recall petition is subject to review for verification, the election superintendent shall be responsible for determining the legal sufficiency of any recall petition within 45 days after it has been filed with him or her. The election superintendent or a designee is granted unrestricted authority to examine the registration records maintained by the board of registrars, to receive evidence and testimony, and to require the personal appearance of any person signing such recall petition for the purpose of determining if the signers are qualified electors eligible to sign the recall petition. If the election superintendent shall not be reasonably able to ascertain that any signature is that of a qualified elector eligible to sign the recall petition, such signature shall not be counted in determining whether the petition contains a sufficient number of signatures as required by law. The nullification of a signature on any sheet of the recall petition shall not affect the validity of other signatures contained on such sheet.

(b) A recall petition shall not be accepted for verification for:

(1) Any state-wide office if more than 90 days have elapsed since the date the official recall petition forms were issued to the sponsors;

(2) Any officer holding an office other than state-wide office and for whom not less than 5,000 signatures are required for the recall petition under paragraph (2) of subsection (a) of Code Section 21-4-4 if more than 45 days have elapsed since the date the official recall petition forms were issued to the sponsor; or

(3) Any officer holding an office other than a state-wide office and for whom less than 5,000 signatures are required under paragraph (2) of subsection (a) of Code Section 21-4-4 if more than 30 days have elapsed since the date the official recall petition forms were issued to the sponsors.
(c)(1) No recall petition shall be amended, supplemented, or returned after it has been filed with the election superintendent for verification.
(2) If a recall petition contains more than one sheet, such recall petition shall, when offered for filing, be bound together and each sheet shall be numbered consecutively at the foot of each page beginning with page one.
(d) Within five days, excluding Saturdays, Sundays, and legal holidays, after the election superintendent has certified the legal sufficiency of a petition, he or she shall immediately notify the Governor or the appropriate official, who shall call the recall election as provided in Code Section 21-4-13.
(e) Upon certifying the legal sufficiency or insufficiency of a recall petition, the election superintendent shall immediately notify the petition chairman and the officeholder in writing of the results and officially file the certification of the petition.

21-4-12.
If an officeholder resigns prior to the holding of a recall election no recall election shall be conducted.

21-4-13.
(a) Within ten days after having received certification of the sufficiency of the recall petition by the election superintendent, a recall election shall be called and published, as provided in this Code section, and shall be conducted not less than 30 days nor more than 45 days after such call; provided, however, that, if a primary or general election is to be held not less than 30 days nor more than 45 days after such call is issued, the recall election shall be conducted on that date.
(b) A recall election shall be called:
(1) By the Governor, if for a state officer;
(2) By the election superintendent of the county, if for a county

officer; or
(3) By the election superintendent of the municipality, if for a municipal officer.
(c) If a recall petition is against an officer who is directed by this Code section to call the election, it shall be called:
(1) By the Secretary of State, if for the Governor; or
(2) By the clerk of the superior court, if for the judge of the probate court and such judge serves as the election superintendent of the county.
(d) The official call for such election shall be published one time as follows:
(1) In a newspaper of general circulation in the electoral district, if such election is for a state officer;
(2) In the official organ of the county, if such election is for a county officer; or
(3) In the official gazette of the municipality, if such election is for a municipal officer.
(e) It shall be the duty of the appropriate official authorized by law to conduct elections to hold and conduct the recall election and to declare and certify the results; provided, however, that if the person sought to be recalled is the official authorized by law to conduct elections, the clerk of the superior court of the county in which such recall election is to be held shall hold and conduct the recall election and declare and certify the results. The ballot for the recall election shall state the name and office of the person whose recall has been petitioned, and the ballot shall be in the form prescribed by law for state, county, or municipal officers. The ballot shall have written or printed thereon the following:
'( ) YES
( ) NO

Shall (name of officeholder), (name of office), be recalled and removed from public office on the grounds that said official has, while holding public office, conducted himself or herself in a manner which relates to and adversely affects the administration of his or her office and adversely affects the rights and interests of the public and on the ground(s) that such official _____________(State the appropriate ground or grounds for recall as set forth in subparagraph (B) of paragraph (7) of Code Section 21-4-3.)?'

If more than one public officer is subject to a recall election in the same precinct, the election superintendent may prepare a recall ballot so as to include on a single ballot separate recall questions for each of the officers sought to be recalled.
(f) Those persons desiring to vote in favor of recall shall vote 'Yes,' and those persons desiring to vote against recall shall vote 'No.' If more than one-half of the votes cast on such question are in favor of recall, the public office in question shall immediately become vacant. Otherwise, the public official named in the recall petition shall continue in office.
(g) A special election shall be called by the appropriate state or local official to fill a vacancy created by recall. The special election shall be called within ten days after the date of the recall election and shall be conducted at least 30 days but not more than 45 days following the call. If no official is specifically designated by law or if the appropriate official has been recalled, the Governor shall issue the call for a special election to fill the vacancy created by recall. Any person who has been recalled from office under this chapter shall be eligible to offer for election to fill the vacancy created by recall.

21-4-14.
(a) After a recall petition and election, no further recall petition shall be filed against the same officer until at least six months have elapsed from the date of the previous recall election; and any other recall petitions against that officer outstanding on the date of the recall election shall be void.
(b) If the election superintendent finds that a recall petition is insufficient and fails to verify the same, no further application for a recall petition shall be filed against the same officer until at least six months have elapsed from the date of the denial of such recall petition; provided, however, that such finding of insufficiency shall not bar the verification of any other recall petition against that officer which is available for signature or

pending verification at the time of such finding of insufficiency.

21-4-15.
The powers, duties, and penalties conferred or imposed by law upon public officials who conduct special elections are conferred and imposed upon public officials conducting recall elections. All such elections shall be conducted in the same manner as special elections and in accordance with Chapters 2 and 3 of this title.

21-4-16.
Any person sponsoring or opposing a recall petition under this chapter shall be subject to Chapter 5 of this title, the 'Ethics in Government Act,' in the same manner as candidates; and the petition chairperson shall file the reports required to be filed under said chapter and shall be subject to the same restrictions, qualifications, and provisions contained in such chapter.

21-4-17.
The Secretary of State is authorized to promulgate such rules and regulations as are necessary to carry out this chapter.

21-4-18.
(a) If the election superintendent fails to comply with this chapter, any elector may apply, within ten days after such refusal, to the superior court for a writ of mandamus to compel the election superintendent to perform his or her official duties. If the court finds that the election superintendent has not complied with this chapter, the court shall issue an order for the election superintendent to comply.
(b) An action against an election superintendent shall be filed in the superior court of the county of such election superintendent, except that an action against the Secretary of State shall be filed in the Superior Court of Fulton County.

21-4-19.
An elector´s eligibility to sign an application for a recall petition

or a petition for recall shall be determined as of the date immediately preceding the date the application or petition is signed by that elector.

21-4-20.

(a) Any person who gives or receives money or any other thing of value for signing a recall application or petition or for signing an affidavit of signature withdrawal shall be guilty of a misdemeanor.

(b) A person who, by menace or threat either directly or indirectly, induces or compels or attempts to induce or compel any other person to sign or subscribe or to refrain from signing or subscribing that person's name to a recall application or petition or, after signing or subscribing that person's name, to have that person's name taken therefrom shall be guilty of a misdemeanor.

(c) A person who signs any name other than his or her own to a recall application or petition, except in a circumstance where he or she signs for a person in the presence of and at the specific request of such person who is incapable of signing that person's own name, or who knowingly signs his or her name more than once for the same recall application or petition or who knowingly is not at the time of signing a qualified elector of the electoral district of the officer sought to be recalled shall be guilty of a misdemeanor.

21-4-21.

This chapter is supplementary to any other methods provided by general law for removing a public official from office; and nothing in this chapter shall be construed as abridging or repealing such laws.

CONSTITUTION OF THE STATE OF IDAHO
Article VI, Section 6.

Recall of Officers Authorized. Every public officer in the state of Idaho, excepting the judicial officers, is subject to recall by the legal voters of the state or of the electoral district from which he is elected. The legislature shall pass the necessary laws to carry this provision into effect.

THE IDAHO CODE
Title 34, Chapter 17, Section 34-1701 et sec.
Beginning with Officers Subject to Recall.

Idaho Code Section 34-1701
Idaho Code Section 34-1702
Idaho Code Section 34-1703
Idaho Code Section 34-1704
Idaho Code Section 34-1705
Idaho Code Section 34-1706
Idaho Code Section 34-1707
Idaho Code Section 34-1708
Idaho Code Section 34-1709
Idaho Code Section 34-1710
Idaho Code Section 34-1711
Idaho Code Section 34-1712
Idaho Code Section 34-1713
Idaho Code Section 34-1714
Idaho Code Section 34-1715

34-1701. OFFICERS SUBJECT TO RECALL. The following public officers, whether holding their elective office by election or appointment, and none other, are subject to recall:

(1) State officers:

(a) The governor, lieutenant-governor, secretary of state, state controller, state treasurer, attorney general, and superintendent of public instruction;

(b) Members of the state senate, and members of the state house of representatives.

(2) County officers:

(a) The members of the board of county commissioners, sheriff, treasurer, assessor, prosecuting attorney, clerk of the district court, and coroner.

(3) City officers:

(a) The mayor;

(b) Members of the city council.

(4) Special district elected officers for whom recall procedure is not otherwise provided by law.

34-1702. REQUIRED SIGNATURES ON PETITION. A petition for recall of an officer shall be instituted by filing with the appropriate official a verified written petition requesting such recall.

(1) If the petition seeks recall of any of the officers named in subsection (1)(a) of section 34-1701, Idaho Code, the petition shall be filed with the secretary of state, and must be signed by registered electors equal in number to twenty percent (20%) of the number of electors registered to vote at the last general election held to elect a governor.

(2) If the petition seeks recall of any of the officers named in subsection (1)(b) of section 34-1701, Idaho Code, the petition shall be filed with the secretary of state, and must be signed by registered electors of the legislative district equal in number to twenty percent (20%) of the number of electors registered to vote at the last general election held in the legislative district at which the member was elected.

(3) If the petition seeks recall of any of the officers named in subsection (2)(a) of section 34-1701, Idaho Code, the petition shall be filed with the county clerk, and must be signed by registered electors of the county equal in number to twenty percent (20%) of the number of electors registered to vote at the last general election held in the county for the election of county officers at which the officer was elected.

(4) If the petition seeks recall of any of the officers named in subsection (3) of section 34-1701, Idaho Code, the petition shall be filed with the city clerk, and must be signed by registered electors of the city equal in number to twenty percent (20%) of the number of electors registered to vote at the last general city election held in the city for the election of officers.

(5) If the petition seeks recall of any of the officers named in subsection (4) of section 34-1701, Idaho Code, the petition

shall be filed with the county clerk of the county wherein the district is located. If the district is located in two (2) or more counties, the clerk in each county shall perform the functions within that county. The petition must be signed by registered electors of the district equal in number to fifty percent (50%) of the number of electors who cast votes in the last election of the district. If no district election has been held in the last six (6) years, the petition must be signed by twenty percent (20%) of the number of electors registered to vote in the district at the time the petition is filed.

34-1703. FORM OF PETITION. (1) The recall petition for state officers other than members of the state legislature shall be in substantially the following form:

RECALL PETITION

To the honorable ...., Secretary of State for the State of Idaho: We, the undersigned citizens and registered electors of the State of Idaho respectfully demand that ...., holding the office of ...., be recalled by the registered electors of this state for the following reasons, to-wit: (setting out the reasons for recall in not more than 200 words); that a special election therefor be called; that we, each for himself say: I am a registered elector of the State of Idaho; my residence, post office address, and the date I signed this petition are correctly written after my name.

Signature
Printed Name
Residence
City or   Date
Street and Post Office Number

(Here follow twenty numbered lines for signatures.)

(2) The recall petition for members of the state legislature shall be in substantially the following form:

RECALL PETITION

To the honorable ...., Secretary of State for the State of Idaho:

We, the undersigned citizens and registered electors of

Legislative District No. ...., respectfully demand that ...., holding the office of ...., be recalled by the registered electors of Legislative District No. .... for the following reasons, to-wit: (setting out the reasons for recall in not more than 200 words); that a special election therefor be called; that we, each for himself say: I am a registered elector of Legislative District No. ...., my residence, post office address, and the date I signed this petition are correctly written after my name.

Signature
Printed Name
Residence
City or Date

Street and Post Office

34-1704. PRINTING OF PETITION AND SHEETS FOR SIGNATURES -- TIME LIMITS
FOR PERFECTING PETITION. (1) Before or at the time of beginning to circulate any petition for the recall of any officer subject to recall, the person or persons, organization or organizations under whose authority the recall petition is to be circulated, shall send or deliver to the secretary of state, county clerk, or city clerk, as the case may be, a copy of such petition duly signed by at least twenty (20) electors eligible to sign such petition. The receiving officer shall immediately examine the petition and specify the form and kind and size of paper on which the petition shall be printed and circulated for further signatures. All petitions for recall and sheets for signatures shall be printed on a good quality bond or ledger paper, on pages eight and one-half (8 1/2) inches in width by thirteen (13) inches in length, with a margin of one and three-fourths (1 3/4) inches at the top for binding, and the sheets for signatures shall have numbered lines thereon from one (1) to twenty (20) for signatures. The petition shall be prepared in sections, with each section numbered consecutively. Each section of a petition must have a printed copy of the petition as the first page, and each section shall have

attached to it not more than ten (10) sheets for signatures.
(2) The secretary of state, county clerk, or city clerk, as the case may be, shall indicate in writing on the recall petition that he has approved it as to form and the date of such approval. Upon approval as to form, the secretary of state, county auditor, or city clerk, shall inform the person or persons, organization or organizations under whose authority the recall petition is to be circulated, in writing, that the petition must be perfected with the required number of certified signatures within sixty (60) days following the date of approval as to form. Any petition that has not been perfected with the required number of certified signatures within the sixty (60) days allowed shall be declared null and void ab initio in its entirety, except for the extension allowed for in section 34-1707, Idaho Code.

34-1705. VERIFICATION ON SHEETS FOR SIGNATURES. Each and every signature sheet of each petition containing signatures shall be verified on the face thereof in substantially the following form by the person who circulated said sheet of the petition, by his or her affidavit thereon, as a part thereof:
State of Idaho
ss.
County of

I, __, swear, under penalty of perjury, that every person who signed this sheet of the foregoing petition signed his or her name thereto in my presence. I believe that each has stated his or her name and the accompanying required information on the signature sheet correctly, and that the person was eligible to sign this petition.
(Signature) ______________
Post office address ______________________
Subscribed and sworn to before me this ___ day of ___, 19__
(Notary Seal)

____
Notary Public
Residing at ___________

34-1706. EXAMINATION AND CERTIFICATION OF SIGNATURES. All petitions with attached signature sheets shall be filed on the same day with the secretary of state, county clerk, or city clerk, as the case may be. The secretary of state or the city clerk shall promptly transmit the petitions and attached signature sheets to the county clerk. An examination to verify whether or not the petition signers are qualified electors shall be conducted by the county clerk as provided in section 34-1807, Idaho Code. This examination shall not exceed fifteen (15) business days from the date of receipt of the petitions.

34-1707. SUFFICIENCY OF PETITION -- NOTIFICATION -- EFFECT OF RESIGNATION
-- SPECIAL ELECTION.

(1) (a) In the event that a petition filed with the secretary of state does not contain the required number of certified signatures after being returned by the county clerks, the secretary of state shall inform the person or organization under whose authority the petition was circulated that the petition is defective for lack of certified signatures, and specify the number of additional signatures required to make the petition valid. The petition must be perfected within thirty (30) days of the date that the secretary of state finds the petition defective for lack of certified signatures. If the petition is not perfected within the thirty (30) day period, the secretary of state shall declare the petition null and void ab initio in its entirety.

(b) In the event that a petition filed with the secretary of state is found by the secretary of state to contain the required number of certified signatures, the secretary of state shall promptly, by certified mail, inform the officer being recalled, and the petitioner, that the recall petition is in proper form.

(i) If the officer being recalled resigns his office within five (5) days after notice from the secretary of state, his resignation shall be accepted and the resignation shall take effect on the day it is offered, and the vacancy shall be filled as provided by law.

(ii) If the officer being recalled does not resign his office within five (5) days after notice from the secretary of state, a special election shall be ordered by the secretary of state, unless he is the officer being recalled, in which event the governor shall order such special election. The special election must be held on the date prescribed in section 34-106, Idaho Code. If the officer being recalled is one (1) specified in section 34-1701(1)(a), Idaho Code, the special election shall be conducted statewide. If the officer being recalled is one (1) specified in section 34-1701(1)(b), Idaho Code, the special election shall be conducted only in the legislative district.

(2) (a) In the event that a petition filed with a county clerk does not contain the required number of certified signatures, the county clerk shall inform the person or organization under whose authority the petition was circulated that the petition is defective for lack of certified signatures, and specify the number of additional signatures required to make the petition valid. The petition must be perfected within thirty (30) days of the date that the clerk finds the petition defective for lack of certified signatures. If the petition is not perfected within the thirty (30) day period, the clerk shall declare the petition null and void ab initio in its entirety.

(b) In the event that a petition filed with the county clerk is found by the county clerk to contain the required number of certified signatures, the county clerk shall promptly, by certified mail, inform the officer being recalled, and the petitioner, that the recall petition is in proper form.

(i) If the officer being recalled resigns his office within five (5) days after notice from the county clerk, his resignation shall be accepted and the resignation shall take effect on the day it is offered, and the vacancy shall be filled as provided by law.

(ii) If the officer being recalled does not resign his office within five (5) days after notice from the county clerk, a special election shall be ordered by the county clerk. The special election must be held on the date prescribed in section 34-106, Idaho Code. The special election shall be conducted county-wide.

(c) In the event that a petition filed with the county clerk concerning the recall of an official of a special district is found by the county clerk to contain the required number of certified signatures, the county clerk shall promptly, by certified mail, inform the officer being recalled, and the petitioner, and the governing board and election officials of the special district that the recall petition is in proper form.

(i) If the officer being recalled resigns his office within five (5) days after notice from the county clerk, his resignation shall be accepted and the resignation shall take effect on the day it is offered, and the vacancy shall be filled as provided by law.

(ii) If the officer being recalled does not resign his office within five (5) days after notice from the county clerk, a special election shall be ordered by the governing board of the special district. The special election must be held on the date prescribed in section 34-106, Idaho Code. The election shall be conducted by the special district in the manner provided in section 34-1401, Idaho Code, and the special district may contract with the county clerk as provided in section 34-1401, Idaho Code.

(3) (a) In the event that a petition filed with a city clerk does not contain the required number of certified signatures, the city clerk shall inform the person or organization under whose authority the petition was circulated that the petition is defective for lack of certified signatures, and specify the number of additional signatures required to make the petition valid. The petition must be perfected within thirty (30) days of the date that the city clerk finds the petition defective for lack of certified signatures. If the petition is not perfected within the thirty (30) day period, the clerk shall declare the petition null and void ab initio in its entirety.

(b) In the event that a petition filed with a city clerk is found by the city clerk to contain the required number of certified signatures, the city clerk shall promptly, by certified mail, inform the officer being recalled, and the petitioner, that the recall petition is in proper form.

(i) If the officer being recalled resigns his office within five (5) days after notice from the city clerk, his resignation shall be accepted and the resignation shall take effect on the day it is offered, and the vacancy shall be filled as provided by law. (ii) If the officer being recalled does not resign his office within five (5) days after notice from the city clerk, a special election shall be ordered by the city clerk. The special election must be held on the date prescribed in section 34-106, Idaho Code. The special election shall be conducted city-wide.

34-1708. FORM OF RECALL BALLOT. The ballot at any recall election shall be headed "RECALL BALLOT" and on the ballot shall be printed in not more than two hundred (200) words the reason for demanding the recall of the officer named in the recall petition, and in not more than two hundred (200) words the officer's justification of his course in office. Then the question of whether the officer should be recalled shall be placed on the ballot in a form substantially similar to the following:

FOR recalling ..... who holds office of ....
AGAINST recalling ..... who holds office of ....

34-1709. OFFICER TO CONTINUE IN OFFICE. The officer named in the recall petition shall continue to perform the duties of his office until the results of the special recall election are officially declared.

34-1710. CONDUCT OF SPECIAL RECALL ELECTION. Special elections for the recall of an officer shall be conducted and the results thereof canvassed and certified in all respects as general elections, except as otherwise provided. Nothing in this chapter shall preclude the holding of a recall election with another election.

34-1711. CANVASS OF RETURNS. (1) The board of county commissioners shall act as the board of canvassers for all special recall elections involving state and county officers that involve elections held wholly or partly within their county. (a) For all special recall elections involving state officers, the board of county commissioners shall meet at 12 noon on the third day after said election to canvass the votes cast at such election, and shall immediately transmit to the secretary of state an abstract of the votes cast.

(i) Within ten (10) days following the special recall election held to recall a state officer, the state board of canvassers shall meet and canvass the votes cast at such election, and the secretary of state shall immediately after the completion thereof, proclaim the results.

(b) For all special recall elections involving county officers, the board of county commissioners shall meet at 12 noon on the third day after said election to canvass the votes cast at such election, and the county clerk shall immediately after the completion thereof, proclaim the results.

(c) For all special recall elections involving city officers, the mayor and council shall meet within five (5) days after said election to canvass the votes cast at such election, and the city clerk shall immediately after the completion thereof, proclaim the results.

34-1712. GENERAL ELECTION LAWS CONTROL. (1) The provisions relating to general elections, including the payment of expenses of conducting the recall election, shall govern special recall elections except where otherwise provided for.

(2) Whenever a special recall election is ordered, notice must be issued and posted in the same manner as for a general election.

(3) To recall any officer, a majority of the votes cast at the special recall election must be in favor of such recall, and additionally, the number of votes cast in favor of the recall must equal or exceed the votes cast at the last general election for that officer. If the officer was appointed or was not required to stand for election, then a majority of the votes cast in the recall election shall be the number necessary for recall.

(4) If recalled, an officer shall be recalled as of the time when the results of the special recall election are proclaimed, and a vacancy in the office shall exist.

(5) If an officer is recalled from his office the vacancy shall be filled in the manner provided by law for filling a vacancy in that office arising from any other cause.

34-1713. TIME WITHIN WHICH RECALL MAY BE FILED -- REMOVAL OF SIGNATURES.
(1) No petition for a recall shall be circulated against any officer until he has actually held his office ninety (90) days.
(2) After one (1) special recall election, no further recall petition shall be filed against the same officer during his current term of office, unless the petitioners first pay into the public treasury which has paid such special recall election expenses the whole amount of the expenses for the preceding recall election. The specific reason for recall in one (1) recall petition cannot be the basis for a second recall petition during that current term of office.
(3) The signer of any recall petition may remove his own name from the petition by crossing out, obliterating, or otherwise defacing his own signature at any time prior to the time when the petition is filed.
(4) The signer of any recall petition may have his name removed from the petition at any time after the petition has been filed, but prior to the time when an election has been ordered, by presenting or submitting to the officer who receives the recall petition, a signed statement, that the signer desires to have his name removed from the petition. The statement shall contain sufficient information to clearly identify the signer. The officer who receives the statement shall immediately strike the signer's name from the petition, and adjust the total of certified signatures on the petition accordingly. The statement shall be attached to, and become a part of the petition for recall.

34-1714. PROHIBITED ACTS -- PENALTIES. (1) A person is guilty of a felony who:
(a) Signs any name other than his own to any recall petition;
(b) Knowingly signs his name more than once on the same recall petition;

(c) Knowingly signs his name to any recall petition for the recall of any state, county or city officer if he is not a registered elector;
(d) Wilfully or knowingly circulates, publishes or exhibits any false statement or representation concerning the contents, purport or effect of any recall petition for the purpose of obtaining any signature to any such petition, or for the purpose of persuading any person to sign any such recall petition;
(e) Presents to any officer for filing any recall petition to which is attached, appended or subscribed any signature which the person so filing such petition knows to be false or fraudulent, or not the genuine signature of the person purporting to sign such petition, or whose name is attached, appended or subscribed thereto;
(f) Circulates or causes to circulate any recall petition, knowing the same to contain false, forged or fictitious names;
(g) Makes any false affidavit concerning any recall petition or the signatures appended thereto;
(h) Offers, proposes or threatens for any pecuniary reward or consideration:
(i) To offer, propose, threaten or attempt to sell, hinder or delay any recall petition or any part thereof or any signatures thereon;
(ii) To offer, propose or threaten to desist from beginning, promoting or circulating any recall petition;
(iii) To offer, propose, attempt or threaten in any manner or form to use any recall petition or any power of promotion or opposition in any manner or form for extortion, blackmail or secret or private intimidation of any person or business interest.
(2) A public officer is guilty of a felony who:
(a) Knowingly makes any false return, certification or affidavit concerning any recall petition, or the signatures appended thereto.
34-1715. REFUSAL TO ACCEPT PETITION – MANDATE – INJUNCTION. If the secretary of state, county clerk, or city clerk, shall refuse to accept and file any petition for the recall of a public officer with the requisite number of eligible signatures, any citizen may apply within ten (10) days after such

refusal to the district court for a writ of mandamus to compel him to do so. If it shall be decided by the court that such petition is legally sufficient, the secretary of state, county clerk, or city clerk shall then accept and file the recall petition, with a certified copy of the judgment attached thereto, as of the date on which it was originally offered for filing in his office, except that the time limitations required by section 34-1704(2), Idaho Code, shall begin to run only as of the date of the court judgment, which shall be so stated in the judgment. On a showing that the petition is not legally sufficient, the court may enjoin the secretary of state, county clerk, or city clerk, and all other officers from certifying or printing any official ballot for a recall election. All such suits shall be advanced on the court docket and heard and decided by the court as quickly as possible. Either party may appeal to the supreme court within ten (10) days after a decision is rendered. The district court of the state of Idaho in and for Ada County shall have jurisdiction in all cases involving the recall of state officers.

CONSTITUTION OF THE STATE OF KANSAS, Article 4, Section 3.

Recall of elected officials. All elected public officials in the state, except judicial officers, shall be subject to recall by voters of the state or political subdivision from which elected. Procedures and grounds for recall shall be prescribed by law.

KANSAS STATUTES ANNOTATED Chapter 25, Article 4301 et sec. Beginning with Officers subject to recall; exceptions.

KSA 25-4301
KSA 25-4302
KSA 25-4303

KSA 25-4304
KSA 25-4305
KSA 25-4306
KSA 25-4307
KSA 25-4308
KSA 25-4309
KSA 25-4310
KSA 25-4311
KSA 25-4312
KSA 25-4314
KSA 25-4315
KSA 25-4316
KSA 25-4317
KSA 25-4318
KSA 25-4319
KSA 25-4320
KSA 25-4321
KSA 25-4322
KSA 25-4323
KSA 25-4324
KSA 25-4325
KSA 25-4326
KSA 25-4328
KSA 25-4329
KSA 25-4330
KSA 25-4331

25-4301. Officers subject to recall; exceptions. All elected public officials in the state, except judicial officers, are subject to recall by the voters of the state or the political subdivision from which elected.

25-4302. Grounds for recall. (a) Grounds for recall are conviction of a felony, misconduct in office or failure to perform duties prescribed by law. No recall submitted to the voters shall be held void because of the insufficiency of the grounds, application, or petition by which the submission was procured.

(b) As used in this section, the term "misconduct in office" means a violation of law by the officer that impacts the officer's ability to perform the official duties of the office.

25-4303. Rules and regulations relating to recall. The secretary of state may adopt rules and regulations for the administration of this act, and such rules and regulations may specify any forms needed therefor.

25-4304. Application of act; state officers; local officers. (a) K.S.A. 25-4305 to 25-4317, inclusive, apply only to recall of the governor, members of the legislature, any public officials elected by the electors of the entire state and members of the state board of education. For the purpose of this act, officers mentioned in this subsection are "state officers."

(b) The provisions of this act do not apply to any judicial officer.

(c) K.S.A. 25-4318 to 25-4331, inclusive, apply only to recall of all elected public officials who are provided by law to be elected at an election conducted by one or more county election officers, except those officers specified in subsections (a) and (b). For the purpose of this act, officers to which this subsection apply are "local officers."

(d) Any person appointed or otherwise designated or elected to fill a vacancy in an office to which subsection (a) applies shall be a state officer for the purpose of this act. Any person appointed or otherwise designated or elected to fill a vacancy in an office to which subsection (c) applies shall be a local officer for the purpose of this act.

25-4305. Recall of state officers; application; deposit; filing, when. The recall of a state officer, except the secretary of state, is proposed by filing an application with the secretary of state. The recall of the secretary of state is proposed by filing an application with the lieutenant governor, who shall perform the duties imposed on the secretary of state in the recall of other state officers. A deposit of $100 must accompany the application. This deposit will be remitted to the state treasurer, in accordance with the provisions of K.S.A. 75-4215, and amendments thereto. Upon receipt of each such remittance, the state treasurer shall deposit the entire amount in the state treasury to the credit of the state general fund if a petition is not properly filed. If a petition is properly filed the deposit shall be refunded. No application for the recall of a state officer may be filed during the first 120 days or the last 200 days of the term of office of such officer.

25-4306. Same; application; form; number of signatures. The application under K.S.A. 25-4305 shall include (a) the name and office of the person sought to be recalled, (b) the grounds for recall described in particular in not more than 200 words, (c) a statement that the sponsors are residents of the state of Kansas and possess the qualifications of an elector of the state of Kansas and who signed the application with the statement of grounds for recall attached, (d) the designation of a recall committee of three sponsors who shall represent all sponsors and subscribers in matters relating to the recall, (e) the designation of at least 100 residents of the state of Kansas who possess the qualifications of electors of the state of Kansas and who subscribe to the application as sponsors for purposes of circulation, and (f) the signatures and addresses of registered electors in the state or election district of the state officer sought to be recalled equal in number to not less than 10% of the votes cast for all candidates for the office of the state officer sought to be recalled, such percentage to be based upon the last general election for the current term of office of the officer sought to be recalled.

25-4307. Same; notice on matters relating to recall. Notice on all matters pertaining to the application and petition may be served on any member of the recall committee in person or by mail addressed to a committee member as indicated on the application. The secretary of state, upon request, shall notify the recall committee of the official number of votes cast for all candidates for the office of the state officer sought to be recalled, such percentage to be based upon the last general election for the current term of office of the officer sought to be recalled. County election officers shall assist the secretary of state as requested by such secretary.

25-4308. Same; certification of application; grounds for refusal of certification; commencement of proceedings concerning recall elections, time limits on. (a) The secretary of state shall review the application and shall either certify such application or notify the recall committee of the grounds of refusal. The secretary of state shall deny certification if the secretary of state determines that:

(1) The facts do not support the grounds for recall as stated in the application;

(2) the application is not substantially in the required form;

(3) the application was filed during the first 120 days of the term of office of the official sought to be recalled or within less than 200 days of the termination of the term of office of the state officer sought to be recalled;

(4) the person named in the application is not a state officer;

(5) there is an insufficient number of required signatures of any kind;

(6) the state officer sought to be recalled has been or is being subjected to another recall election during such officer's current term of office; or

(7) the application does not conform to any other requirement of this act.

(b) All mandamus proceedings to compel a recall election and all injunction proceedings to restrain a recall election shall be commenced not less than 30 days after the secretary of state's decision.

25-4309. Same; petition; form; certain acts crimes. (a) If the secretary of state certifies the application, he or she shall prescribe the form of, and prepare, a petition containing (1) the name and office of the person to be recalled, (2) the statement of the grounds for recall included in the application, (3) the statement of warning required in subsection (b), (4) sufficient space for signatures and addresses, and (5) other specifications prescribed by the secretary of state to assure proper handling and control. Petitions, for purposes of circulation, shall be prepared by the secretary of state in a number reasonably calculated to allow full circulation throughout the state or throughout the election district of the state officer sought to be recalled. The secretary of state shall number each petition and shall keep a record of the petitions delivered to each sponsor.

(b) Any person who signs a name other than that person's own name to a petition for recall of a state officer, or who knowingly signs more than once for the same proposition at one election, or who signs the petition knowing he or she is not a registered elector is guilty of a class B misdemeanor. Each page of the petition shall include a statement of warning of this crime.

25-4310. Same; petition; circulation; signatures; withdrawal. The petitions may be circulated only by a sponsor who is a resident of the state of Kansas and possesses the qualifications of an elector of the state of Kansas and only in person throughout the state or election district of the state officer sought to be recalled. No copy of a petition shall be circulated in more than one county, and the county election officer of the county in which each petition is circulated shall certify to the secretary of state the sufficiency of the signatures on the petition. Any registered elector of such election district or of the state, as the case may be, may subscribe to the petition by signing the elector's name and address as the same appears on the voter registration books. A person who has signed the petition may withdraw such person's name only by giving written notice to the secretary of state before the date the petition is filed. The necessary signatures on a petition shall be secured within 90 days from the date that the petitions prepared by the secretary of state pursuant to

K.S.A. 25-4309, and amendments thereto, are delivered to the recall committee. The petition shall be signed only in ink. Illegible signatures unless accompanied by a legible printed name may be rejected by the secretary of state or by any county election officer assisting the secretary of state.

25-4311. Same; petition; affidavit; filing, when; number of signatures. Before being filed, each petition shall be certified by an affidavit by the sponsor who personally circulated the petition. The affidavit shall state in substance that (a) the person signing the affidavit is a sponsor, (b) the person is the only circulator of that petition or copy, (c) the signatures were made in the petition circulator's actual presence, (d) to the best of the petition circulator's knowledge, the signatures are those of the persons whose names they purport to be, and (e) the person circulated the petition in the manner provided by this act. In determining the sufficiency of the petition, the secretary of state and county election officers assisting the secretary of state shall not count subscriptions on petitions not properly certified. Only one election may be held for the recall of a particular state officer in a single term of office, and no application for a second recall election within a single term shall be approved nor shall any petition therefor be circulated. No petition may be filed within less than 180 days of the termination of the term of office of the state officer sought to be recalled. The recall committee may file the petition only if signed by registered electors in the state or in the election district of the state officer sought to be recalled equal in number to not less than 40% of the votes cast for all candidates for the office of the state officer sought to be recalled, such percentage to be based upon the last general election for the current term of office of the state officer sought to be recalled.

25-4312. Same; petition; determination of sufficiency; when improperly filed. The secretary of state with the assistance and co-operation of each county election officer involved shall determine the sufficiency of each application and petition for recall of a state officer. Within thirty (30) days of the date of filing, the secretary of state shall review the petition and shall notify the recall committee and the person sought to be recalled whether the petition was properly or improperly filed. The secretary of state shall notify the committee that the petition was improperly filed if he or she determines that (a) there is an insufficient number of subscribing qualified registered electors, (b) the petition was filed within less than one hundred and eighty (180) days of the termination of the term of office of the state officer sought to be recalled or (c) the petition does not conform to any other requirement of this act.

25-4314. Same; election; time; ballot form. If the secretary of state determines the petition is properly filed and if the office is not vacant, he or she shall prescribe the ballot form and shall call a special election to be held on a date not less than sixty (60), nor more than ninety (90), days after the date that notification is given that the petition was properly filed. If a primary or general election is to be held not less than sixty (60), nor more than ninety (90), days after the date that notification is given that the petition was properly filed, the special election shall be held on the date of the primary or general election. The ballot shall be designed with the question of whether the state officer shall be recalled, placed on the ballot in the following manner: "Shall (name of official) be recalled from the office of ____________?". Provision shall be made for marking the question "Yes" or "No." Except as otherwise specifically provided by this act, laws applicable to question submitted elections shall apply to elections held under this section.

25-4315. Same; election; public inspection of statements. The secretary of state shall provide each county election officer in the state or in the election district of the state officer sought to be recalled with one copy of the statement of the grounds for recall included in the application and one copy of the statement of not more than 200 words made by the state officer sought to be recalled in justification of such state officer's conduct in office. The state officer sought to be recalled may provide the secretary of state with such state officer's statement within 10 days after the date the secretary of state gave notification that the petition was properly filed. Each county election officer shall maintain such statements for public inspection.

25-4316. Same; determination and certification of election results; filling of vacancy. If a majority of the votes cast on the question of recall favor the recall of the state officer, the state board of canvassers shall so determine and the secretary of state shall so certify and the office shall be vacant on the day after the date of certification. A vacancy caused by a recall shall be filled as a vacancy caused by other means.

25-4317. Same; action to have determinations relating to recall reviewed. Any person aggrieved by a determination made by the secretary of state or lieutenant governor with respect to recall of a state officer may bring an action to have such determination reviewed within thirty (30) days of the date on which notice of determination was given by action in the district court of Shawnee county or of the county of the legal residence of state officer.

25-4318. Recall of local officers; petition, filing. The recall of a local officer is proposed by filing a petition with the county election officer of the county in which all or the greater part of the population of the election district of the local officer is located, if not a school district, or the home county of the school district, if the election district of the local officer is a school district. The recall of a county election officer (if elected) is proposed by filing a petition with the county attorney of his or her county who shall perform the duties imposed on the county election officer in the recall of other local officers.

25-4319. Same; conduct of election. Subject to rules and

regulations of the secretary of state, the recall election of a local officer shall be conducted by the county election officer of the county in which the petition is required to be filed. Other county election officers of counties in which any part of the election district of the officer sought to be recalled shall assist the county election officer conducting such election.

25-4320. Petitions for recall of local officers; petition; contents; circulation; form; sample from election officer on request; affidavit. (a) Each petition for recall of a local officer shall include: (1) The name and office of the local officer sought to be recalled; (2) the grounds for recall described in particular in not more than 200 words; (3) a statement that the petition signers are registered electors of the election district of the local officer sought to be recalled; (4) the names and addresses of three registered electors of the election district of the officer sought to be recalled who shall comprise the recall committee; (5) the statement of warning required in K.S.A. 25-4321, and amendments thereto; and (6) a statement that a list of all sponsors authorized to circulate recall petitions for such recall may be examined in the office of the county election officer where the petition is required to be filed. Each sponsor shall be a resident of the state of Kansas and possess the qualifications of an elector of the state of Kansas.

(b) Each page of a petition for recall of a local officer shall be in substantially the following form:

I, the undersigned, hereby seek the recall of ____________ from the office of ________________________, on the ground(s) that

____

_______, (state specific grounds) and declare that I am a registered electer of __________________ County, Kansas, and of the election district of the officer named above. Street Number Name of or RR Name of Signer (as Registered) City Date of Signing _______ _______________ _______ _______________ _______ _______________ _______

NOTE:
1. It is a class B misdemeanor to sign a name other than your own name to this petition, to knowingly sign more than once for the recall of the same officer at the same election or to sign this petition knowing you are not a registered elector.

2. The following comprise the recall committee:
(names and resident addresses)

3. A list of all sponsors authorized to circulate petitions for this recall may be examined in the office of the ___________ County election officer.

(c) A county election officer shall provide a sample of the form prescribed by subsection (b) upon request by any person.

(d) The affidavit required by K.S.A. 25-4325, and amendments thereto, shall be appended to each petition for recall of a local officer.

25-4321. Same; certain acts crimes. Any person who signs a name other than that person's own name to a petition for recall of a local officer, or who knowingly signs more than once for the same proposition at one election, or who signs the petition knowing he or she is not a registered elector is guilty of a class B misdemeanor. Each page of the petition shall include a statement of warning of this crime.

25-4322. Same; petition; filing of copy before circulation; notice on matters relating to recall; determination of sufficiency of petition, procedure; commencement of proceedings concerning recall elections, time limits on. (a) Before any petition for recall of a local officer is circulated, a copy thereof accompanied by names and addresses of the recall committee and sponsors shall be filed in the office of the county election officer with whom the petitions are required to be filed. The copy of the petition so filed shall be subscribed by the members of the recall committee in the presence of such county election officer. The recall committee shall represent all sponsors and subscribers in matters relating to the recall. Notice on all matters pertaining to the recall may be served on any member of the recall committee in person or by mail addressed to a committee member as indicated on the petition so filed. The county election officer, upon request, shall notify the recall committee of the official number of votes cast for all candidates for the office of the local officer sought to be recalled, such percentage to be based upon the last general election for the current term of office of the officer sought to be recalled.

(b) Before any petition for recall of a local officer is circulated, the county election officer shall transmit a copy of such petition to the county or district attorney or to the attorney designated pursuant to subsection (c) for determination of the sufficiency of the grounds stated in the petition for recall. Within five days of receipt of the copy of the petition from the county election officer, the county or district attorney or the attorney designated pursuant to subsection (c) shall make such determination and notify the county election officer and the recall committee of such determination. Such determination shall include whether:

(1) The facts do not support the grounds for recall as stated in the petition for recall;

(2) the petition is not substantially in the required form;

(3) the petition was filed during the first 120 days of the term of office of the official sought to be recalled or within less than 180 days of the termination of the term of office of the officer sought to be recalled;

(4) the person named in the petition is not a local officer;

(5) there is an insufficient number of required signatures of any kind;

(6) the local officer sought to be recalled has been or is being subjected to another recall election during such officer's current term of office; or

(7) the application does not conform to any other requirement of this act.

(c) In the case of a recall of the county or district attorney, a judge of the district court of such county shall designate an attorney to determine the sufficiency of the grounds stated in the petition for recall. Such attorney shall perform the duties imposed on the county or district attorney in the recall of other local officers.

(d) All mandamus proceedings to compel a recall election and all injunction proceedings to restrain a recall election shall be commenced not less than 30 days after the county or district attorney's decision.

25-4323. Same; petition; filing, when; limitations. (a) No petition for recall of a local officer may be filed during the first one hundred and twenty (120) days of the term of office of the local officer sought to be recalled or within less than one hundred and eighty (180) days of the termination of the term of office of the local officer sought to be recalled.

(b) Only one recall election may be held to recall a particular local officer in a single term of office, and no petition for a second recall election within a single term shall be approved or circulated.

(c) The number of local officers serving on the same governing body which may be subject to recall at the same time shall not exceed a majority of the members of the governing body minus one, and no petition for recall of a local officer serving on a governing body shall be approved if petitions for the recall of other local officers serving on the same governing body have been properly filed and elections thereon have not been held and the number of such other local officers equals a majority of the members of the governing body minus one.

25-4324. Same; petition; circulation; signatures; withdrawal. The petitions shall be circulated in person by a sponsor. No petition shall be circulated in more than one county. The county election officer of the county in which each petition is circulated shall certify to the county election officer where petitions are required to be filed the sufficiency of the signatures on the petition. Any registered elector of such election district may subscribe to the petition by signing such elector's name and address. A person who has signed the petition may withdraw such person's name only by giving written notice to the county election officer where petitions are to be filed before the date filed. The necessary signatures on a petition shall be secured within 90 days from the date that the recall committee receives notice that the county or district attorney has determined that the grounds for recall as stated in the petition are sufficient as required by K.S.A. 25-4322, and amendments thereto. The petition shall be signed only in ink. Illegible signatures unless accompanied by a legible printed name may be rejected by the county election officer.
25-4325. Recall of local officers; petition; affidavit, form, number of signatures. Before being filed, each petition shall be certified by an affidavit by the sponsor who personally circulated the petition. The affidavit shall state in substance that (a) the person signing the affidavit is a sponsor, (b) the person is the only circulator of that petition or copy, (c) the signatures were made in such person's actual presence, (d) to the best of such person's knowledge, the signatures are those of the persons whose names they purport to be, (e) the person circulated the petition in the manner provided by this act and (f) the person signing the affidavit, being duly sworn, on oath states that the statements of grounds for recall contained in the recall petition are true. In determining the sufficiency of the petition, the county election officer shall not count signatures on petitions not properly certified. The

recall committee may file the petition only if signed by registered electors in the election district of the local officer sought to be recalled equal in number to not less than 40% of the votes cast for all candidates for the office of the local officer sought to be recalled, such percentage to be based upon the last general election for the current term of office of the local officer sought to be recalled. If more than one person was elected to such office at such election the number of signatures required shall be equal to not less than 40% of the votes cast at such election for all candidates for the office divided by the number of persons elected to such office.

25-4326. Same; petition; determination of sufficiency; when improperly filed. The county election officer of the county where petitions are required to be filed, with the assistance and cooperation of each other county election officer involved, shall determine the sufficiency of each petition for recall of a local officer. Within thirty (30) days of the date of filing, such county election officer shall review the petition and shall notify the recall committee and the local officer sought to be recalled whether the petition was properly or improperly filed. Such county election officer shall notify the recall committee that the petition was improperly filed if he or she determines that (a) there is an insufficient number of subscribing qualified registered electors, (b) the petition was filed within less than one hundred and eighty (180) days of the termination of the term of office of the local officer sought to be recalled, (c) the local officer sought to be recalled has been or is being subjected to another recall election during his or her current term of office, (d) petitions for the recall of other local officers serving on the same governing body have been properly filed and elections thereon have not been held and the number of such local officers equals a majority of the members of the governing body minus one or (e) the petition does not conform to any other requirement of this act.

25-4328. Same; election; form of ballot; vacancy in office. If the county election officer of the county where petitions are required to be filed determines the petition is properly filed and if the office is not vacant, such election officer shall prepare the ballots and shall call a special election to be held on a date not less than 60, nor more than 90, days after the date that notification is given that the petition was properly filed. If a vacancy occurs in the office held by the local officer sought to be recalled at any time after the date that notification is given that the petition therefor was properly filed, the county election officer, if such officer determines that unnecessary election expenses may be avoided thereby, may cancel such special election. The county election officer shall immediately notify the recall committee and any other county election officer involved of such vacancy and determination and take such other action as may be necessary to withdraw such proposition from submission to election. If a primary or general election is to be held not less than 60, nor more than 90, days after the date that notification is given that the petition was properly filed, the special election shall be held on the date of the primary or general election. If an election at which all or some of the residents of the district are entitled to vote, is to be held more than 90 days but not more than 120 days after the date notification is given that the petition was properly filed, the recall election may be held on the date of such election. The ballot shall be designed with the question of whether the local officer shall be recalled, placed on the ballot in the following manner: "Shall (name of official) be recalled from the office of ______________?". Provision shall be made for marking the question "Yes" or "No." Except as otherwise specifically provided by this act, laws applicable to question submitted elections shall apply to elections held under this section.

25-4329. Same; election; public inspection of statements. Within 10 days after the date the county election officer gave notification that the recall petition was properly filed, the person sought to be recalled may provide to the county election officer such person's statement, containing not more than 200 words, in justification of such person's conduct in office. The county election officer shall maintain such statement for public inspection.

25-4330. Same; election results; certification; vacancies; disqualification for appointment to governing body. If a majority of the votes cast on the question of recall favor the recall of the local officer, the county board of canvassers shall so determine and the county election officer shall so certify and the office shall be vacant on the day after the date of certification. A vacancy caused by a recall shall be filled as a vacancy caused by other means. No local officer who has been recalled, or who has resigned after a petition for recall has been filed to recall such officer, shall be eligible for appointment to fill such vacancy, and if the officer is a member of a governing body, the person so resigning shall be ineligible for appointment to any other position or office on such governing body until the current term of that office has expired.

25-4331. Same; action to have determinations relating to recall reviewed. Any person aggrieved by a determination made by the county election officer or county attorney of the county where petitions are required to be filed may bring an action to have the determination reviewed within thirty (30) days of the date on which notice of determination was given by action in the district court of such county.

CONSTITUTION OF LOUISIANA
Article X, Section 26.

The legislature shall provide by general law for the recall by election of any state, district, parochial, ward, or municipal official except judges of the courts of record. The sole issue at a recall election shall be whether the official shall be recalled.

LOUISIANA REVISED STATUTES ANNOTATED,
Section 1300.1 et. sec.
Beginning with Recall Authorized.

La. R.S. 18:1300.1
La. R.S. 18:1300.2
La. R.S. 18:1300.3
La. R.S. 18:1300.4
La. R.S. 18:1300.5
La. R.S. 18:1300.6
La. R.S. 18:1300.7
La. R.S. 18:1300.8
La. R.S. 18:1300.9
La. R.S. 18:1300.10
La. R.S. 18:1300.11
La. R.S. 18:1300.12
La. R.S. 18:1300.13
La. R.S. 18:1300.14
La. R.S. 18:1300.15
La. R.S. 18:1300.16
La. R.S. 18:1300.17

1300.1. Recall authorized

Any public officer, excepting judges of the courts of record, may be recalled in accordance with the provisions of this Chapter. However, no recall petition may be submitted for certification to or accepted for certification by the registrar of voters or any other official if less than six months remain in the term of office.

1300.2. Petition for Recall Election immediately before "A.(1)

A.(1) Whenever the recall of any public officer is sought, a petition shall be directed to the governor. The petition shall be limited to the request that an election be called and held in the voting area for the purpose of recalling the officer. No recall petition shall seek an election for the recall of more than one public officer, individually, in the same recall petition.

(2) The secretary of state shall provide a form approved by the attorney general to be used for the petition for a recall election. Such form shall be in conformity with the provisions of this Chapter and R.S. 18:3. All recall petitions shall be on an approved form or on a form which contains the same information as required by the approved form and any petition not on such a form shall be invalid.

B. All signatures on recall petitions shall be handwritten. This petition shall be signed by a number of the electors of the voting area as will in number equal not less than thirty-three and one-third percent of the number of the total electors of the voting area wherein and for which a recall election is petitioned; however, where fewer than one thousand qualified electors reside within the voting area, the petition shall be signed by not less than forty percent of said electors.

C.(1) Prior to the entering of any signatures on a petition, the chairman designated to represent the petitioners shall file with the secretary of state a copy of the recall petition which will be used and upon receipt of the recall petition the secretary of state shall endorse thereon the fact and the date of filing. A copy shall be transmitted by the secretary of state to the registrar of voters for each parish in which the recall election is to be held. The chairman shall list on the petition every parish which is wholly or partially within the voting area in which the recall election is to be held. The petition shall be deemed filed when it is received in the office of the secretary of state, or at the time it is postmarked by the United States Postal Service or is receipted on a return receipt request form, if it is subsequently received in the office of the secretary of state.

(2) The signed and dated petition shall be submitted to the

registrar of voters for each parish within the voting area not later than one hundred eighty days after the day on which the copy of the petition was filed with the secretary of state. If the final day for submitting the signed and dated petition falls on a Saturday, Sunday, or legal holiday, the deadline for filing such petition shall be on the next day which is not a Saturday, Sunday, or legal holiday.

(3) The chairman shall file notice with the registrar on the third day before the petition is submitted to the registrar that he will submit the petition and the date of such submission, unless such submission is made within three days prior to the expiration of the period for submitting such petition. Such notice of submission shall be a public record. If the notice filed with the registrar on the third day before the petition is submitted includes a date for submitting the signed and dated petition which falls on a Saturday, Sunday, or other legal holiday, the registrar shall so inform the chairman and advise the chairman of the next day which is not a Saturday, Sunday, or other legal holiday and on which the petition is to be submitted.

D. Each elector, at the time of signing the petition, shall enter his address and the date on which he signed beside or underneath his signature; however, if a person is unable to write, as provided in R.S. 18:1300.4, the two witnesses shall date their signatures. In addition, each petition shall be in compliance with the provisions of R.S. 18:3. In determining the number of qualified electors who signed the petition in any parish, the registrar of voters shall not count any signature which is undated or bears a date prior to the date on which the copy of the petition initially was filed with the secretary of state or after the date of the submission of the petition to the registrar except as otherwise provided in R.S. 18:1300.3(B). The registrar shall not receive or certify a petition submitted to him for certification unless it is submitted to him timely.

E. The secretary of state shall notify the Supervisory Committee on Campaign Finance Disclosure of the filing of a copy of a recall petition to be used to seek the recall of a public officer, including the date of such filing, the officer who is the subject of the petition, and the names and addresses of the chairman and vice chairman designated on the petition. The Campaign Finance Disclosure Act shall be applicable to persons supporting or opposing the recall of a public officer as provided in R.S. 18:1486.

1300.3. Certification of Registrar of Voters.

A. The registrar of voters of each parish in the voting area wherein a recall election is sought shall certify on the recall petition, within fifteen working days after it is presented to him for that purpose, the number of names appearing thereon, the number of qualified electors of the voting area within the parish whose handwritten signatures appear on the petition, and also the total number of electors of the voting area within the parish as of the date of the filing of the petition with the secretary of state. However, if any parish wholly or partially within the voting area has more than fifty thousand registered voters, the registrar of voters for each parish within the voting area shall complete such certification on the recall petition within twenty working days after it is presented to him for that purpose. Each registrar also shall indicate on the petition the names appearing thereon who are not electors of the voting area. Each person who participates in the review of the names on the petition for certification by the registrar as required in this Section shall initial each of those portions of the petition which he reviews for certification by the registrar.

B. The registrar of voters shall honor the written request of any voter who either desires to have his handwritten signature stricken from the petition or desires to have his handwritten signature added to the petition at any time after receipt of the signed petition as provided in R.S.

18:1300.2(C) but prior to certification of the petition or within five days after receipt of such signed petition, whichever is earlier.

C. When there is no registrar of voters, or deputy registrar of voters in any parish, or in case of the absence or inability of that officer, the clerk of the district court of the parish shall execute the certificate. Immediately after the recall petition is certified a copy of the petition shall be made and the original recall petition shall be sent to the governor by the officer executing the certificate. Such copy shall be retained in the office of the registrar of voters in each parish affected by the petition and shall be a public record.

D. When any officer designated in this Chapter refuses to execute the certificates provided for, any signer of a recall petition, or the chairman or vice chairman designated to represent the signers, may compel the execution of the certificates by summary process in the district court having jurisdiction over the officer.

E. The registrar of voters shall comply with the provisions of R.S. 18:3(C) when determining the number of qualified electors of the voting area who signed the petition.

1300.4. Signature to recall petition
No person may sign any name to a recall petition other than his own, except in a case where a person is unable to write, in which case the incapacitated person shall affix his mark to the petition and the person circulating the petition shall affix the name and address of the incapacitated person, as well as the date on which the incapacitated person affixed his mark to the petition, provided he does so in the presence of two witnesses who shall also sign their names as witnesses to the mark.

1300.5. Chairman and vice chairman designated in petition; petition designated as a public record.

A. The recall petition shall designate a chairman to act for the signers of the petition in all matters, and a vice chairman to act on order of the chairman or in case of the death, disability, absence, or resignation of the chairman. The petition shall include the full name and residence address of the chairman and the vice chairman. The chairman and vice chairman each shall be a qualified voter in the voting area from which the public official whose recall is being sought is elected.

B. Upon the signature of the first elector, the recall petition, including the name, address, and signature of each elector who has signed thereon, shall be a public record. The chairman, or the vice chairman when acting as the chairman, shall be the custodian thereof. The petition and the custodian shall be subject to all of the provisions of R. S. 44:31 et. seq.

C. Upon the filing of the petition pursuant to R.S. 18:1300.2(C)(2), the chairman, or the vice chairman when acting as chairman, shall no longer be the custodian thereof.

1300.6. Acts prohibited; penalty

A. It shall be unlawful for any person to circulate recall petitions or seek handwritten signatures to a recall petition within any polling place being used in an election on election day or within any place wherein absentee voting is being conducted, or within a radius of six hundred feet of the entrance to any polling place being used in an election on election day or any place wherein absentee voting is being conducted.

B. Whoever violates any provision of this Section shall be fined not more than five hundred dollars or be imprisoned for not more than six months, or both. On a second offense or any succeeding offense, the penalty shall be a fine of not more than one thousand dollars or imprisonment for not more than one year, or both.

1300.7. Governor to order election; proclamation; publication

A. If the required number of qualified electors of the voting area sign the petition for recall, the governor shall issue a proclamation ordering an election to be held for the purpose of voting on the question of the recall of the officer. The total number of registered voters in the voting area and the total number of registered voters in the voting area signing the petition shall be calculated from the totals on the certificates of all of the registrars of voters received by the governor. The governor shall issue such proclamation within fifteen days after he receives the certified petitions from all of the registrars of voters in the voting area who have received petitions for certification. The proclamation shall order the election to be held on the next available date specified in R.S. 18:402(F). If the election is to be held on a primary election date, the proclamation shall be issued on or before the last day for candidates to qualify in the election. If the election is not to be held on a primary election date, then the proclamation shall be issued on or before the forty-sixth day prior to the election.

B. Immediately after the issuance of the proclamation, the governor shall publish the proclamation in the official journal of each parish in which the election is to be held. Within twenty-four hours after issuing the proclamation, the governor shall send a copy of the petition and proclamation, by registered or certified mail, to the clerk of the district court for each parish in which the election is to be held. If the election is to be held in Orleans Parish, the city of New Orleans, the copy of the petition and proclamation shall be mailed to the clerk of the criminal district court. A copy of the petition and proclamation also shall be sent to the secretary of state. Within twenty-four hours after he receives the copies, the secretary of state shall notify all other election officials having any duty to perform in connection with a recall election, including the parish board of election supervisors for the parish or parishes in which the election is held.

1300.8. Voting area

A. The voting area for an election to recall an officer is the area which composes the state, district, parish, municipality, or ward that the officer represents as of the date the petition is filed with the secretary of state.
B. This area is the basis on which to determine whether the handwritten signatures to the recall petition are sufficient and proper; the number of handwritten signatures required is determined by calculation of the number of electors of the voting area as set forth in R.S. 18:1300.2.

1300.9. Recall elections, conduct in accordance with Election Code

Elections for the recall of any public officer shall be held under and in accordance with the applicable provisions of the Louisiana Election Code, except as otherwise specifically provided in this Chapter.

MICHIGAN CONSTITUTION
Article II, Section 8.

Laws shall be enacted to provide for the recall of all elective officers except judges of courts of record upon petition of electors equal in number to 25 percent of the number of persons voting in the last preceding election for the office of governor in the electoral district of the officer sought to be recalled. The sufficiency of any statement of reasons or grounds procedurally required shall be a political rather than a judicial question.

MICHIGAN ELECTION LAW
Article 116, Section 168.69 et sec.
Beginning with Governor or lieutenant governor; recall.

MCL 168.69

MCL 168.180
MCL 168.951
MCL 168.952
MCL 168.952a
MCL 168.954
MCL 168.955
MCL 168.957
MCL 168.958
MCL 168.958a
MCL 168.959
MCL 168.961a
MCL 168.963
MCL 168.964
MCL 168.966
MCL 168.967
MCL 168.968
MCL 168.969
MCL 168.970
MCL 168.971
MCL 168.972
MCL 168.973
MCL 168.974
MCL 168.975
MCL 168.976

168.69 Governor or lieutenant governor; recall.

Any person elected to the office of governor or lieutenant governor shall be subject to recall as provided in chapter 36 of this act and in section 8 of article 2 of the state constitution.

168.180 State senators and representatives; recall.

Any person elected to the office of state senator or representative shall be subject to recall as provided in chapter 36 of this act and in section 8 of article 2 of the state constitution.

168.951 Officers subject to recall; time for filing recall petition; performance of duties until result of recall election certified.

Every elective officer in the state, except a judicial officer, is subject to recall by the voters of the electoral district in which the officer is elected as provided in this chapter. A petition shall not be filed against an officer until the officer has actually performed the duties of the office to which elected for a period of 6 months during the current term of that office. A petition shall not be filed against an officer during the last 6 months of the officer's term of office. An officer sought to be recalled shall continue to perform duties of the office until the result of the recall election is certified.

168.952 Recall petitions; requirements; submission to board of county election commissioners; determination; notice; meeting; presentation of arguments; appeal; validity of petition.

(1) A petition for the recall of an officer shall meet all of the following requirements:

(a) Comply with section 544c(1) and (2).

(b) Be printed.

(c) State clearly each reason for the recall. Each reason for the recall shall be based upon the officer's conduct during his or her current term of office. The reason for the recall may be typewritten.

(d) Contain a certificate of the circulator. The certificate of the circulator may be printed on the reverse side of the petition.

(e) Be in a form prescribed by the secretary of state.

(2) Before being circulated, a petition for the recall of an officer shall be submitted to the board of county election commissioners of the county in which the officer whose recall is

sought resides.

(3) The board of county election commissioners, not less than 10 days or more than 20 days after submission to it of a petition for the recall of an officer, shall meet and shall determine whether each reason for the recall stated in the petition is of sufficient clarity to enable the officer whose recall is sought and the electors to identify the course of conduct that is the basis for the recall. Failure of the board of county election commissioners to comply with this subsection shall constitute a determination that each reason for the recall stated in the petition is of sufficient clarity to enable the officer whose recall is being sought and the electors to identify the course of conduct that is the basis for the recall.

(4) The board of county election commissioners, not later than 24 hours after receipt of a petition for the recall of an officer, shall notify the officer whose recall is sought of each reason stated in the petition and of the date of the meeting of the board of county election commissioners to consider the clarity of each reason.

(5) The officer whose recall is sought and the sponsors of the petition may appear at the meeting and present arguments on the clarity of each reason.

(6) The determination by the board of county election commissioners may be appealed by the officer whose recall is sought or by the sponsors of the petition drive to the circuit court in the county. The appeal shall be filed not more than 10 days after the determination of the board of county election commissioners.

(7) A petition that is determined to be of sufficient clarity under subsection (1) or, if the determination under subsection (1) is appealed pursuant to subsection (6), a petition that is determined by the circuit court to be of sufficient clarity is

valid for 180 days following the last determination of sufficient clarity under this section. A recall petition that is filed under section 959 or 960 after the 180-day period described in this subsection is not valid and shall not be accepted pursuant to section 961. This subsection does not prohibit a person from resubmitting a recall petition for a determination of sufficient clarity under this section.

168.952a Recall petitions; blank forms; substantial compliance.

The county clerk shall retain blank forms of recall petitions for use by the electors in the county. A person may print his or her own recall petitions if those petitions comply substantially with the form prescribed by the secretary of state and the requirements of section 544c(2).

168.954 Recall petitions; eligibility of signers.
The petitions shall be signed by registered and qualified electors of the electoral district of the official whose recall is sought. In a school district where school electors are not required to be registered, the signers of the petition shall not be required to be registered electors and the term "registered and qualified electors" shall mean "qualified electors". Each signer of the petition shall affix his signature, address, and the date of signing. The persons signing the petition shall be registered and qualified electors of the governmental subdivision designated in the heading of the petition.

168.955 Recall petition; number of signatures; certification.

The petitions shall be signed by registered and qualified electors equal to not less than 25% of the number of votes cast for candidates for the office of governor at the last preceding general election in the electoral district of the officer sought to be recalled. Upon written demand, the county clerk, within 5 days, shall certify the minimum number of signatures required for the recall of an officer in the governmental unit in which recall is sought.

168.957 Recall petitions; qualifications and certificate of circulator; false statement; penalty.

A person circulating a petition shall be a qualified and registered elector in the electoral district of the official sought to be recalled and shall attach thereto his certificate stating that he is a qualified and registered elector in the electoral district of the official sought to be recalled and shall state the city or the township wherein he resides and his post-office address; further, that signatures appearing upon the petition were not obtained through fraud, deceit, or misrepresentation and that he has neither caused nor permitted a person to sign the petition more than once and has no knowledge of a person signing the petition more than once; that all signatures to the petition were affixed in his presence; and that to the best of his knowledge, information, and belief, the signers of the petition are qualified and registered electors and the signatures appearing thereon are the genuine signatures of the persons of whom they purport to be. A person who knowingly makes a false statement in the certificate hereby required is guilty of a misdemeanor.

168.958 Recall petition sheet; signature of qualified and registered electors; location for signing; signature of person not qualified and registered elector.

A petition sheet shall contain only the signatures of qualified and registered electors of the city or township listed in its heading. For recall of a village officer the petition shall be signed by qualified and registered electors of the village. A qualified and registered elector may sign the petition sheet in any location at which the petition sheet is available. A petition is not invalid if it contains the signature of a person who is not a qualified and registered elector of the appropriate city, township, or village listed in the heading of that petition sheet.

168.958a Separate petitions required.

A separate petition shall be circulated for each officer sought to be recalled.

168.959 Recall of senators, representatives, elective state officers, county officials, or secretary of state; filing petitions.

Petitions demanding the recall of United States senators, members of congress, state senators and representatives in the state legislature, elective state officers except the secretary of state, and county officials except county commissioners, shall be filed with the secretary of state. Petitions for the recall of the secretary of state shall be filed with the governor.

168.961 Recall petition; filing; receipt; duties of filing official; duties of city or township clerk; certificate; duties of village clerk; use of qualified voter file.
(1) A recall petition shall be filed with the filing officer provided in section 959 or 960. The filing official shall give a receipt showing the date of filing, the number of petition sheets filed, and the number of signatures claimed by the filer. This shall constitute the total filing, and additional petition sheets for this filing shall not be accepted by the filing official.

(2) Within 7 days after a recall petition is filed, the filing official with whom the petition was filed shall examine the recall petition. The filing official shall determine if the recall petition is in proper form and shall determine the number of signatures of the petition. In determining the number of signatures, the filing official shall not count signatures on a petition sheet if 1 or more of the following apply:

(a) The execution of the certificate of circulator is not in compliance with this act.

(b) The heading of the petition sheet is improperly completed.

(c) The reasons for recall are different than those determined by the board of county election commissioners to be of sufficient clarity to enable the officer whose recall is sought and the electors to identify the course of conduct which is the basis for this recall.

(d) The signature was obtained before the date of determination by the board of county election commissioners or more than 90 days before the filing of the petition.

(3) If the filing official determines that the form of the petition is improper or that the number of signatures is less than the minimum number required in section 955, the filing official shall proceed as provided in section 963(1).

(4) If the filing official determines that the number of signatures is in excess of the minimum number required in section 955, the filing official shall determine the validity of the signatures by verifying the registration of signers pursuant to subsection (6) or shall forward each petition sheet to the clerk of the city or township appearing on the head of the petition sheet. However, the petition shall not be forwarded to the secretary of a school district.

(5) Subject to subsection (6), the city or township clerk shall compare the names on the petition with the city or township registration records. The clerk may compare with the signatures on the original registration record or with the name or address on registration lists on file in the clerk's office. Within 15 days after receipt of the petition, the city or township clerk shall attach to the petition a certificate indicating the number of signers on each petition sheet that are registered electors in the city or township and in the governmental unit for which the recall is sought. The certificate shall be on a form approved by the secretary of state and may be a part of the petition sheet. If the recall petition is for the recall of a village official, the county clerk shall forward the petition to the clerk of the village, and the duties and responsibilities of the city or township clerk as set forth in this section shall be performed by the village clerk.

(6) The qualified voter file may be used to determine the validity of petition signatures by verifying the registration of signers. If the qualified voter file indicates that, on the date the elector signed the petition, the elector was not registered to vote, there is a rebuttable presumption that the signature is invalid. If the qualified voter file indicates that, on the date the elector signed the petition, the elector was not registered to vote in the city or township designated on the petition, there is a rebuttable presumption that the signature is invalid.

168.963 Sufficiency or insufficiency of recall petition; determination; notice; submission of proposed date for special election; effect of petition filed under § 168.959.

(1) Within 35 days after the filing of the recall petition, the filing official with whom the recall petition is filed shall make an official declaration of the sufficiency or insufficiency of the petition. If the recall petition is determined to be insufficient, the filing official shall notify the person or organization sponsoring the recall of the insufficiency of the petition. It is not necessary to give notification unless the person or organization sponsoring the recall files with the filing official a written notice of sponsorship and a mailing address.

(2) Immediately upon determining that the petition is sufficient, but not later than 35 days after the date of filing of the petition, the county clerk with whom the petition is filed shall submit to the county election scheduling committee a proposed date for a special election to be held within 60 days after the submission to the county scheduling committee to determine whether the electors will recall the officer whose recall is sought.

(3) If a petition is filed under section 959, the officer with whom the petition is filed shall not submit a proposed date to the county election scheduling committee but shall call the special election subject to the time limitations set out in this section.

168.964 Recall election; procedure; notice; ballots; election supplies; assignment of precinct election officials.

The procedure governing the election on the question of the recall of an officer shall be the same, so far as possible and unless otherwise provided in this act, as that by which the officer is elected to office. If the official with whom the petition is filed is not required to give public notice of an election concerning the office in question, the official shall give notice to the official or officials required by the general election, the school, or the library laws of this state or a city charter to give public notice of the election, cause the ballots to be printed, provide election supplies, and do all things necessary to conduct the election in the manner provided in this act. Fewer precinct election officials than the number otherwise required under the general election laws of this state may be assigned to duty if it appears that the votes to be cast will not necessitate the number of precinct election officials otherwise so required.

168.966 Recall ballot; contents.

(1) The reason for demanding the recall of the officer as set forth in the petition shall be printed on the recall ballot used at the election in not more than 200 words. If the statement of reason set forth in the petition shall contain more than 200 words, then the statement shall be condensed by the sponsor of the petition for use on the ballot. If the sponsor fails to furnish the condensed statement within 48 hours following written demand, then the statement shall be condensed by the official preparing the ballots.

(2) The official preparing the ballot shall provide in writing the officer whose recall is sought the statement of reason which shall appear on the ballot. The officer whose recall is sought, in not more than 200 words, may submit a justification of conduct in office. The justification shall be submitted to the official preparing the ballot within 72 hours after receipt of the notification. If submitted in the prescribed time,

the justification shall be printed on the ballot.

(3) The statement "Vote no on the recall" or "Vote yes on the recall" or words of similar import shall not be permitted on the ballot. A part of the reason for demanding the recall of the officer or the officer's justification of conduct in office shall not be emphasized by italics, underscoring, or in any other manner.

(4) There shall be printed on the recall ballot the following questions:

Shall (Name the person against whom the recall petition is filed) be recalled from the office of (title of the office)? Printed below the question in separate lines in easily legible type shall be the words "Yes[ ]" and "No[ ]"or in a form as may be prescribed by the secretary of state.

168.967 Recall election; payment of expenses.

The expenses of the recall election shall be payable in the same manner as are the costs of a regular election to fill the office in question.

168.968 Canvass of recall election; certification of results; office vacant upon certification; notice.

If a petition is filed under section 960, the board of county canvassers in the county where the petition is filed shall conduct the canvass of the recall election. The canvass of other recall elections shall be by the board of state canvassers. If a board of canvassers determines that a majority of the votes are in favor of recall, the board of canvassers immediately upon the determination shall certify the result to the officer with whom the recall petition was filed. Upon certification, the office is vacant. The officer with whom the recall petition was filed shall immediately upon receipt of the certification notify the clerk or secretary of the electoral district or, if the electoral district is a district library district, the district library board from which the official was recalled and the recalled official of the results of the recall election and the date and time of the certification.

168.969 Further recall petition; filing, condition.

After filing such recall petition and after such special election, no further recall petition shall be filed against the same incumbent of such office during the term for which he is elected unless such further petitioners shall first pay into the public treasury, which has paid such election expenses, the whole amount of election expenses for the preceding special election held for the recall of said incumbent.

MINNESOTA CONSTITUTION
Article VIII, Section 6.

A member of the senate or the house of representatives, an executive officer of the state identified in section 1 of article V of the constitution, or a judge of the supreme court, the court of appeals, or a district court is subject to recall from office by the voters. The grounds for recall of a judge shall be established by the supreme court. The grounds for recall of an officer other than a judge are serious malfeasance or nonfeasance during the term of office in the performance of the duties of the office or conviction during the term of office of a serious crime. A petition for recall must set forth the specific conduct that may warrant recall. A petition may not be issued until the supreme court has determined that the facts alleged in the petition are true and are sufficient grounds for issuing a recall petition. A petition must be signed by a number of eligible voters who reside in the district where the officer serves and who number not less than 25 percent of the number of votes cast for the office at the most recent general election. Upon a determination by the secretary of state that a petition has been signed by at least the minimum number of eligible voters, a recall election must be conducted in the manner provided by law. A recall election may not occur less than six months before the end of the officer's term. An officer who is removed from office by a recall election or who resigns from office after a petition for recall issues may not be appointed to fill the vacancy that is created.

MINNESOTA STATUTES
Chapter 211C, Section 211C.01 et. sec.
Beginning with Definitions

MS, Section 211C.01
MS, Section 211C.02
MS, Section 211C.03
MS, Section 211C.04
MS, Section 211C.05
MS, Section 211C.06
MS, Section 211C.07
MS, Section 211C.08
MS, Section 211C.09

211C.01 Definitions.

Subdivision 1. Application. The definitions in this section and in chapter 200 apply to this chapter.

Subd. 2. Malfeasance. "Malfeasance" means the intentional commission of an unlawful or wrongful act by a state officer other than a judge in the performance of the officer's duties that is substantially outside the scope of the authority of the officer and that substantially infringes on the rights of any person or entity.

Subd. 3. Nonfeasance. "Nonfeasance" means the intentional, repeated failure of a state officer other than a judge to perform specific acts that are required duties of the officer.

Subd. 4. Serious crime. (a) "Serious crime" means a crime that is punished as a gross misdemeanor, as defined in section 609.02, and that involves assault, intentional injury or threat of injury to person or public safety, dishonesty, stalking, aggravated driving while intoxicated, coercion, obstruction of justice, or the sale or possession of controlled substances. (b) "Serious crime" also means a crime that is punished as a misdemeanor, as defined in section 609.02, and that involves assault, intentional injury or threat of injury to person or public safety, dishonesty, coercion, obstruction of justice, or the sale or possession of controlled substances.

Subd. 5. State officer. "State officer" means an individual occupying an office subject to recall under the Minnesota Constitution, article VIII, section 6.

211C.02 Grounds.

The grounds for recall of a judge shall be established by the Supreme Court. A state officer other than a judge may be subject to recall for serious malfeasance or nonfeasance during the term of office in the performance of the duties of the office or conviction during the term of office for a serious crime.

211C.03 Petition for recall; form and content.

The secretary of state shall prescribe by rule the form required for a recall petition. Each page of the petition must contain the following information:

(1) the name and office held by the state officer who is the subject of the recall petition and, in the case of a representative, senator, or district judge, the district number in which

the state officer serves;

(2) the specific grounds upon which the state officer is sought to be recalled and a concise, accurate, and complete synopsis of the specific facts that are alleged to warrant recall on those grounds;

(3) a statement that a recall election, if conducted, will be conducted at public expense;

(4) a statement that persons signing the petition:

(i) must be eligible voters residing within the district where the state officer serves or, in the case of a statewide officer, within the state;

(ii) must know the purpose and content of the petition; and
(iii) must sign of their own free will and may sign only once; and

(5) a space for the signature and signature date; printed first, middle, and last name; residence address, including municipality and county; and date of birth of each signer.

The secretary of state shall make available sample recall petition forms upon request.

211C.04 Proposed petition; submittal.

A petition to recall a state officer may be proposed by 25 or more persons, who must be eligible to sign and shall sign the proposed petition for the recall of the officer. The persons submitting the petition must designate in writing no more than three individuals among them to represent all petitioners in matters relating to the recall. The proposed petition must be submitted to the secretary of state in the manner and form required by the secretary of state and be accompanied by a fee of $100. After the secretary of state issues a petition to recall a state officer under section 211C.06, the secretary of state may not accept a proposed petition to recall the same officer until either the earlier petition is dismissed by the secretary of state for a deficiency of signatures under section 211C.06, or the recall election brought about by the earlier petition results in the officer retaining the office. Upon receiving a proposed petition that satisfies the requirements of this section, the secretary of state shall immediately notify in writing the state officer named and forward the proposed petition to the clerk of the appellate courts for action under section 211C.05.

211C.05 Supreme Court review of proposed petition.

Subdivision 1. Assignment for hearing. Upon receiving a proposed petition from the secretary of state, the clerk of the appellate courts shall submit it immediately to the chief justice of the Supreme Court, or, if the chief justice is the subject of the proposed petition, to the most senior associate justice of the Supreme Court. The persons proposing the petition shall provide to the reviewing judge any materials supporting the petition. The officer who is named in the proposed petition may submit materials in opposition. The justice, or a designee if the justice has a conflict of interest or is unable to conduct the review in a timely manner, shall review the proposed petition to determine whether it alleges specific facts that, if proven, would constitute grounds for recall of the officer under the Minnesota Constitution, article VIII, section 6, and section 211C.02. If it does not, the justice shall immediately issue an order dismissing the petition and indicating the reason for dismissal. If the proposed petition does allege specific facts that, if proven, would constitute grounds for recall, the justice shall assign the case to a special master for a public hearing. The special master must be an active or retired judge. The justice shall complete the review under this section and dismiss the proposed petition or assign the case for hearing within ten days.

Subd. 2. Hearing; report. A public hearing on the allegations of a proposed petition must be held within 21 days after issuance of the order of the justice assigning the case to a special master. The special master shall report to the court within seven days after the end of the public hearing. In the report, the special master shall determine:

(1) whether the persons proposing the petition have shown by a preponderance of the evidence that the factual allegations supporting the petition are true; and

(2) if so, whether the persons proposing the petition have shown that the facts found to be true are sufficient grounds for issuing a recall petition.

If the special master determines that these standards have been met, the report must include a statement of the specific facts and grounds for the recall petition.

Subd. 3. Supreme Court; decision. The Supreme Court shall review the report of the special master and make a decision on the petition within 20 days. If the court decides that the standard expressed in subdivision 2 has not been met, the court shall dismiss the petition. If the court decides that the standard for decision expressed in subdivision 2 has been met, the court shall prescribe, by order to the secretary of state, the statement of the specific facts and grounds that must appear on the petition for recall issued under section 211C.06.

If the court dismisses a petition under this section because the persons proposing the petition have acted in bad faith in violation of section 211C.09, the court may assess the persons proposing the petition for reasonable costs of conducting the proceeding.

211C.06 Issuing, circulating, and verifying petition.

Upon receipt of the order from the Supreme Court, the secretary of state shall issue a recall petition. When the required number of signatures on the petition have been secured, the petition may be filed with the secretary of state. The petition must be filed within 90 days after the date of issuance. Upon the filing of the petition, the secretary of state shall verify the number and eligibility of signers in the manner provided by the secretary of state. If the secretary of state determines that a petition has been signed by a sufficient number of eligible voters, the secretary of state shall certify the petition and immediately notify in writing the governor, the petitioners, and the state officer named in the petition. If the petition is not signed by a sufficient number of eligible voters, the secretary of state shall dismiss the petition.

211C.07 Governor; writ of election; election.

Within five days of receiving certification of a petition under section 211C.06, the governor shall issue a writ calling for a recall election, unless the election cannot be held before the deadline specified in the Minnesota Constitution, article VIII, section 6. A recall election must be conducted, and the results canvassed and returned, in the manner provided by law for the state general election.

211C.08 Election result; removal from office.

If a majority of the votes cast in a recall election favor the removal of the state officer, upon certification of that result the state officer is removed from office and the office is vacant.

211C.09 Recall petition; corrupt practices.

A person proposing a petition may not allege any material fact in support of the petition that the person knows is false or has alleged with reckless disregard of whether it is false. A person may not intentionally make any false entry on a petition or aid, abet, counsel, or procure another to do so. A person may not use threat, intimidation, coercion, or other corrupt means to interfere or attempt to interfere with the right of any eligible voter to sign or not to sign a recall petition of their own free will. A person may not, for any consideration, compensation, gift, reward, or thing of value or promise thereof, sign or not sign a recall petition.

The Supreme Court may dismiss a proposed petition for violation of this section. Notwithstanding section 645.241, the sole remedy for a violation of this section is dismissal of the petition by the Supreme Court.

RECALL NOT COVERED IN MONTANA CONSTITUTION

MONTANA CODE ANNOTATED

Title 2, Chapter 16, Part 6 (Montana Recall Act), Section 2-16-601 et sec. Beginning with short title.

MCA 2-16-601
MCA 2-16-602
MCA 2-16-603
MCA 2-16-611
MCA 2-16-612
MCA 2-16-613
MCA 2-16-614
MCA 2-16-615
MCA 2-16-616
MCA 2-16-617
MCA 2-16-618
MCA 2-16-619
MCA 2-16-620
MCA 2-16-621
MCA 2-16-622

MCA 2-16-631
MCA 2-16-632
MCA 2-16-633
MCA 2-16-634
MCA 2-16-635

2-16-601. Short title. This part shall be cited as the "Montana Recall Act".

2-16-602. Definitions. As used in this part, the following definitions apply:
(1) "Political subdivision" means a local government unit including but not limited to a county, city, or town established under authority of Article XI, section 1, of The Constitution of the State of Montana or a school district.
(2) "Public office" means a position of duty, trust, or authority created by the constitution or by the legislature or by a political subdivision through authority conferred by the constitution or the legislature that meets the following criteria:
(a) the position must possess a delegation of a portion of the sovereign power of government to be exercised for the benefit of the public;
(b) the powers conferred and the duties to be discharged must be defined, directly or impliedly, by the constitution, the legislature, or by a political subdivision through legislative authority;
(c) the duties must be performed independently and without control of a superior power other than the law, unless the legislature has created the position and placed it under the general control of a superior office or body; and
(d) the position must have some permanency and continuity and not be only temporary or occasional.
(3) "State-district" means a public service commission district, a legislative representative or senatorial district, or a judicial district.

2-16-603. Officers subject to recall -- grounds for recall. (1)

Every person holding a public office of the state or any of its political subdivisions, either by election or appointment, is subject to recall from such office.
(2) A public officer holding an elective office may be recalled by the qualified electors entitled to vote for his successor. A public officer holding an appointive office may be recalled by the qualified electors entitled to vote for the successor or successors of the elective officer or officers who have the authority to appoint a person to that position.
(3) Physical or mental lack of fitness, incompetence, violation of his oath of office, official misconduct, or conviction of a felony offense enumerated in Title 45 is the only basis for recall. No person may be recalled for performing a mandatory duty of the office he holds or for not performing any act that, if performed, would subject him to prosecution for official misconduct.

2-16-611. Method of removal cumulative. The recall is cumulative and additional to, rather than a substitute for, other methods for removal of public officers.

2-16-612. Persons qualified to petition -- penalty for false signatures. (1) Every person who is a qualified elector of this state may sign a petition for recall of a state officer.
(2) Every person who is a qualified elector of a district of the state from which a state-district officer is elected may sign a petition for recall of a state-district officer of that district or appointed by an officer or the officers of that election district.
(3) Every person who is a qualified elector of a political subdivision of this state may sign a petition for recall of an officer of that political subdivision. However, if a political subdivision is divided into election districts, a person must be a qualified elector in the election district to be eligible to sign a petition to recall an officer elected from that election district.
(4) Any person signing any name other than his own to any petition or knowingly signing his name more than once for the recall or who is not at the time of the signing a qualified elector or any person who knowingly makes a false entry

upon an affidavit required in connection with the filing of a petition for the recall of an officer is guilty of unsworn falsification or tampering with public records or information, as appropriate, and is punishable as provided in 45-7-203 or 45-7-208, as applicable.

2-16-613. Limitations on recall petitions. (1) A recall petition may not name more than one officer to be recalled.
(2) No recall petition against an officer may be approved for circulation, as required in 2-16-617(3), until he has held office for 2 months.
(3) No recall petition may be filed against an officer for whom a recall election has been held for a period of 2 years during his term of office unless the state or political subdivision or subdivisions financing such recall election is first reimbursed for all expenses of the preceding recall election.

2-16-614. Number of electors required for recall petition. Recall petitions for elected or appointed state officers shall contain the signatures of qualified electors equaling at least 10% of the number of persons registered to vote at the preceding state general election. A petition for the recall of a state-district officer must contain the signatures of qualified electors equaling at least 15% of the number of persons registered to vote in the last preceding election in that district. Recall petitions for elected or appointed county officers shall contain the signatures of qualified electors equaling at least 15% of the number of persons registered to vote at the preceding county general election. Recall petitions for elected or appointed officers of municipalities or school districts shall contain the signatures of qualified electors equaling at least 20% of the number of persons registered to vote at the preceding election for the municipality or school district.

2-16-615. Filing of recall petitions -- mandamus for refusal. (1) Recall petitions for elected officers shall be filed with the official who is provided by law to accept the declaration of nomination or petition for nomination for such office. Recall

petitions for appointed state officers shall be filed with the secretary of state and for appointed county or municipal officers shall be filed with the county election administrator. Recall petitions for appointed officers from other political subdivisions shall be filed with the county election administrator if the boundaries of the political subdivisions lie wholly within one county or otherwise with the secretary of state.
(2) If the secretary of state, county election administrator or other filing official refuses to accept and file any petition for recall with the proper number of signatures of qualified electors, any elector may within 10 days after such refusal apply to the district court for a writ of mandamus. If it is determined that the petition is sufficient, the district court shall order the petition to be filed with a certified copy of the writ attached thereto, as of the date when it was originally offered for filing. On a showing that any filed petition is not sufficient, the court may enjoin certification, printing, or recall election.
(3) All such suits or appeals therefrom shall be advanced on the court docket and heard and decided by the court as expeditiously as possible.
(4) Any aggrieved party may file an appeal within 10 days after any adverse order or decision as provided by law.

2-16-616. Form of recall petition. (1) The form of the recall petition shall be substantially as follows:

WARNING
A person who knowingly signs a name other than his own to this petition or who signs his name more than once upon a petition to recall the same officer at one election or who is not, at the time he signs this petition, a qualified elector of the state of Montana entitled to vote for the successor of the elected officer to be recalled or the successor or successors of the officer or officers who have the authority to appoint a person to the position held by the appointed officer to be recalled is punishable by a fine of no more than $500 or imprisonment in the county jail for a term not to exceed 6

months, or both, or imprisonment in the state prison for a term not to exceed 10 years, or both.

RECALL PETITION

To the Honorable ________, Secretary of State of the State of Montana (or name and office of other filing officer): We, the undersigned qualified electors of the State of Montana (or name of appropriate state-district or political subdivision) respectfully petition that an election be held as provided by law on the question of whether ________, holding the office of ________, should be recalled for the following reasons: (Setting out a general statement of the reasons for recall in not more than 200 words). By his signature each signer certifies: I have personally signed this petition; I am a qualified elector of the state of Montana and (name of appropriate political subdivision); and my residence and post-office address are correctly written after my name to the best of my knowledge and belief.
(2) Numbered lines shall follow the above heading. Each numbered line shall contain spaces for the signature, post-office address, and printed last name of the signer. Each separate sheet of the petition shall contain the heading and reasons for the proposed recall as prescribed above.

2-16-617. Form of circulation sheets. (1) The signatures on each petition shall be placed on sheets of paper known as circulation sheets. Each circulation sheet shall be substantially 8 1/2 x 14 inches or a continuous sheet may be folded so as to meet this size limitation. Such circulation sheets shall be ruled with a horizontal line 1 1/2 inches from the top thereof. The space above such line shall remain blank and shall be for the purpose of binding.
(2) The petition, for purposes of circulation, may be divided into sections, each section to contain not more than 25 circulation sheets.
(3) Before a petition may be circulated for signatures, a sample circulation sheet must be submitted to the officer with

whom the petition must be filed in the form in which it will be circulated. The filing officer shall review the petition for sufficiency as to form and approve or reject the form of the petition, stating his reasons therefor, within 1 week of receiving the sheet.
(4) The petition form submitted must be accompanied by a written statement containing the reasons for the desired recall as stated on the petition. The truth of purported facts contained in the statement shall be sworn to by at least one of the petitioners before a person authorized to administer oaths.
(5) The filing officer shall serially number all approved petitions continuously from year to year.

2-16-618. Forms not mandatory. The forms prescribed in this part are not mandatory, and if substantially followed, the petition shall be sufficient, notwithstanding clerical and merely technical errors.

2-16-619. Submission of circulation sheets -- certification of signatures. (1) Signed circulation sheets or sections of a petition for recall must be submitted to the officer responsible for registration of electors in the county in which the signatures were obtained within 3 months of the date the form of the petition was approved under 2-16-617.
(2) An affidavit, in substantially the following form, must be attached to each circulation sheet or section submitted to the county officer:
(Name of person circulating petition), being first sworn, deposes and says: I circulated or assisted in circulating the petition to which this affidavit is attached, and I believe that the signatures on the petition are genuine and are the signatures of the persons whose names they purport to be and that the signers knew the contents of the petition before signing the petition.
(Signature)______________________________________
Subscribed and sworn before me this ___ day of ____,20___
(Person authorized to take oaths)
Seal_____________ (Title or notarial information)

2-16-620. County clerk to verify signatures. (1) The county clerk in each county in which such a petition is signed shall verify and compare the signatures of each person who has signed the petition to assure that he is an elector in such county and, if satisfied the signatures are genuine, certify that fact to the officer with whom the recall petition is to be filed, in substantially the following form:

To the Honorable ———, Secretary of State of the State of Montana (or name and title of other officer):

I, ______, ______ (title) of _____ County certify that I have compared the signatures on ...... sheets (specifying number of sheets) of the petition for recall No. ...... attached, in the manner prescribed by law, and I believe ...... (number) signatures are valid for the purpose of the petition. I further certify that the affidavit of the circulator of the (sheet) (section) of the petition is attached and that the post-office address is completed for each valid signature.

Signed: ________ (Date) _______________(Signature)
Seal __________ (Title)

(2) Such certificate is prima facie evidence of the facts stated therein, and the secretary of state or other officer receiving the recall petition may consider and count only such signatures as are certified. However, the officer with whom the recall petition is filed shall consider and count any remaining signatures of the registered voters which prove to be genuine, and such signatures shall be considered and counted if they are attested to in the manner and form as provided for initiative and referendum petitions.

(3) The county clerk may not retain any portion of a petition for more than 30 days following the receipt of that portion. At the expiration of such period the county clerk shall certify the valid signatures on that portion of the petition and deliver the same to the person with whom the petition is required to be filed.

2-16-621. Notification to officer -- statement of justification. Upon filing the petition or a portion of the petition containing the number of valid signatures required under 2-16-614, the official with whom it is filed shall immediately give written notice to the officer named in the petition. The notice shall state that a recall petition has been filed, shall set forth the reasons contained therein, and shall notify the officer named in the recall petition that he has the right to prepare and have printed on the ballot a statement containing not more than 200 words giving reasons why he should not be recalled. No such statement of justification shall be printed on the ballot unless it is delivered to the filing official within 10 days of the date notice is given.

2-16-622. Resignation of officer -- proclamation of election. (1) If the officer named in the petition for recall submits his resignation in writing, it shall be accepted and become effective the day it is offered. The vacancy created by such resignation shall be filled as provided by law, provided that the officer named in the petition for recall may not be appointed to fill such vacancy. If the officer named in the petition for recall refuses to resign or does not resign within 5 days after the petition is filed, a special election shall be called unless the filing is within 90 days of a general election, in which case the question shall be placed on a separate ballot at the same time as the general election.
(2) The call of a special election shall be made by the governor in the case of a state or state-district officer or by the board or officer empowered by law to call special elections for a political subdivision in the case of any officer of a political subdivision of the state.

2-16-631. Notice of recall election. The notice of a recall election shall be in substantially the following form:
NOTICE OF RECALL ELECTION

Notice is hereby given pursuant to law that a recall election will be held on _____ (Date) for the purpose of voting upon the recall of ______ who holds the office of _________

DATED at ______, ______ (Date)

2-16-632. Conduct of special elections. A special election for recall shall be conducted and the results canvassed and certified in the same manner that the law in effect at the time of the election for recall requires for an election to fill the office that is the subject of the recall petition, except as herein otherwise provided. In the case of an official holding a nonelective office, the election shall be conducted and the results canvassed and certified in the same manner that the law in effect at the time of the election for recall requires for an election to fill the office of the person who has the power to appoint such official. The powers and duties conferred or imposed by law upon boards of election, registration officers, canvassing boards, and other public officials who conduct general elections are conferred and imposed upon similar officers conducting recall elections under the provisions of this section together with the penalties prescribed for the breach thereof.

2-16-633. Form of ballot. (1) The ballot at such recall election shall set forth the statement contained in the recall petition stating the reasons for demanding the recall of such officer and the officer's statement of reasons why he should not be recalled. Then the question of whether the officer should be recalled shall be placed on the ballot in a form similar to the following:

[ ] FOR recalling ______ who holds the office of ________

[ ] AGAINST recalling ____ who holds the office of _____

(2) The form of the ballot shall be approved as provided in the election laws of this state.

2-16-634. Expenses of election. Expenses of a recall election shall be paid in the same manner as the expenses for any other election. The expenditure of such funds constitutes an emergency expenditure of funds, and the political subdivision affected may fund the costs of such an election through emergency funding procedures. In the event a recall election is held for a state or state-district officer, the legislature shall appropriate funds to reimburse the counties involved for costs incurred in running the election.

2-16-635. Officer to remain in office until results declared -- filling of vacancy. The officer named in the recall petition continues in office until he resigns or the results of the recall election are officially declared. If a majority of those voting on the question vote to remove the officer, the office becomes vacant and the vacancy shall be filled as provided by law, provided that the officer recalled may in no event be appointed to fill the vacancy.

THE CONSTITUTION OF THE STATE OF NEVADA
Article 2, Section 9. Recall of public officers: Procedure and limitations.

Recall of public officers: Procedure and limitations. Every public officer in the State of Nevada is subject, as herein provided, to recall from office by the registered voters of the state, or of the county, district, or municipality which he represents. For this purpose, not less than twenty-five per cent (25%) of the number who actually voted in the state or in the county, district, or municipality which he represents, at the election in which he was elected, shall file their petition, in the manner herein provided, demanding his recall by the people. They shall set forth in said petition, in not exceeding two hundred (200) words, the reasons why said recall is demanded. If he shall offer his resignation, it shall be accepted and take effect on the day it is offered, and the vacancy thereby caused shall be filled in the manner provided by law. If he shall not resign within five (5) days after the petition is filed, a special election shall be ordered to be held within thirty (30) days after the issuance of the call therefore, in the state, or county, district, or municipality electing said officer, to determine whether the people will recall said officer. On the ballot at said election shall be printed verbatim as set forth in the recall petition, the reasons for demanding the recall of said officer, and in not more than two hundred (200) words, the officer's justification of his course in office. He shall continue to perform the duties of his office until the result of said election shall be finally declared. Other candidates for the office may be nominated to be voted for at said special election. The candidate who shall receive highest number of votes at said special election shall be deemed elected for the remainder of the term, whether it be the person against whom the recall petition was filed, or another. The recall petition shall be filed with the officer with whom the petition for nomination to such office shall be filed, and the same officer shall order the special election when it is required. No such petition shall be circulated or filed against any officer until he has actually held his office six (6) months, save and except that it may be filed against a senator or assemblyman in the legislature at any time after ten (10) days from the beginning of the first session after his election. After one such petition and special election, no further recall petition shall be filed against the same officer during the term for which he was elected, unless such further petitioners shall pay into the public treasury from which the expenses of said special election have been paid, the whole amount paid out of said public treasury as expenses for the preceding special election. Such additional legislation as may aid the operation of this section shall be provided by law.

NEVADA REVISED STATUTES
Chapter 306, Section 306.005 et. sec.
Beginning with Informational Pamphlet describing requirements of chapter; fee.

NRS 306-005
NRS 306-011
NRS 306.015

NRS 306.017
NRS 306.020
NRS 306.025
NRS 306.030
NRS 306.035
NRS 306.040
NRS 306.045
NRS 306.060
NRS 306.070
NRS 306.080
NRS 306.110
NRS 306.120
NRS 306.130

NRS 306.005 Informational pamphlet describing requirements of chapter; fee.

1. The Secretary of State shall prepare an informational pamphlet describing the requirements for filing and circulating a petition to recall a public officer pursuant to this chapter. The pamphlet must include:

(a) A copy of Section 9 of Article 2 of the Constitution of the State of Nevada;

(b) A copy of chapter 306 of NRS and any regulations adopted pursuant to that chapter;

(c) A copy of all other relevant provisions of NRS;

(d) A sample petition to demonstrate an acceptable format for such a petition; and

(e) Such other information as the Secretary of State deems necessary.

2. A copy of the pamphlet must be distributed to any person who requests such information upon payment of any

applicable fee. The Secretary of State may charge a fee for the pamphlet which must not exceed the cost of preparing and printing the pamphlet.

NRS 306.011 Regulations. The Secretary of State shall adopt such regulations as are necessary to carry out the provisions of this chapter.

NRS 306.015 Contents and filing of notice of intent to circulate petition for recall; penalty for failure to submit timely petition; procedure for removing name from petition; person who signs notice of intent or petition immune from civil liability for certain conduct.

1. Before a petition to recall a public officer is circulated, the persons proposing to circulate the petition mustfile a notice of intent with the filing officer.

2. The notice of intent:
(a) Must be signed by three registered voters who actually voted in this state or in the county, district or municipality electing the officer at the last preceding general election.

(b) Must be signed before a person authorized by law to administer oaths that the statements and signatures contained in the notice are true.

(c) Is valid until the date on which the call for a special election is issued, as set forth in NRS 306.040.

3. The petition may consist of more than one document. The persons filing the notice of intent shall submit the petition that was circulated for signatures to the filing officer within 90 days after the date on which the notice of intent was filed. The filing officer shall immediately submit the petition to the county clerk for verification pursuant to NRS 306.035. Any person who fails to submit the petition to the filing officer as required by this subsection is guilty of a

misdemeanor. Copies of the petition are not valid for any subsequent petition.

4. The county clerk shall, upon completing the verification of the signatures on the petition, file the petition with the filing officer.

5. Any person who signs a petition to recall any public officer may request that the county clerk remove his name from the petition by submitting a request in writing to the county clerk at any time before the petition is submitted for the verification of the signatures thereon pursuant to NRS 306.035.

6. A person who signs a notice of intent pursuant to subsection 1 or a petition to recall a public officer is immune from civil liability for conduct related to the exercise of his right to participate in the recall of a public officer.

7. As used in this section, "filing officer" means the officer with whom the public officer to be recalled filed his declaration of candidacy or acceptance of candidacy pursuant to NRS 293.185, 293C.145 or 293C.175.

NRS 306.017 Employment of independent legal counsel to provide advice concerning recall of public officer who is legal adviser. If a notice of intent to circulate a petition to recall any public officer who is a legal adviser for the State or for a county, district or municipality is filed, the officer with whom the notice is filed may employ independent legal counsel to provide advice concerning the recall, at the expense of the State or the county, district or municipality electing that public officer.

NRS 306.020 Public officers subject to recall from office; contents of petition for recall.
1. Every public officer in the State of Nevada is subject to recall from office by the registered voters of the State or of the county, district or municipality from which he was elected,

as provided in Section 9 of Article 2 of the Constitution of the State of Nevada and this chapter. A public officer who is appointed to an elective office is subject to recall in the same manner as provided for an officer who is elected to that office.

2. The petition must, in addition to setting forth the reason why the recall is demanded:
(a) Contain the residence addresses of the signers and the date that the petition was signed;
(b) Contain a statement of the minimum number of signatures necessary to the validity of the petition;
(c) Contain at the top of each page and immediately above the signature line, in at least 10-point bold type, the words "Recall Petition";

(d) Include the date that a notice of intent was filed; and

(e) Have the designation: "Signatures of registered voters seeking the recall of .... (name of public officer for whom recall is sought)" on each page if the petition contains more than one page.

NRS 306.025 Misrepresenting intent or content of petition for recall prohibited; penalty.

1. A person shall not misrepresent the intent or content of a petition for the recall of a public officer which is circulated pursuant to the provisions of this chapter.

2. Any person who violates the provisions of subsection 1 is guilty of a misdemeanor.

NRS 306.030 Petition for recall may consist of number of copies; verification.

1. The petition may consist of any number of copies which are identical in form with the original, except for the name of

the county and the signatures and addresses of the residences of the signers. The pages of the petition with the signatures and of any copy must be consecutively numbered. Each page must bear the name of a county, and only registered voters of that county may sign the page.

2. Every copy must be verified by the circulator thereof, who shall swear or affirm, before a person authorized by law to administer oaths, that the statements and signatures contained in the petition are true to the best of his knowledge and belief. The verification must also contain a statement of the number of signatures being verified by the circulator.

NRS 306.035 Signatures must be submitted to county clerk for verification before petition for recall may be filed.

1. Before a petition to recall a state officer who is elected statewide is filed with the Secretary of State pursuant to subsection 4 of NRS 306.015, each county clerk must verify, pursuant to NRS 293.1276 to 293.1279, inclusive, the document or documents which were circulated for signature within his county.

2. Before a petition to recall a State Senator, Assemblyman, or a county, district or municipal officer is filed pursuant to subsection 4 ofNRS 306.015, the county clerk must verify, pursuant to NRS 293.1276 to 293.1279, inclusive, the document or documents which were circulated for signatures within his county.

3. If more than one document was circulated, all the documents must be submitted to the clerk at the same time.

NRS 306.040 Notification that number of signatures is sufficient; striking of names from petition; call for special election; legal challenge.

1. Upon determining that the number of signatures on a

petition to recall is sufficient pursuant to NRS 293.1276 to 293.1279, inclusive, the Secretary of State shall notify the county clerk, the officer with whom the petition is to be filed pursuant to subsection 4 of NRS 306.015and the public officer who is the subject of the petition.

2. After the verification of signatures is complete, but not later than the date a complaint is filed pursuant to subsection 5 or the date the call for a special election is issued, whichever is earlier, a person who signs a petition to recall may request the Secretary of State to strike his name from the petition. If the person demonstrates good cause therefor and the number of such requests received by the Secretary of State could affect the sufficiency of the petition, the Secretary of State shall strike the name of the person from the petition.

3. Not sooner than 10 days nor more than 20 days after the Secretary of State completes the notification required by subsection 1, if a complaint is not filed pursuant to subsection 5, the officer with whom the petition is filed shall issue a call for a special election in the jurisdiction in which the public officer who is the subject of the petition was elected to determine whether the people will recall him.

4. The call for a special election pursuant to subsection 3 or 6 must include, without limitation:
(a) The last day on which a person may register to vote to qualify to vote in the special election; and

(b) The last day on which a petition to nominate other candidates for the office may be filed.

5. The legal sufficiency of the petition may be challenged by filing a complaint in district court not later than 5 days, Saturdays, Sundays and holidays excluded, after the Secretary of State completes the notification required by subsection 1. All affidavits and documents in support of the challenge must be filed with the complaint. The court shall

set the matter for hearing not later than 30 days after the complaint is filed and shall give priority to such a complaint over all other matters pending with the court, except for criminal proceedings.

6. Upon the conclusion of the hearing, if the court determines that the petition is sufficient, it shall order the officer with whom the petition is filed to issue a call for a special election in the jurisdiction in which the public officer who is the subject of the petition was elected to determine whether the people will recall him. If the court determines that the petition is not sufficient, it shall order the officer with whom the petition is filed to cease any further proceedings regarding the petition.

NRS 306.045 Effect of resignation by officer. If a public officer who is subject to a recall petition resigns his office:

1. Before the call for a special election is issued:
(a) The official with whom the petition to recall is filed shall cease any further proceedings regarding the petition;

(b) A vacancy occurs in that office; and

(c) The vacancy thereby created must be filled in the manner provided by law.

2. After the call for a special election is issued, the special election must be conducted.

NRS 306.060 Ballots for recall: Printing of officer's justification; printing of reason for demanding recall and officer's justification on sample ballot required if mechanical voting system used.

1. If the officer against whom the petition is filed furnishes no justification of his course in office, none need appear on the ballot at the election upon his recall.

2. Where a mechanical voting system is used, the reason for demanding the recall of the officer and the officer's justification need not be printed on the ballot, but must be printed on sample ballots, which must be presented to registered voters upon their application to vote.

NRS 306.070 Form of proposal on ballots for recall; names of nominees.

1. If there are no other candidates nominated to be voted for at the special election, there must be printed on the ballot the name of the officer sought to be recalled, the office which he holds, and the words "For Recall" and "Against Recall."

2. If there are other candidates nominated for the office to be voted for at the special election, there must be printed upon the ballot the name of the officer sought to be recalled, and the office which he holds, and the name or names of such other candidates as may be nominated to be voted for at the special election, and the words "For Recall" and "Against Recall" must be omitted.

3. In other respects the ballot must conform with the requirements of this title.

NRS 306.080 Vacancy in office created if no other candidates voted upon in special election. If any officer is recalled upon a special election and other candidates are not nominated to be voted for at the special election, the vacancy thereby created must be filled in the manner provided by law. (Added to NRS by 1960, 283; A 1981, 23)

NRS 306.110 Nominating petition for successors; verification of signatures; acceptance of candidacy.

1. A petition to nominate other candidates for the office must be signed by registered voters of the State, or of the

county, district or municipality holding the election, equal in number to 25 percent of the number of registered voters who voted in the State, or in the county, district or municipality holding the election at the general election at which the public officer was elected. Each petition may consist of more than one document. Each document must bear the name of one county and must not be signed by a person who is not a registered voter of that county.

2. The nominating petition must be filed, at least 20 days before the date of the special election, with the officer with whom the recall petition is filed. Each document of the petition must be submitted for verification pursuant to NRS 293.1276 to 293.1279, inclusive, to the county clerk of the county named on the document.

3. Each candidate who is nominated for office must file an acceptance of candidacy with the appropriate filing officer and pay the fee required by NRS 293.193 or by the governing body of a city at least 20 days before the date of the special election.

NRS 306.120 Conduct of special election. Any special election must be conducted pursuant to the provisions of:

1. Chapter 293 of NRS for primary and general elections.

2. Chapter 293C of NRS for primary city elections and general city elections.

NRS 306.130 Applicability of laws governing elections. The general election laws of this state, so far as applicable, shall apply to all elections held under this chapter.

NEW JERSEY STATE CONSTITUTION
Article I, Section 2b.

The people reserve unto themselves the power to recall, after at least one year of service, any elected official in this State or representing this State in the United States Congress. The Legislature shall enact laws to provide for such recall elections. Any such laws shall include a provision that a recall election shall be held upon petition of at least 25% of the registered voters in the electoral district of the official sought to be recalled. If legislation to implement this constitutional amendment is not enacted within one year of the adoption of the amendment, the Secretary of State shall, by regulation, implement the constitutional amendment, except that regulations adopted by the Secretary of State shall be superseded by any subsequent legislation consistent with this constitutional amendment governing recall elections. The sufficiency of any statement of reasons or grounds procedurally required shall be a political rather than a judicial question.

NEW JERSEY PERMANENT STATUTES
Title 19, Section 27A-1 et sec.
Beginning with Short Title.

NJPS 19:27A-1
NJPS 19:27A-2
NJPS 19:27A-3
NJPS 19:27A-4
NJPS 19:27A-5
NJPS 19:27A-6
NJPS 19:27A-7
NJPS 19:27A-8
NJPS 19:27A-9
NJPS 19:27A-10
NJPS 19:27A-11
NJPS 19:27A-12
NJPS 19:27A-13
NJPS 19:27A-14
NJPS 19:27A-15

NJPS 19:27A-16
NJPS 19:27A-17
NJPS 19:27A-18

19:27A-1. Short title

This act shall be known and may be cited as the "Uniform Recall Election Law."

19:27A-2. Recall of United States Senator or Representative authorized

Pursuant to Article I, paragraph 2b. of the New Jersey Constitution, the people of this State shall have the power to recall, after at least one year of service in the person's current term of office, any United States Senator or Representative elected from this State or any State or local elected official in the manner provided herein.

19:27A-3. Definitions

As used in this act:

"circulator" means an individual, whether paid or unpaid, who solicits signatures for a recall petition;

"elected official" means any person holding the office of United States Senator or member of the United States House of Representatives elected from this State, or any person holding a State or local government office which, under the State Constitution or by law, is filled by the registered voters of a jurisdiction at an election, including a person appointed, selected or otherwise designated to fill a vacancy in such office, but does not mean an official of a political party;

"jurisdiction" means the electoral jurisdiction, including but not limited to the State, or any county or municipality thereof, within which the voters reside who are qualified to vote for an elected official who is sought to be recalled;

"notice of intention" means the notice filed with the recall election official by a recall committee for the purpose of initiating a recall effort;

"recall committee" means a committee formed by persons sponsoring the recall of an elected official which represents the sponsors and signers of a recall petition in matters relating to the recall effort;

"recall election" means an election held for the purpose of allowing the voters of a jurisdiction to decide whether an elected official shall be recalled from office;

"recall election official" means the official authorized by law to receive nominating petitions for an elective office, except that with respect to the recall of the county clerk, it means the Secretary of State;

"recall petition" means a petition prepared and circulated by a recall committee as provided by this act for the purpose of gathering a sufficient number of valid signatures of registered voters to cause a recall election to be called; and

"sponsors" means the proponents of a recall effort who establish a recall committee.

19:27A-4. Time of election; statement of reasons or grounds; commencement of proceedings

a. An elected official shall be recalled from office upon the affirmative vote of a majority of those voting on the question of recall at a recall election which shall have been held after the officeholder shall have served one year of the term of office from which the person is sought to be recalled. A person serving to fill a vacancy in the term of an elective office shall be subject to recall at such an election after one year of such service. No election to recall an elected official shall be held after the date occurring six months prior to the general election or regular election for that office, as appropriate, in the final year of the official's term.

No statement of reasons or grounds for the holding of a recall election or for the recall at such an election of an elected official shall be required in connection with the preparation or circulation of a recall petition, with the transmittal of any notice required under the provisions of this act, [FN1] with the submission to the voters of the question of the recall of an elected official, or with any other action or procedure relating to such a recall, and to the extent that any such statement of reasons or grounds is offered by the sponsors of a recall petition or by any other person, the sufficiency of that statement shall be a political rather than a judicial question.

b. The procedures established in this act to initiate the calling of a recall election may be commenced not earlier than the 50th day preceding the completion of the first year of the term of office by the official sought to be recalled. In the case of an official serving to fill a vacancy in the term of an elective office, the procedures established in this act to initiate the calling of a recall election may be commenced not earlier than the 50th day preceding the completion of the first year of such service. However, the recall election itself shall not be held until after the official has completed one year of such term or service, as appropriate.

19:27A-5. Petition; number of signatures; filing; number of officials cited

A recall petition demanding that an election be held for the purpose of deciding whether an elected official shall be recalled from office shall be signed by a number of registered voters of the jurisdiction of the official sought to be recalled equal to at least 25% of the persons registered to vote in that jurisdiction on the date of the general election preceding the date on which the sponsors of the petition file a notice of intention pursuant to section 6 of this act. [FN1] A recall petition shall be filed with the appropriate recall election official. No recall petition shall demand the holding of an election to recall more than one elected official.

19:27A-6. Notice of intention
Prior to collecting any signatures, the sponsors of a recall petition shall file a notice of intention with the appropriate recall election official. The notice of intention shall contain the following information:

a. the name and office of the elected official sought to be recalled;

b. the name and business or residence address of at least three sponsors of the recall petition who shall constitute a recall committee which shall represent the sponsors and signers of the recall petition in matters relating to the recall effort, provided that no recall committee shall sponsor the recall of more than one officeholder and, if a recall effort fails at the ballot, the sponsoring recall committee and the members thereof shall not again sponsor, nor shall the recall committee again finance, an effort to recall the targeted officeholder during the same term of office in which the failed recall effort was attempted;

c. the name of the recall committee, which shall be expressed in the following form: "COMMITTEE TO RECALL [name of the official sought to be recalled] FROM THE OFFICE OF [name of the office]";

d. a statement certified by each member of the recall committee that the member is registered to vote in the jurisdiction of the official sought to be recalled and that the member supports the recall of the named official and accepts the responsibilities associated with serving on the recall committee;

e. at the option of the recall committee, a statement, not in excess of 200 words, of the reasons for the recall; and

f. a statement as to whether the recall election shall be held at the next general election or regular election, as appropriate, or at a special election, as provided in section 13 of this act.

19:27A-7. Duties of recall election official; answer of official cited

a. Upon receiving a notice of intention, the recall election official shall review it for compliance with the provisions of section 6 of this act. [FN1] If the notice of intention is found to be in compliance, the recall election official shall imprint on the face of that notice a statement of the official's approval thereof, which statement shall identify the public office held by the official and include the signature of the official and the date on which the approval was given, and shall, within three business days of receiving the notice, return a certified copy of the approved notice to the recall committee. If the recall committee has requested that the recall election be held at a special election, the recall election official shall also prepare, within that same three-day period, an estimate of the cost of conducting the recall election which shall be added to the notice of intention and printed on the first page of each section of the petition as required by section 8 of this act. [FN2] The official shall retain, and shall hold available for public inspection and copying, the original notice so approved for a period of not less than five years from the date of such approval. If the notice of intention is found not to be in compliance, the recall election official shall, within that period of three business days, return the notice, together with a written statement indicating the reasons for that finding, to the recall committee, which shall have the opportunity to file a corrected notice of intention.

b. Within five business days of approving a notice of intention, the recall election official shall serve a copy of the approved notice of intention on the official sought to be recalled by personal delivery or certified mail, and within two weeks of approving the notice of intention shall cause a copy thereof to be printed in a newspaper published in the jurisdiction or, if none exists, in a newspaper generally circulated within the jurisdiction, and affix to the approved notice of intention previously filed an affidavit of the time and manner of service and proof of publication. The copy of the notice of intention which is published shall be abbreviated to include information on only three members of the recall committee who shall be designated for that purpose by the committee. The recall election official shall retain on file the affidavit and proof for so long as the approved notice of intention is retained.

c. Within five business days of being served with a notice of intention, the official sought to be recalled may file an answer to the proposed recall, not to exceed 200 words, with the recall election official if the notice of intention contained a statement of the reasons for the recall. An answer shall be used solely to provide information to the voters and shall be printed on the first page of each section of the petition in the manner provided by section 8 of this act. If the notice of intention did not contain a statement of the reasons for the recall or the official sought to be recalled chooses not to file an answer, that official shall instead provide the recall election official with a written acknowledgment of receipt of a copy of the notice of intention. Within two business days of the filing of such an answer or acknowledgment, the recall election official shall by personal delivery or certified mail serve a copy of that answer or acknowledgment on the recall committee. If no such answer or acknowledgment is filed within the period of time allowed therefor, the recall election official, within two business days of the expiration of that time period, shall by personal delivery or certified mail transmit to the recall committee a signed statement in writing that no such answer or acknowledgment was timely filed with the recall election official.

19:27A-8. Petition; form of and signatures on

a. No signature appearing on any document other than a recall petition prepared in accordance with the provisions of this section shall be counted among the signatures required under section 5 of this act [FN1] to determine whether a recall election shall be held.

b. A recall petition shall be prepared by the recall committee in accordance with a format, consistent with the provisions of this act, which shall have been approved for such purpose by the Secretary of State. A petition may consist of any number of separate sections which shall be identical except with respect to information required to be entered thereon by the signers and circulators and as otherwise provided herein. The size of the paper used in a recall petition and the number of pages included in each section thereof shall be determined by the recall committee. The back and the front of a piece of paper shall each constitute a page and signatures may be affixed to each such page.

c. Each page of each section of a recall petition shall be sequentially numbered and shall include, printed in bold letters in at least 10-point type, the heading "PETITION FOR THE RECALL OF [name of the official sought to be recalled] FROM THE OFFICE OF [name of the office]" and, where appropriate, the information required by subsection e. of this section. The first page of each section also shall bear, in type of uniform size but not less than 8-point type, (1) the information contained in the notice of intention, including any cost estimate prepared and the statement of the reasons for the recall, if one was provided, or a declaration that no such statement of reasons was provided, except that information on only three members of the recall committee need be listed; and (2) a copy of the answer provided by the official sought to be recalled, if one was provided, or a declaration that no such answer was provided, except that no such answer or declaration shall be included if a statement of the reasons for the recall was not provided.

d. Each page of a recall petition shall be arranged so that each signer of the petition shall personally affix the signer's signature; printed name and residence address, including street and number, or a designation of residence which is adequate to readily determine location; the municipality of residence; and the date on which the signer signed the petition. A space at least one inch wide shall be left blank after each name for use in verifying signatures when appropriate, as provided by this act. A box shall be provided after each name for the signer to indicate that the signer has had the opportunity to review the information on the first page of that section of the petition.

e. (1) Whenever the official sought to be recalled is the Governor or a United States Senator, separate sections of the petition shall be prepared for use by signers registered to vote in each county. Each page of a section shall bear in not less than 10-point type the name of the county in which that section is to be used and the statement, "Only eligible persons residing in (name of county) County shall sign this page." A signer shall not affix the signer's signature to any page of any section unless it bears the name of the county in which the signer is registered to vote.

(2) Whenever the official sought to be recalled is a member of the Legislature or a member of the United States House of Representatives and the official's jurisdiction includes parts of more than one county, separate sections of the petition shall be prepared for use by signers registered to vote in each county included within the member's jurisdiction. Each page of a section shall bear in not less than 10-point type the name of the county in which that section is to be used and the statement, "Only eligible persons residing in (name of county) County shall sign this page." A signer shall not affix the signer's signature to any page of any section unless it bears the name of the county in which the signer is registered to vote.

(3) The signature of any person to a page of a recall petition bearing the name of a county in which the person is not registered to vote shall be invalid, but the invalidity of such a signature shall not invalidate or otherwise impair the section wherein or page whereon that signature appears, nor shall it invalidate or otherwise impair any other signature to that or any other section of the petition.

f. Prior to use, the sections of a recall petition shall be reviewed by the recall election official for compliance with the provisions of this act. The recall election official shall complete the review of the petition within three business days of receipt. No section of a recall petition shall be used to solicit signatures unless it has been so approved and a statement of such approval, signed by the recall election official, has been printed on the first page of that section.

g. No obstruction shall be placed over any portion of a page of a petition section at the time that page is presented to a voter to be signed.

h. Every member of a recall committee circulating a recall petition and every circulator of that petition shall sign the petition. If any member of the committee shall fail to sign the petition, the petition shall be deemed void. In the event that the signature to the petition of a member of the recall committee shall be deemed invalid, then notwithstanding the provisions of subsection e. of this section, the petition shall be deemed void.

i. If a solicitation for signatures to a recall petition is presented to prospective petition signers by a paid print advertisement or paid mailing, or if a recall petition is presented to such a prospective signer by a paid circulator, the solicitation or petition, respectively, shall disclose prominently in a statement printed in at least 10-point type (1) the identity of the person paying for the printed or personal solicitation, and (2) that the circulator is paid. The Election Law Enforcement

Commission shall promulgate such rules and regulations as are necessary to implement the provisions and effectuate the purposes of this subsection.

j. No person who is ineligible to sign a recall petition shall, with knowledge of that ineligibility, sign such a petition. No person shall offer to pay or pay another to sign or to refrain from signing a recall petition or to vote or to refrain from voting in a recall election. A person who violates any of the foregoing provisions of this subsection is guilty of a crime of the fourth degree.

19:27A-9. Responsibilities of circulators

a. No person shall act as the circulator of a petition who is not a registered voter in the jurisdiction from which the official sought to be recalled was elected.

b. Each completed page of any section of a recall petition which is filed with the recall election official shall include at the bottom of that page an affidavit signed by the circulator of that section which sets forth the following:

(1) the printed name of the circulator;

(2) the address of the circulator;

(3) a statement that the circulator assumed responsibility for circulating that section, that the circulator witnessed the signing of that page by each person whose signature appears thereon, that, to the best information and belief of the circulator, the signers are legal residents of the State and of the county in which the section was circulated, and that the section was circulated in absolute good faith for the purpose of causing the recall of the elected official named in the petition;

(4) the dates between which all signatures to that page were collected; and

(5) a statement, signed by the circulator, as to the truth and correctness of the aforesaid information.

19:27A-10. Deadlines; resignation of official

a. A recall committee shall collect the required number of signatures and file a completed petition with the recall election official within the following time periods calculated from the date that the recall petition receives final approval for circulation from the recall election official:

(1) 320 days, when the Governor or a United States Senator is sought to be recalled; and

(2) 160 days, when any other elected official is sought to be recalled.

b. If a completed petition is not filed within the applicable time period, the petition shall be void. No part of a void petition shall be used in connection with any other recall effort.

c. If the official sought to be recalled resigns from office, the collection of signatures shall cease and the petition shall be void.

19:27A-11. Filing of entire petition; determining number of signatures

All sections of a completed recall petition shall be filed with the recall election official at the same time. When a petition is presented for filing, the recall election official, within 10 business days, shall determine the total number of signatures affixed thereto and whether the completed petition complies with the other provisions of this act. A petition which contains an insufficient number of signatures or otherwise fails to comply with the provisions of this act shall be void.

19:27A-12. Challenges to determination of number of signatures

The determination of the recall election official as to whether a recall petition is signed by a sufficient number of registered voters and otherwise complies with the provisions of this act may, within 10 business days of issuance, be challenged by the official sought to be recalled or by the recall committee by filing a written objection thereto with the recall election official. Upon the request of either of those parties, the recall election official shall provide the party with a duly certified copy of the recall petition and shall allow examination of the original recall petition during regular business hours. The recall election official shall pass upon the validity of an objection in an expedited manner. The decision of the recall election official may be contested, within 10 business days, by filing an action in the Superior Court, which shall hear the matter on an expedited basis and issue an order or determination as soon as possible after filing of the action. Whenever the decision of a recall election official with respect to a recall petition requiring more than 1,000 names is challenged by the official sought to be recalled or by a recall committee, the parties shall be permitted to introduce evidence that, under a random sample method which employs the theory, assumptions and methods of standard statistical analysis, the petition contains either a sufficient or an insufficient number of signatures. The introduction of such evidence shall create a rebuttable presumption that a petition is valid or invalid, as the case may be.

19:27A-13. Certificate of sufficiency; calling of election

a. (1) If the recall election official determines that a petition contains the required number of signatures and otherwise complies with the provisions of this act and if the official sought to be recalled makes no timely challenge to that determination, or if the official makes such a challenge but the original determination is confirmed by the recall election official or the court, the recall election official shall forthwith issue a certificate as to the sufficiency of the petition to the recall committee. A copy of the certificate shall be served by the recall election official on the elected official sought to be recalled by personal service or certified mail. If, within five business days of service of the certification, the official has not resigned from office, the recall election official shall order and fix the holding of a recall election on the date indicated in the certificate.

(2) In the case of an office which is ordinarily filled at the general election, a recall election shall be held at the next general election occurring at least 55 days following the fifth business day after service of the certification, unless it was indicated in the notice of intention that the recall election shall be held at a special election in which case the recall election official shall order and fix the date for holding the recall election to be the next Tuesday occurring during the period beginning with the 55th day and ending on the 61st day following the fifth business day after service of the certification of the petition or, if that Tuesday falls on, or during the 28-day period before or after, a day on which any general, primary, nonpartisan municipal, school district or other recall election is to be held or shall have been held within all or any part of the jurisdiction, then the first Tuesday thereafter which does not fall within such period. In the case of an office which is ordinarily filled at an election other than the general election, a recall election shall be held at the next general election or the next regular election for that office occurring at least 55 days following the fifth business day after service of the certification, unless it was indicated in the notice of intention that the recall election shall be held at a special election in which case the recall election official shall order and fix the date for holding the recall election to be the next Tuesday occurring during the period beginning with the 55th day and ending on the 61st day following the fifth business day after service of the certification of the petition or, if that Tuesday falls on, or during the 28-day period before or after, a day on which any general, primary, nonpartisan municipal, school district or other recall election is to be held or shall have been held within all or any part of the jurisdiction, then the first Tuesday thereafter which does not fall

within such period. A recall election to be held at a special election shall not be scheduled on the same day as a primary election. The date for a recall election shall not be fixed, and no recall election shall be held, after the date occurring six months prior to the general election or regular election for the office, as appropriate, in the final year of an official's term.

(3) A vacancy in an elective office resulting from the resignation of an elective official sought to be recalled prior to the expiration of the five-day period shall be filled in the manner provided by law for filling vacancies in that office.

b. The certificate issued by the recall election official shall contain: (1) the name and office of the official sought to be recalled;

(2) the number of signatures required by law to cause a recall election to be held for that office;

(3) a statement to the effect that a valid recall petition, determined to contain the required number of signatures, has been filed with the recall election official and that a recall election will be held; and

(4) the date and time when the election will be held if the official does not resign.

c. The recall election official shall transmit a copy of the certificate to the officer or public body designated by law to be responsible for publishing notice of any other election to be held in the jurisdiction on the same day as the recall election, and that officer or body shall cause notice of the recall election, including all of the information contained in the certificate as prescribed by subsection b. of this section, to be printed in a newspaper published in the jurisdiction of the official sought to be recalled or, if none exists, in a newspaper generally circulated in the jurisdiction. The notice of the recall election shall appear on the same schedule applicable to the notice of such other election. In the event that the recall election is to be held as a special election, the recall election official shall transmit a copy of the certificate to the county board or boards of elections, and the county board or boards shall cause notice of the recall election to be printed, in the manner hereinbefore prescribed, once during the 30 days next preceding the day fixed for the closing of the registration books for the recall election and once during the calendar week next preceding the week in which the recall election is held.

19:27A-14. Conduct of election

A recall election shall be conducted in accordance with the provisions of Title 19 of the Revised Statutes which apply to all elections, except that in the case of an election to recall a member of the governing body of a municipality operating under the provisions of the "Uniform Nonpartisan Elections Law," P.L.1981, c. 379 (C.40:45-5 et al.), or a member of the school board in a Type II school district, or any other elected official elected under the provisions of another title, the election shall be conducted in accordance with the appropriate provisions of that other title to the extent not inconsistent with the provisions of this act.

Notwithstanding the provisions of any other law to the contrary, for any election at which the question of the recall of an elected official is submitted to the voters, the county clerk or other appropriate officer shall cause samples of the entire ballot to be voted upon at that election to be printed and distributed to the voters of the jurisdiction wherein the recall election is to be held in the same manner as prescribed for the printing and distribution of sample ballots at the general election as provided by article 2 of chapter 14 of Title 19 of the Revised Statutes, [FN1] except that in the case of an election other than the general election, any period of time calculated under the provisions of that article from the date of the general election shall be calculated instead from the date on which such other election is to be held.

19:27A-15. Filling of vacancies; recall ballot

a. Whenever the elected official sought to be recalled is the Governor or a member of the Legislature, the question of whether or not the Governor or member of the Legislature shall be recalled shall appear on the ballot but no candidates to succeed the Governor or member of the Legislature in the event the recall is successful shall be listed thereon. A vacancy in the office of Governor resulting from a recall election shall be filled pursuant to Article V, Section I of the State Constitution in the same manner as any other vacancy occurring in that office. A vacancy in the office of member of the Legislature resulting from a recall election shall be filled pursuant to Article IV, Section IV, paragraph 1 of the State Constitution in the same manner as any other vacancy occurring in that office, except that no member who is recalled shall be eligible to be selected to fill the vacancy created as a result of the recall.

b. Whenever the elected official sought to be recalled is other than the Governor or a member of the Legislature, candidates to succeed the elected official in the event the recall is successful may be nominated within nine days after the fifth business day following service of the certification of the petition by each political party in the manner prescribed in R.S. 19:13-20 for selecting candidates to fill vacancies among candidates nominated at primary elections. Candidates may also be nominated within that time period by petition in a manner similar to that used for direct nomination by petition for a general election. In the case of offices in nonpartisan units of government, nomination shall be by petition. An elected official who is the subject of a recall election shall be eligible to be elected as that official's own successor in the event that the election results in the official's recall.

c. The ballot used at a recall election shall pose the following question to the voters: "Shall (insert name of elected official sought to be recalled) be recalled from the office of (insert title of office)?" To the right of the question, the words "Yes" and "No" shall appear and each voter shall indicate the voter's choice of one. A recall election sample ballot, but not the actual ballot, shall contain the statement of the reasons for the recall prepared by the recall committee and the answer thereto, if any, which appeared on the petition.

d. Whenever a successor is to be chosen at a recall election in the event the recall is successful, the ballot shall indicate: "Nominees for successor to [insert name and title of the elected official sought to be recalled] in the event he (or she) is recalled." The names of all persons nominated as successors shall appear immediately thereafter in such manner as will allow each voter to vote for one.

19:27A-16. Election results; further petitions

a. If a majority of votes cast on the question of the recall of an elected official are in the affirmative, the term of office of the elected official shall terminate upon the certification of the election results. Where nominees to succeed the recalled official are voted on at the same election, the successor receiving the greatest number of votes shall succeed to the office of the recalled official upon certification of the election results and shall serve for the remainder of the unexpired term.

b. If a majority of votes cast on the question of recall of an elected official are in the negative, the official shall continue in office as if no recall election had been held and the vote for the successor of such officer shall be void.

c. An elected official sought to be recalled who is not recalled as the result of a recall election shall not again be subject to recall until after having served one year of a term calculated from the date of the recall election.

19:27A-17. Campaign committees and contributions

a. Except as otherwise provided in this section, a recall

committee shall be treated as a candidate committee for the purposes of "The New Jersey Campaign Contributions and Expenditures Reporting Act," P.L.1973, c. 83 (C. 19:44A-1 et seq.), except that all contributions received by a recall committee shall be used only for (1) the payment of campaign expenses incurred in the course of and directly related to the committee's effort to promote the recall or the passage of the question of recall at the recall election, (2) the payment of overhead and administrative expenses related to the operation of the committee, or (3) the pro-rata repayment of contributors.

b. Except as provided in subsection c. of this section:

(1) an elected official sought to be recalled who receives contributions and makes expenditures for the purpose of opposing a recall effort shall establish a "recall defense committee," which shall be separate from, but subject to the same organizational and filing requirements and limitations on the receipt of contributions applicable to, any candidate committee under "The New Jersey Campaign Contributions and Expenditures Reporting Act," P.L.1973, c. 83 (C. 19:44A-1 et seq.), except that a recall defense committee shall be permitted to receive without limit contributions from the candidate committee or joint candidates committee of the elected official sought to be recalled. A recall defense committee, for all purposes relating to campaign finance, shall be in addition to any candidate committee or joint candidates committee which an official sought to be recalled may by law establish. If an elected official sought to be recalled transfers funds from the official's candidate committee or joint candidates committee to the official's recall defense committee, a new election cycle shall be deemed to begin with respect to the candidate committee or joint candidates committee after the recall election is held or the recall effort fails and such official shall be permitted to solicit and receive contributions thereto, including contributions from prior contributors, up to the limits imposed by P.L.1973, c. 83 (C. 19:44A-1 et

seq.). A recall defense committee may be formed at any time after an official sought to be recalled is served with either form of notice provided for by subsection e. of this section. All contributions received by a recall defense committee shall be used only for (a) the payment of campaign expenses incurred in the course of and directly related to the committee's effort to oppose the recall effort or the passage of the question of recall at the recall election, (b) the payment of the overhead and administrative expenses related to the operation of the committee, or (c) the pro-rata repayment of contributors; and

(2) any nominee to succeed that elected official shall be treated as a candidate for the purposes of "The New Jersey Campaign Contributions and Expenditures Reporting Act," P.L.1973, c. 83 (C. 19:44A-1 et seq.).

c. The limits on contributions established by 2 U.S.C. ß 441a shall apply to a federal elected official sought to be recalled, a candidate to succeed such an official and a recall committee seeking to recall a federal elected official.

d. A Governor who is sought to be recalled shall not be entitled to public support pursuant to P.L.1974, c. 26 (C. 19:44A-27 et seq.) for the purpose of opposing the recall effort.

e. Neither a recall committee nor a recall defense committee shall solicit or accept contributions in connection with a recall effort until after either: (1) the recall committee serves written notice of the recall effort on the official sought to be recalled by personal service or certified mail, with a copy thereof filed with the recall election official; or (2) a copy of an approved notice of intention is served on the official sought to be recalled as provided in subsection b. of section 7 of this act. [FN1] If a recall committee notifies an official sought to be recalled of its intention to initiate a recall effort by the method described in paragraph (1) of this subsection, it must file a notice of intention within 30 days of the date the notice is served on the official or cease the solicitation, acceptance and expenditure of funds.

f. Contributions to a recall committee by a candidate committee or joint candidates committee of a candidate who was defeated by the official sought to be recalled at the last election for that office shall be subject to the limits on contributions established by "The New Jersey Campaign Contributions and Expenditures Reporting Act," P.L.1973, c. 83 (C. 19:44A-1 et seq.).

g. A recall committee shall submit, at the time of its initial filing with the Election Law Enforcement Commission, in addition to its depository account registration information, a registration statement which includes:

(1) the complete name or identifying title of the committee and the general category of entity or entities, including but not limited to business organizations, labor organizations, professional or trade associations, candidates for or holders of public offices, political parties, ideological groups or civic associations, the interests of which are shared by the leadership, members, or financial supporters of the committee;

(2) the mailing address of the committee and the name and resident address of a resident of this State who shall have been designated by the committee as its agent to accept service of process; and

(3) a descriptive statement prepared by the organizers or officers of the committee that identifies:

(a) the names and mailing addresses of the persons having control over the affairs of the committee, including but not limited to persons in whose name or at whose direction or suggestion the committee solicits funds;

(b) the name and mailing address of any person not included among the persons identified under subparagraph (a) of this paragraph who, directly or through an agent, participated in the initial organization of the committee;

(c) in the case of any person identified under subparagraph (a) or subparagraph (b) who is an individual, the occupation of that individual, the individual's home address, and the name and mailing address of the individual's employer, or, in the case of any such person which is a corporation, partnership, unincorporated association, or other organization, the name and mailing address of the organization; and

(d) any other information which the Election Law Enforcement Commission may, under such regulations as it shall adopt pursuant to the provisions of the "Administrative Procedure Act," P.L.1968, c. 410 (C. 52:14B-1 et seq.), require as being material to the fullest possible disclosure of the economic, political and other particular interests and objectives which the committee has been organized to or does advance. The commission shall be informed, in writing, of any change in the information required by this paragraph within three days of the occurrence of the change.

h. In accordance with the Election Law Enforcement Commission's regular reporting schedule, the commission may, by regulation, require a recall committee or a recall defense committee to file during any calendar year one or more additional cumulative reports of such contributions received and expenditures made to ensure that no more than three months shall elapse between the last day of a period covered by one such report and the last day of the period covered by the next such report.

19:27A-18. Repealer
On the effective date of this act, sections 88 through 98 of P.L. 1972, c. 154 (C. 40:41A-88 et seq.); sections 17-19 through 17-29 of P.L.1950, c. 210 (C. 40:69A-168 et seq.);

R.S. 40:75-25 through R.S. 40:75-44; R.S. 40:81-6; and R.S. 40:84-12 through R.S. 40:84-19 shall become inoperative and shall have no force or effect unless a court of competent jurisdiction issues a final order invalidating the provisions of Article I, paragraph 2b. of the New Jersey Constitution, providing for the recall of elected officials, and the provisions of this act which permit the recall of county or municipal officials, in which case the aforesaid laws shall again become operative and shall have full force and effect as of the date of the court's ruling.

Current through L.2003, c. 1 to 315

CONSTITUTION OF NORTH DAKOTA
Article III, Section 10.

Any elected official of the state, of any county or of any legislative or county commissioner district shall be subject to recall by petition of electors equal in number to twenty-five percent of those who voted at the preceding general election for the office of governor in the state, county, or district in which the official is to be recalled.

The petition shall be filed with the official with whom a petition for nomination to the office in question is filed, who shall call a special election if he finds the petition valid and sufficient. No elector may remove his name from a recall petition.

The name of the official to be recalled shall be placed on the ballot unless he resigns within ten days after the filing of the petition. Other candidates for the office may be nominated in a manner provided by law. When the election results have been officially declared, the candidate receiving the highest number of votes shall be deemed elected for the remainder of the term. No official shall be subject twice to recall during the term for which he was elected.

NORTH DAKOTA CENTURY CODE ANNOTATED
Section 16.1-01-09.1 et sec.
Beginning with Recall petitions – Signature-Form-Circulation.

16.1-01-09.1 Recall Petitions – Signature – Form – Circulation

1. A person may not sign a recall petition circulated pursuant to article III of the Constitution of North Dakota or section 44-08-21 unless the person is a qualified elector. A person may not sign a petition more than once, and each signer shall add the signer's complete residential, rural route, or general delivery address and the date of signing. Every qualified elector signing a petition must do so in the presence of the person circulating the petition. A petition must be in substantially the following form:

RECALL PETITION

We, the undersigned, being qualified electors request that __________(name of the person being recalled) the _________(office of person being recalled) be recalled for the reason or reasons of _________.
RECALL SPONSORING COMMITTEE

The following are the names and addresses of the qualified electors of the state of North Dakota and the political subdivision who, as the sponsoring committee for the petitioners, represent and act for the petitioners in accordance with law:

Complete Residential,
Rural Route,
Name or General Delivery Address

1. ____________(Chairman)

____

2.

____

3.

____

4.

____

5.

____

INSTRUCTIONS TO PETITION SIGNERS

You are being asked to sign a petition. You must be a qualified elector. This means you are eighteen years old, you have lived in North Dakota for thirty day, and you are a United States citizen. All signers must add their complete residential, rural route, or general delivery address and date of signing. Every qualified elector signing a petition must do so in the presence of the person circulating the petition.

QUALIFIED ELECTORS

Month, Day, Year	Name of Qualified Elector	Complete Residential, Rural Route, or or General Delivery Address City,State

1.______________________________
2.______________________________
3.______________________________
4.______________________________
5.______________________________
6.______________________________
7.______________________________
8.______________________________

The number of signature lines on each page of a printed petition may vary if necessary to accommodate other required textual matter.

2. Each copy of a petition provided for in this section, before being filed, must have attached an affidavit executed by the circulator in substantially the following form:

State of North Dakota
ss.
County of___________________
(county where signed)
I. ______________________being sworn, say that I am a qualified elector; that I
(circulator's name)
reside at __________________________;
(address)
that each signature contained on the attached petition was executed in my presence; and that to the best of my knowledge and belief each person whose signature appears on the attached petition is a qualified elector; and that each signature contained on the attached petition is the genuine signature of the person whose name it purports to be.

____
(signature of circulator)

Subscribed and sworn to before me on
_______________,_______at
______________, North Dakota
(city)
(Notary seal)_____________________________________
(signature of notary)
Notary Public
My commission expires______________

3. A petition for recall must include, before the signature lines for the qualified electors as provided in subsection 1, the name of the person being recalled, the office from which that person is being recalled, and a list of the names and addresses of not less than five qualified electors of the state,

political subdivision , or district in which the official is to be recalled who are sponsoring the recall.

4. A petition may not be circulated under the authority of article III of the Constitution of North Dakota or section 44-08-21 by a person who is less than eighteen years of age, nor may the affidavit called for by subsection 2 be executed by a person who is less than eighteen years of age at the time of signing. All petitions circulated under the authority of the constitution and of this section must be circulated in their entirety

5. When recall petitions are delivered to the secretary of state or other filing officer with whom a petition for nomination to the office in question is filed, the chairman of the sponsoring committee shall submit to the secretary of state or other filing officer an affidavit stating that to the best of that person's knowledge, the petitions contain at least the required number of signatures.

6. The filing officer has a reasonable period, not to exceed thirty days, in which to pass upon the sufficiency of a recall petition. The filing officer may conduct a representative random sampling of the signatures contained in the petitions by the use of questionnaires, postcards, telephone calls, personal interviews, or other accepted information, gathering techniques, or any combinations thereof, to determine the validity of the signatures. Signatures determined by the filing officer to be invalid may not be counted and all violations of law discovered by the filing officer must be reported to the state's attorney for possible prosecution.

16.1-01.10. Secretary of state to pass upon sufficiency of petitions – Method-Time limit.

The secretary of state shall have a reasonable period, not to exceed thirty-five days, in which to pass upon the sufficiency of any petition mentioned in section 16.1-01-09. The secretary of state shall conduct a representative random sampling of the signatures contained in the petitions by the use of questionnaires, postcards, telephone calls, personal interviews, or other accepted information gathering techniques, or any combinations thereof, to determine the validity of the signatures. Signatures determined by the secretary of state to be invalid may not be counted and all violations of law discovered by the secretary of state must be reported to the attorney general for prosecution.

CONSTITUTION OF OREGON
Article 2, Section 18.

Recall; meaning of words "the legislative assembly shall provide."

(1) Every public officer in Oregon is subject, as herein provided, to recall by the electors of the state or of the electoral district from which the public officer is elected.

(2) Fifteen per cent, but not more, of the number of electors who voted for Governor in the officer's electoral district at the most recent election at which a candidate for Governor was elected to a full term, may be required to file their petition demanding the officer's recall by the people.
(3) They shall set forth in the petition the reasons for the demand.

(4)If the public officer offers to resign, the resignation shall be accepted and take effect on the day it is offered, and the vacancy shall be filled as may be provided by law. If the public officer does not resign within five days after the petition is filed, a special election shall be ordered to be held within 35 days in the electoral district to determine whether the people will recall the officer.

(5)On the ballot at the election shall be printed in not more than 200 words the reasons for demanding the recall of the officer as set forth in the recall petition, and, in not more than 200 words, the officer's justification of the officer's course in office. The officer shall continue to perform the duties of office until the result of the special election is officially declared. If an officer is recalled from any public office the vacancy shall be filled immediately in the manner provided by law for filling a vacancy in that office arising from any other cause.

(6)The recall petition shall be filed with the officer with whom a petition for nomination to such office should be filed, and the same officer shall order the special election when it is required. No such petition shall be circulated against any officer until the officer has actually held the office six months, save and except that it may be filed against a senator or representative in the legislative assembly at any time after five days from the beginning of the first session after the election of the senator o representative.

(7)After one such petition and special election, no further recall petition shall be filed against the same officer during the term for which the officer was elected unless such further petitioners first pay into the public treasury which has paid such special election expenses, the whole amount of its expenses for the preceding special election.
(8)Such additional legislation as may aid the operation of this section shall be provided by the legislative assembly, including provision for payment by the public treasury of the reasonable special election campaign expenses of such officer. But the words, "the legislative assembly shall provide," or any similar or equivalent words in this constitution or any amendment thereto, shall not be construed to grant to the legislative assembly any exclusive power of lawmaking nor in any way to limit the initiative and referendum powers reserved by the people.

OREGON REVISED STATUTES
Section 249.865 et sec. Beginning with Filing prospective petition; contents of petition; statement regarding payment of petition circulators; effect of violation.

Or. Rev. Stat. 249.865 Filing prospective petition; contents of petition; statement regarding payment of petition circulators; effect of violation.

(1)Pursuant to section 18, Article II of the Oregon Constitution, an elector of the electoral district from which the public officer is elected may file a petition demanding the recall of the public officer. Before the petition is circulated for signatures, the chief petitioner of the petition shall file with the officer authorized to order the recall election:
(a)A copy of the prospective petition signed by the chief petitioner;
(b)A statement of organization conforming to ORS 260.083 of contributions received and expenditures made by or on behalf of the chief petitioner and political committee the chief petitioner represents, if any, to the date of filing the prospective petition.
(c)A statement conforming to ORS 260.083 of contributions received and expenditures made by or on behalf of the chief petitioner and political committee the chief petitioner represents, if any, to the date of filing the prospective petition.
(2)The chief petitioner shall include with the prospective petition a statement declaring whether one or more persons will be paid money or other valuable consideration for obtaining signatures of electors of electors on the recall petition. After the prospective petition is filed, the chief petitioner shall notify the filing officer not later than the 10th day after the chief petitioner first has knowledge or should have had knowledge that:
(a)Any person is being paid for obtaining signatures, when the statement included with the prospective petition declared that no such person would be paid.

(b)No person is being paid for obtaining signatures, when the statement included with the prospective petition declared that one or more such persons would be paid.

(3)Each sheet of the recall petition shall contain:

(a)The words "Petition for recall of," (name and title of officer) and the date of the filing under subsection (a) of this section, and
(b)The name and address of the treasurer of the political committee the chief petitioner represents, or if there is not a political committee, the name and address of the chief petitioner.

(4)Not more than 20 signatures on each sheet of the recall petition shall be counted. The circulator shall certify on each signature sheet that the individuals signed the sheet in the presence of the circulator and that the circulator believes each individual is an elector.

(5)Any intentional or willful violation of subsection (1) or (2) of this section by a chief petitioner of the recall petition or by the treasurer of the political committee the chief petitioner represents, if any, shall invalidate the prospective petition before it is circulated for signatures.

249.870 Number of signers on recall petition.
The requisite number of signers on a recall petition is 15 percent of the total votes cast in the electoral district for all candidates for Governor at the most recent election at which a candidate for Governor was elected to a full term next preceding the filing of the petition for verification of signatures.

249.875 Time for completing filing; verification of signatures.

(1)A recall petition shall be void unless completed and filed not later than the 100th day after filing the prospective petition described in ORS 249.865. Not later than the 90th day after filing the prospective petition the petition shall be submitted to the filing officer who shall verify the signatures not later than the 10th days after the submission. The filed petition shall contain only original signatures. A recall petition shall not be accepted for signature verification if it contains less than 100 percent of the required number of signatures. The petition shall not be accepted for filing until 100 percent of the required number of signatures of electors have been verified.

(2)The provisions for verification of signatures on an initiative or referendum petition contained in ORS 250.105, are applicable to the verification of signatures on a recall petition.

249.876 Elector may not remove signature after petition submitted for verification.

After a recall petition is submitted for signature verification, no elector who signed the petition may remove the signature of the elector from the petition.

249.877 Statement of justification by public officer.

(1)A public officer against whom a recall petition has been filed may submit to the filing officer, in not more than 200 words, a statement of justification of the public officer's course in office. The statement must be filed not later than the fifth day after the recall petition is filed.

(2)The county clerk shall have the statement printed on the official and sample ballots for the recall election.

CONSTITUTION OF RHODE ISLAND
Article IV, Section 1.

Section 1. Election and terms of governor, lieutenant governor, secretary of state, attorney-general, general treasurer, and general assembly members. -- The governor, lieutenant governor, secretary of state, attorney-general, general treasurer shall be elected on the Tuesday after the first Monday in November, quadrennially commencing A.D. 1994, and every four (4) years thereafter, and shall severally hold their offices, subject to recall as provided herein, for four (4) years from the first Tuesday of January next succeeding their election and until their successors are elected and qualified. No person shall serve consecutively in the same general office for more than two (2) full terms, excluding any partial term of less than two (2) years previously served. The senators and representatives in the general assembly shall be elected on the Tuesday after the first Monday in November, biennially in even numbered years, and shall severally hold their offices for two (2) years from the first Tuesday of January next succeeding their election and until their successors are elected and qualified. Recall is authorized in the case of a general officer who has been indicted or informed against for a felony, convicted of a misdemeanor, or against whom a finding of probable cause of violation of the code of ethics has been made by the ethics commission. Recall shall not, however be instituted at any time during the first six (6) months or the last year of an individual's term of office. Such a recall may be instituted by filing with the state board of elections an application for issuance of a recall petition against said general officer which is signed by duly qualified electors equal to three percent (3%) of the total number of votes cast at the last preceding general election for that office. If, upon verification, the application is determined to contain signatures of the required number of electors, the state board of elections shall issue a recall petition for circulation amongst the electors of the state. Within ninety (90) days of issuance, recall petitions containing the signatures of duly qualified electors constituting fifteen percent (15%) of the total number of votes cast in the last preceding general election for said office must be filed with the state board of elections. The signatures to the application and to the recall petition need not all be on one (1) sheet of paper, but each such application and petition must contain an identical statement naming the person to be recalled, the general office held by said person, and the grounds for such recall set forth in a statement of one hundred (100) words or less approved by the board of elections. Each signatory must set forth his or her signature as it appears on the voting list, the date of signing, and his or her place of residence. The person witnessing the signatures of each elector on said petition must sign a statement under oath on said sheet attesting that the signatures thereon are genuine and were signed in his or her presence. If the requisite number of signatures are not obtained within said ninety (90) days period, the recall effort shall terminate. Upon verification of the requisite number of signatures, a special election shall be scheduled at which the issue of removing said office holder and the grounds therefor shall be placed before the electors of the state. If a majority of those voting support removal of said office holder, the office shall be immediately declared vacant and shall be filled in accordance with the constitution and laws of the state. The person so removed shall not be eligible to fill the unexpired portion of the term of office. The general assembly shall provide by statute for implementation of the recall process.

Section 2. Election by plurality. -- In all elections held by the people for state, city, town, ward or district officers, the person or candidate receiving the largest number of votes cast shall be declared elected.

Section 3. Filling vacancy caused by death, removal, refusal to serve, or incapacity of elected officers -- Election when no candidate receives plurality. -- When the governor-elect shall die, remove from the state, refuse to serve; become insane, or be otherwise incapacitated, the lieutenant governor-elect shall be qualified as governor at the beginning of the term for which the governor was elected. When both the governor and lieutenant governor-elect, or either the lieutenant governor, secretary of state, attorney-general, or general treasurer-elect, are so incapacitated, or when there has been a failure to elect any one or more of the officers mentioned in this section, the general assembly shall upon its organization meet in grand committee and elect some person or persons to fill the office or offices, as the case may be, for which such incapacity exists or as to which such failure to elect occurred. When the general assembly shall elect any of said officers because of the failure of any person to receive a plurality of the votes cast, the election in each case shall be made from the persons who received the same and largest number of votes.

Section 4. Temporary appointment to fill vacancies in office of secretary of state, attorney-general, or general treasurer. -- In case of a vacancy in the office of the secretary of state, attorney-general, or general treasurer from any cause, the general assembly in grand committee shall elect some person to fill the same; provided, that if such vacancy occurs when the general assembly is not in session the governor shall appoint some person to fill such vacancy until a successor elected by the general assembly is qualified to act. exists or as to which such failure to elect occurred. When the general assembly shall elect any of said officers because of the failure of any person to receive a plurality of the votes cast, the election in each case shall be made from the persons who received the same and largest number of votes.

Section 5. Special elections to fill general assembly vacancies. – When a senator or representative-elect shall die, remove from the state, refuse to serve, become insane, or be otherwise incapacitated, or when at an election for any senator or representative no person shall receive a plurality of the votes cast, a new election shall be held. A vacancy in the senate or house of representatives shall be filled at a new election. The general assembly shall provide by general law for the holding of such elections at such times as to insure that each town and city shall be fully represented in the general assembly during the whole of every session thereof so far as is practicable. Every person elected in accordance with this section shall hold office for the remainder of the term or for the full term, as the case may be, of the office which that person is elected to fill, and until a successor is elected and qualified. same and largest number of votes.

Section 6. Elections in grand committee -- Majority vote -- Term of elected official. -- In elections by the general assembly in grand committee the person receiving a majority of the votes shall be elected. Every person elected by the general assembly to fill a vacancy, or pursuant to section 3 of this article, shall hold office for the remainder of the term or for the full term, as the case may be, and until a successor is elected and qualified. elected to fill, and until a successor is elected and qualified.

Section 7. Elections in grand committee -- Quorum -- Permitted activities. -- A quorum of the grand committee shall consist of a majority of all the members of the senate and a majority of all the members of the house of representatives duly assembled pursuant to an invitation from one of said bodies which has been accepted by the other, and the acceptance of which has been communicated by message to the body in which such invitation originated, and each house shall be attended by its secretaries and clerks. No act or business of any kind shall be done in grand committee other than that which is distinctly specified in the invitation by virtue of which such grand committee is assembled, except to take a recess or to dissolve; provided, that the grand committee may appoint a subcommittee of its own members to count any ballots delivered to it and report the result of such count.

Section 8. Voter registration lists. -- It shall not be necessary for the town or ward clerks to keep and transmit to the general assembly a list or register of all persons voting for general officers; but the general assembly shall have power to pass such laws on the subject as it may deem expedient. appoint a subcommittee of its own members to count any ballots delivered to it and report the result of such count.

Section 9. Reports of campaign contributions and expenses. -- The general assembly shall require each candidate for general office in any primary, general or special election to report to the secretary of state all contributions and expenditures made by any person to or on behalf of such candidate, provided however, that the general assembly may limit such disclosure to contributions or expenditures in excess of such an amount as the general assembly shall specify.

Section 10. Limitations on campaign contributions -- Public financing of campaign expenditures of general officers. -- The general assembly shall adopt limitations on all contributions to candidates for election to state and local office in any primary, general or special election and shall provide for the adoption of a plan of voluntary public financing and limitations on total campaign expenditures of campaigns for governor and such other general officers as the general assembly shall specify.

NO STATUTORY PROVISION ON RECALL IN RHODE ISLAND

WASHINGTON STATE CONSTITUTION
Article 1, Section 33 and Section 34.

Section 33. Recall of Elective Officers.

Every elective public officer of the state of Washington expect (except) judges of courts of record is subject to recall and discharge by the legal voters of the state, or of the political subdivision of the state, from which he was elected whenever a petition demanding his recall, reciting that such officer has committed some act or acts of malfeasance or misfeasance while in office, or who has violated his oath of office, stating the matters complained of, signed by the percentages of the qualified electors thereof, hereinafter provided, the percentage required to be computed from the total number of votes cast for all candidates for his said office to which he was elected at the preceding election, is filed with the officer with whom a petition for nomination, or certificate for nomination, to such office must be filed under the laws of this state, and the same officer shall call a special election as provided by the general elections laws of this state, and the result determined as therein provided.

Section 34. Same.

The legislature shall pass the necessary laws to carry out the provisions of Section thirty-three (33) of this article, and to facilitate its operation and effect without delay: Provided, That the authority hereby conferred upon the legislature shall not be construed to grant to the legislature any exclusive power of lawmaking nor in any way limit the initiative and referendum powers reserved by the people. The percentages required shall be, state officer, other than judges, senators and representatives, city officers of cities of the first class, school district boards in cities of the first class; county officers of counties of the first, second and third classes, twenty-five per cent. Officers of all other political subdivisions, cities, towns, townships, precincts and school districts not herein mentioned, and state senators and representatives, thirty-five per cent.

WASHINGTON REVISED CODE
Chapter 29A, Section 29A.56.110 et sec.
Beginning with Initiating recall proceedings.

RCW 29A.56.110

RCW 29A.56.120
RCW 29A.56.130
RCW 29A.56.140
RCW 29A.56.160
RCW 29A.56.170
RCW 29A.56.210
RCW 29A.56.220
RCW 29A.56.230
RCW 29A.56.240
RCW 29A.56.250
RCW 29A.56.260
RCW 29A.56.270

RCW 29A.56.110
Initiating proceedings – Statement – Contents – Verification – Definitions.

Whenever any legal voter of the state or of any politicalsubdivision thereof, either individually or on behalf of anorganization, desires to demand the recall and discharge of any elective public officer of the state or of such political subdivision, as the case may be, under the provisions of sections33 and 34 of Article 1 of the Constitution, the voter shall prepare a typewritten charge, reciting that such officer, naminghim or her and giving the title of the office, has committed an act or acts of malfeasance, or an act or acts of misfeasance while in office, or has violated the oath of office, or has been guilty of any two or more of the acts specified in the Constitution as grounds for recall. The charge shall state theact or acts complained of in concise language, give a detailed description including the approximate date, location, and nature of each act complained of, be signed by the person or persons making the charge, give their respective post office addresses, and be verified under oath that the person or persons believe the charge or charges to be true and have knowledge of the alleged facts upon which the stated grounds for recall are based. For the purposes of this chapter: (1) "Misfeasance" or "malfeasance" in office means any wrongful conduct that affects, interrupts, or interferes with the performance of official duty; (a) Additionally, "misfeasance" in office means the performance of a duty in an improper manner; and (b) Additionally, "malfeasance" in office means the commission of an unlawful act; (2) "Violation of the oath of office" means the neglect orknowing failure by an elective public officer to performfaithfully a duty imposed by law.

RCW 29A.56.120
Petition -- Where filed.
Any person making a charge shall file it with the elections officer whose duty it is to receive and file a declaration of candidacy for the office concerning the incumbent of which the recall is to be demanded. The officer with whom the charge is filed shall promptly (1)serve a copy of the charge upon the officer whose recall is demanded, and (2) certify and transmit the charge to the preparerof the ballot synopsis provided in RCW 29A.56.130. The manner of service shall be the same as for the commencement of a civil action in superior court.

SRCW 29A.56.130
Ballot synopsis.

(1) Within fifteen days after receiving a charge, the officer specified below shall formulate a ballot synopsis of the charge of not more than two hundred words. (a) Except as provided in (b) of this subsection, if there call is demanded of an elected public officer whose political jurisdiction encompasses an area in more than one county, the attorney general shall be the preparer, except if the recall is demanded of the attorney general, the chief justice of thesupreme court shall be the preparer. (b) If the recall is demanded of an elected public officer whose political jurisdiction lies wholly in one county, or if there call is demanded of an elected public officer of a district whose jurisdiction encompasses more than one county but whose declaration of candidacy is filed with a county auditor in one of the counties, the prosecuting

attorney of that county shall be the preparer, except that if the prosecuting attorney is the officer whose recall is demanded, the attorney general shall be the preparer. (2) The synopsis shall set forth the name of the person charged, the title of the office, and a concise statement of the elements of the charge. Upon completion of the ballot synopsis, the preparer shall certify and transmit the exact language of the ballot synopsis to the persons filing the charge and the officer subject to recall. The preparer shall additionally certify and transmit the charges and the ballot synopsis to the superior court of the county in which the officer subject to recall resides and shall petition the superior court to approve the synopsis and to determine the sufficiency of the charges.

RCW 29A.56.140
Determination by superior court – Correction of ballot synopsis.

Within fifteen days after receiving the petition, the superior court shall have conducted a hearing on and shall have determined, without cost to any party, (1) whether or not the acts stated in the charge satisfy the criteria for which a recall petition may be filed, and (2) the adequacy of the ballot synopsis. The clerk of the superior court shall notify the person subject to recall and the person demanding recall of the hearing date. Both persons may appear with counsel. The court may hear arguments as to the sufficiency of the charges and the adequacy of the ballot synopsis. The court shall not consider the truth of the charges, but only their sufficiency. An appeal of a sufficiency decision shall be filed in the supreme-court as specified by RCW 29A.56.270. The superior court shall correct any ballot synopsis it deems inadequate. Any decision regarding the ballot synopsis by the superior court is final. The court shall certify and transmit the ballot synopsis to the officer subject to recall, the person demanding the recall, and either the secretary of state or the county auditor, as appropriate.

RCW 29A.56.150

Filing supporting signatures – Time limitations.

(1) The sponsors of a recall demanded of any public officer shall stop circulation of and file all petitions with the appropriate elections officer not less than six months before the next general election in which the officer whose recall is demanded is subject to reelection. (2) The sponsors of a recall demanded of an officer elected to a statewide position shall have a maximum of two hundred seventy days, and the sponsors of a recall demanded of any other officer shall have a maximum of one hundred eighty days, in which to obtain and file supporting signatures after the issuance of a ballot synopsis by the superior court. If the decision of the superior court regarding the sufficiency of the charges is not appealed, the one hundred eighty or two hundred seventy day period for the circulation of signatures begins on the sixteenth day following the decision of the superior court. If the decision of the superior court regarding the sufficiency of the charges is appealed, the one hundred eighty or two hundred seventy day period for the circulation of signatures begins on the day following the issuance of the decision by the supreme court.

RCW 29A.56.160
Petition – Form.

Recall petitions must be printed on single sheets of paper of good writing quality (including but not limited to newsprint) not less than eleven inches in width and not less than fourteen inches in length. No petition may be circulated or signed prior to the first day of the one hundred eighty or two hundred seventy day period established by RCW 29A.56.150 for that recall petition. The petitions must be substantially in the following form: The warning prescribed by RCW 29A.72.140; followed by: Petition for the recall of (here insert the name of the office and of the person whose recall is petitioned for) to the Honorable (here insert the name and title of the officer with whom the charge is filed). We, the undersigned citizens and legal voters of (the state of

Washington or the political subdivision in which the recall is to be held), respectfully direct that a special election be called to determine whether or not (here insert the name of the person charged and the office which he or she holds) be recalled and discharged from his or her office, for and on account of (his or her having committed the act or acts of malfeasance or misfeasance while in office, or having violated his or her oath of office, as the case may be), in the following particulars: (here insert the synopsis of the charge); and each of us for himself or herself says: I have personally signed this petition; I am a legal voter of the State of Washington in the precinct and city (or town) and county written after my name, and my residence address is correctly stated, and to my knowledge, have signed this petition only once. The petition must include a place for each petitioner to sign and print his or her name, and the address, city, and county at which he or she is registered to vote.

RCW 29A.56.170
Petition – Size.

Each recall petition at the time of circulating, signing, and filing with the officer with whom it is to be filed, must consist of not more than five sheets with numbered lines for not more than twenty signatures on each sheet, with the prescribed warning, title, and form of petition on each sheet, and a full, true, and correct copy of the original statement of the charges against the officer referred to therein, printed on sheets of paper of like size and quality as the petition, firmly fastened together.

RCW 29A.56.180
Number of signatures required.

When the person, committee, or organization demanding the recall of a public officer has secured sufficient signatures upon the recall petition the person, committee, or organization may submit the same to the officer with whom the charge was filed for filing in his or her office. The number of signatures required shall be asfollows: (1) In the case of a state officer, an officer of a city of the first class, a member of a school board in a city of the first class, or a county officer of a county with a population of forty thousand or more – signatures of legal voters equal to twenty-five percent of the total number of votes cast for all candidates for the office to which the officer whose recall is demanded was elected at the preceding election. (2) In the case of an officer of any political subdivision, city, town, township, precinct, or school district other than those mentioned in subsection (1) of this section, and in the case of a state senator or representative – signatures of legalvoters equal to thirty-five percent of the total number of votes cast for all candidates for the office to which the officer whose recall is demanded was elected at the preceding election.

RCW 29A.56.190
Canvassing signatures – Time of – Notice.

Upon the filing of a recall petition, the officer with whom the charge was filed shall stamp on each petition the date of filing, and shall notify the persons filing them and the officer whose recall is demanded of the date when the petitions will be canvassed, which date must be not less than five or more than ten days from the date of its filing.

RCW 29A.56.200
Verification and canvass of signatures – Procedure – Statistical sampling.

(1) Upon the filing of a recall petition, the elections officer shall proceed to verify and canvass the names of legal voters on the petition. (2) The verification and canvass of signatures on the petition may be observed by persons representing the advocates and opponents of the proposed recall so long as they make no record of the names, addresses, or other information on the petitions or related records

during the verification process except upon the order of the superior court. The elections officer may limit the number of observers to not fewer than two on each side, if in his or her opinion a greater number would cause undue delay or disruption of the verification process. Any such limitation shall apply equally to both sides. If the elections officer finds the same name signed to more than one petition, he or she shall reject all but the first such valid signature. (3) Where the recall of a statewide elected official is sought, the secretary of state may use any statistical sampling techniques for verification and canvassing which have been adopted by rule for canvassing initiative petitions under RCW 29A.72.230. No petition will be rejected on the basis of any statistical method employed. No petition will be accepted on the basis of any statistical method employed if such method indicates that the petition contains less than the number of signatures of legal voters required by Article I, section 33 (Amendment 8) ofthe state Constitution.

RCW 29A.56.210
Fixing date for recall election – Notice.

If, at the conclusion of the verification and canvass, it is found that a petition for recall bears the required number of signatures of certified legal voters, the officer with whom the petition is filed shall promptly certify the petitions assufficient and fix a date for the special election to determine whether or not the officer charged shall be recalled and discharged from office. The special election shall be held not less than forty-five nor more than sixty days from the certification and, whenever possible, on one of the dates provided in RCW 29A.04.330, but no recall election may be held between the date of the primary and the date of the general election in any calendar year. Notice shall be given in themanner as required by law for special elections in the state orin the political subdivision, as the case may be.

RCW 29A.56.220
Response to petition charges.

When a date for a special recall election is set the certifying officer shall serve a notice of the date of the election to the officer whose recall is demanded and the person demanding recall. The manner of service shall be the same as for the commencement of a civil action in superior court. After having been served a notice of the date of the election and the ballot synopsis, the officer whose recall is demanded may submit to the certifying officer a response, not to exceed two hundred fifty words in length, to the charge contained in the ballot synopsis. Such response shall be submitted by the seventh consecutive day after service of the notice. The certifying officer shall promptly send a copy of the response to the person who filed the petition.

RCW 29A.56.230
Destruction of insufficient recall petition.

If it is found that the recall petition does not contain the requisite number of signatures of certified legal voters, the officer shall so notify the persons filing the petition, and at the expiration of thirty days from the conclusion of the count the officer shall destroy the petitions unless prevented therefrom by the injunction or mandate of a court.

RCW 29A.56.240
Fraudulent names – Record of.

The officer making the canvass of a recall petition shall keep a record of all names appearing on it that are not certified to be legal voters of the state or of the political subdivision, as the case may be, and of all names appearing more than once, and shall report the same to the prosecuting attorneys of the respective counties where the names appear to have been signed, to the end that prosecutions may be had for the violation of this chapter.

RCW 29A.56.250
Conduct of election – Contents of ballot.

The special election for the recall of an officer shall beconducted in the same manner as a special election for that jurisdiction. The county auditor shall conduct the recall election. The ballots at any recall election shall contain a full, true, and correct copy of the ballot synopsis of the charge and the officer's response to the charge if one has been filed.

RCW 29A.56.260
Ascertaining the result – When recall effective.

The votes on a recall election must be counted, canvassed, and the results certified in the manner provided by law for counting, canvassing, and certifying the results of an election for the office from which the officer is being recalled. However, if the officer whose recall is demanded is the officer to whom, under the law, returns of elections are made, the returns must be made to the officer with whom the charge is filed, and who called the special election. In the case of an election for the recall of a state officer, the county canvassing boards of the various counties shall canvass and return the result of the election to the officer calling the special election. If a majority of all votes cast at the recall electionis for the recall of the officer charged, the officer is thereupon recalled and discharged from the office, and the office there upon is vacant.

RCW 29A.56.270
Enforcement provisions – Mandamus – Appellate review.

The superior court of the county in which the officer subject to recall resides has original jurisdiction to compel the performance of any act required of any public officer or toprevent the performance by any such officer of any act inrelation to the recall not in compliance with law. The supreme court has like original jurisdiction in relation to state officers and revisory jurisdiction over the decisions of the superior courts. Any proceeding to compel or prevent the performance of any such act shall be begun within ten days from the time the cause of complaint arises, and shall be considered an emergency matter of public concern and take precedence over other cases, and be speedily heard and determined. Appellate review of a decision of any superior court shall be begun and perfected within fifteen days after its decision in a recall election case and shall be considered an emergency matter of public concern by the supreme court, and heard and determined within thirty days after the decision of the superior court.

WISCONSIN CONSTITUTION
Article XIII, Section 12.

Recall of elective officers. Section 12. The qualified electors of the state, of any congressional, judicial or legislative district or of any county may petition for the recall of any incumbent elective officer after the first year of the term for which the incumbent was elected, by filing a petition with the filing officer with whom the nomination petition to the office in the primary is filed, demanding the recall of the incumbent.

12(1) The recall petition shall be signed by electors equaling at least twenty-five percent of the vote cast for the office of governor at the last preceding election, in the state, county, or district which the incumbent represents.

12(2) The filing officer with whom the recall petition is filed shall call a recall election for the Tuesday of the 6th week after the date of filing the petition or, if that Tuesday is a legal holiday, on the first day after that Tuesday which is not a legal holiday.

12(3) The incumbent shall continue to perform the duties of the office until the recall election results are officially declared.

12(4) Unless the incumbent declines within 10 days after the filing of the petition, the incumbent shall without filing be deemed to have filed for the recall election. Other candidates may file for the office in the manner provided by law for special elections. For the purpose of conducting elections under this section

(4)(a) When more than 2 persons compete for a nonpartisan office, a recall primary shall be held. The 2 persons receiving the highest number of votes in the recall primary shall be the 2 candidates in the recall election, except that if any candidate receives a majority of the total number of votes cast in the recall primary, that candidate shall assume the office for the remainder of the term and a recall election shall not be held.

(4)(b) For any partisan office, a recall primary shall be held for each political party which is by law entitled to a separate ballot and from which more than one candidate competes for the party's nomination in the recall election. The person receiving the highest number of votes in the recall primary for each political party shall be that party's candidate in the recall election. Independent candidates and candidates representing political parties not entitled by law to a separate ballot shall be shown on the ballot for the recall election only.

(4)(c) When a recall primary is required, the date specified under sub. (2) shall be the date of the recall primary and the recall election shall be held on the Tuesday of the 4th week after the recall primary or, if that Tuesday is a legal holiday, on the first day after that Tuesday which is not a legal holiday.

12(5) The person who receives the highest number of votes in the recall election shall be elected for the remainder of the term.

12(6) After one such petition and recall election, no further recall petition shall be filed against the same officer during the term for which he was elected.

12(7) this section shall be self-executing and mandatory. Laws may be enacted to facilitate its operation but no law shall be enacted to hamper, restrict or impair the right of recall.

WISCONSIN STATUTES ANNOTATED
Chapter 9, Section 9.10 et sec. Beginning with Recall.

WSA 9.10(1)
WSA 9.10(2)
WSA 9.10(3)
WSA 9.10(4)
WSA 9.10(5)
WSA 9.10(6)

9.10 Recall. (1) RIGHT TO RECALL; PETITION SIGNATURES. (a) The qualified electors of the state, of any county, city, village, town, of any congressional, legislative, judicial or school district, or of any prosecutorial unit may petition for the recall of any incumbent elective official by filing a petition with the same official or agency with whom nomination papers or declarations of candidacy for the office are filed demanding the recall of the officeholder.

(b) Except as provided in par.

(c), a petition for recall of a state, congressional, legislative, judicial or county officer shall be signed by electors equal to at least 25% of the vote cast for the office of governor at the last election within the same district or territory as that of the officeholder being recalled. Except as provided in par. (c), a petition for the recall of a city, village, town or school district officer shall be signed by electors equal to at least 25% of the vote cast for the office of president at the last election within the same district or territory as that of the officeholder being recalled. (c) If no statistics are available to calculate the required number of signatures on a petition for recall of an officer, the number of signatures shall be determined as follows:

1. The area of the district in square miles shall be divided by the area of the municipality in square miles in which it lies.

2. The vote for governor or president, as required, at the last general election in the municipality within which the district lies shall be multiplied by 25% of the quotient determined under subd. 1. to determine the required number of signatures.

3. If a district is in more than one municipality, the method of determination under subds. 1. and 2. shall be used for each part of the district which constitutes only a fractional part of any area for which election statistics are kept.

(d) The official or agency with whom declarations of candidacy are filed for each office shall determine and certify to any interested person the number of signatures required on a recall petition for that office.

(2) PETITION REQUIREMENTS. (a) Every recall petition shall have on the face at the top in bold print the words "RECALL PETITION". Other requirements as to preparation and form of the petition shall be governed by s. 8.40.

(b) A recall petition for a city, village, town or school district office shall contain a statement of a reason for the recall which is related to the official responsibilities of the official for whom removal is sought.

(c) A petition requesting the recall of each elected officer shall be prepared and filed separately.

(d) No petition may be offered for filing for the recall of an officer unless the petitioner first files a registration statement under s. 11.05 (1) or (2) with the filing officer with whom the petition is filed. The petitioner shall append to the registration a statement indicating his or her intent to circulate a recall petition, the name of the officer for whom recall is sought and, in the case of a petition for the recall of a city, village, town or school district officer, a statement of a reason for the recall which is related to the official responsibilities of the official for whom removal is sought. No petitioner may circulate a petition for the recall of an officer prior to completing registration. The last date that a petition for the recall of a state, congressional, legislative, judicial or county officer may be offered for filing is 5 p.m. on the 60th day commencing after registration. The last date that a petition for the recall of a city, village, town or school district officer may be offered for filing is 5 p.m. on the 30th day commencing after registration. After the recall petition has been offered for filing, no name may be added or removed. No signature may be counted unless the date of the signature is within the period provided in this paragraph.

(e) An individual signature on a petition sheet may not be counted if: 1. The signature is not dated.

2. The signature is dated outside the circulation period.

3. The signature is dated after the date of the certification contained on the petition sheet.

4. The residency of the signer of the petition sheet cannot be determined by the address given.

5. The signature is that of an individual who is not a resident of the jurisdiction or district from which the elective official being recalled is elected.

6. The signer has been adjudicated not to be a qualified elector on grounds of incompetency or limited incompetency as provided in s. 6.03 (3).

7. The signer is not a qualified elector by reason of age.

8. The circulator knew or should have known that the signer, for any other reason, was not a qualified elector.

(em) No signature on a petition sheet may be counted if:

1. The circulator fails to sign the certification of circulator.

2. The residency of the circulator cannot be determined by the information given on the petition.

(f) The filing officer or agency shall review a verified challenge to a recall petition if it is made prior to certification.
(g) The burden of proof for any challenge rests with the individual bringing the challenge.

(h) Any challenge to the validity of signatures on the petition shall be presented by affidavit or other supporting evidence demonstrating a failure to comply with statutory requirements.

(i) If a challenger can establish that a person signed the recall petition more than once, the 2nd and subsequent signatures may not be counted.

(j) If a challenger demonstrates that someone other than the elector signed for the elector, the signature may not be counted, unless the elector is unable to sign due to physical disability and authorized another individual to sign in his or her behalf.

(k) If a challenger demonstrates that the date of a signature is altered and the alteration changes the validity of the signature, the signature may not be counted.

(L) If a challenger establishes that an individual is ineligible to sign the petition, the signature may not be counted.

(m) No signature may be stricken on the basis that the elector was not aware of the purpose of the petition, unless the purpose was misrepresented by the circulator.

(n) No signature may be stricken if the circulator fails to date the certification of circulator.

(p) If a signature on a petition sheet is crossed out by the petitioner before the sheet is offered for filing, the elimination of the signature does not affect the validity of other signatures on the petition sheet.

(q) Challenges are not limited to the categories set forth in pars. (i) to (L).

(r) A petitioner may file affidavits or other proof correcting insufficiencies, including but not limited to:

4. Failure of the circulator to sign the certification of circulator.

5. Failure of the circulator to include all necessary information.

(s) No petition for recall of an officer may be offered for filing prior to the expiration of one year after commencement of the term of office for which the officer is elected.

(3) STATE, COUNTY, CONGRESSIONAL, LEGISLATIVE AND JUDICIAL OFFICES. (a) This subsection applies to the recall of all elective officials other than city, village, town and school district officials. City, village, town and school district officials are recalled under sub. (4).

(b) Within 10 days after the petition is offered for filing, the officer against whom the petition is filed may file a written challenge with the official, specifying any alleged insufficiency. If a challenge is filed, the petitioner may file a written rebuttal to the challenge with the official within 5 days after the challenge is filed. If a rebuttal is filed, the officer against whom the petition is filed may file a reply to any new matter raised in the rebuttal within 2 days after the rebuttal is filed. Within 14 days after the expiration of the time allowed for filing a reply to a rebuttal, the official shall file the certificate or an amended certificate. Within 31 days after the petition is offered for filing, the official with whom the petition is offered for filing shall determine by careful examination whether the petition on its face is sufficient and so state in a certificate attached to the petition. If the official finds that the amended petition is sufficient, the official shall file the petition and call a recall election to be held on the Tuesday of the 6th week commencing after the date of filing of the petition. If Tuesday is a legal holiday, the recall election shall be held on the first day after Tuesday which is not a legal holiday. If the official finds that the petition is insufficient, the certificate shall state the particulars creating the insufficiency. The petition may be amended to correct any insufficiency within 5 days following the affixing of the original certificate. Within 5 days after the offering of the amended petition for filing, the official with whom the petition is filed shall again carefully examine the face of the petition to determine sufficiency and shall attach a certificate stating the findings. Upon showing of good cause, the circuit court for the county in which the petition is offered for filing may grant an extension of any of the time periods provided in this paragraph.

(bm) Within 7 days after an official makes a final determination of sufficiency or insufficiency of a recall petition under par. (b), the petitioner or the officer against whom the recall petition is filed may file a petition for a writ of mandamus or prohibition with the circuit court for the county where the recall petition is offered for filing. Upon filing of such a petition, the only matter before the court shall be whether the recall petition is sufficient. The court may stay the effect of the official's order while the petition is under advisement and may order the official to revise the election schedule contained in the order if a revised schedule is necessitated by judicial review. Whenever the recall petitioner files a petition under this paragraph, the officer against whom the recall petition is filed shall be a party to the proceeding. The court shall give the matter precedence over other matters not accorded similar precedence by law.

(c) The official against whom the recall petition is filed shall be a candidate at the recall election without nomination unless the official resigns within 10 days after the original filing of the petition. Candidates for the office may be nominated under the usual procedure of nomination for a special election by filing nomination papers not later than 5 p.m. on the 4th Tuesday preceding the election and have their names placed on the ballot at the recall election.

(d) If more than 2 persons compete for a nonpartisan office, a recall primary shall be held. The names of the 2 persons receiving the highest number of votes in the recall primary shall be certified to appear on the ballot in the recall election, but if any person receives a majority of the total number of votes cast in the recall primary, a recall election shall not be held. If the incumbent receives a majority of the votes cast, the incumbent shall be retained in office for the remainder of the term. If another candidate receives a majority of the votes cast, that candidate shall be elected to serve for the residue of the unexpired term of the incumbent. Write–in votes are permitted only at a recall primary or at a recall election in which no primary is held.

(e) For any partisan office, a recall primary shall be held for each political party which is entitled to a separate ballot under s. 5.62 (1) (b) or (2) and from which more than one candidate competes for the party's nomination in the recall election. The primary ballot shall be prepared in accordance with s. 5.62, insofar as applicable. The person receiving the highest number of votes in the recall primary for each political party shall be that party's candidate in the recall election. Independent candidates shall be shown on the ballot for the recall election only.

(f) If a recall primary is required, the date specified under par. (b) shall be the date of the recall primary and the recall election shall be held on the Tuesday of the 4th week commencing after the recall primary or, if that Tuesday is a legal holiday, on the first day after that Tuesday which is not a legal holiday.

(4) CITY, VILLAGE, TOWN AND SCHOOL DISTRICT OFFICES. (a) Within 10 days after a petition for the recall of a city, village, town or school district official, is offered for filing, the officer against whom the petition is filed may file a written challenge with the municipal clerk or board of election commissioners or school district clerk with whom it is filed, specifying any alleged insufficiency. If a challenge is filed, the petitioner may file a written rebuttal to the challenge with the clerk or board of election commissioners within 5 days after the challenge is filed. If a rebuttal is filed, the officer against whom the petition is filed may file a reply to any new matter raised in the rebuttal within 2 days after the rebuttal is filed. Within 14 days after the expiration of the time allowed for filing a reply to a rebuttal, the clerk or board of election commissioners shall file the certificate or an amended certificate. Within 31 days after the petition is offered for filing, the clerk or board of election commissioners shall determine by careful examination of the face of the petition whether the petition is sufficient and shall so state in a certificate attached to the petition. If the petition is found to be insufficient, the certificate shall state the particulars creating the insufficiency. The petition may be amended to correct any insufficiency within 5 days following the affixing of the original certificate. Within 2 days after the offering of the amended petition for filing, the clerk or board of election commissioners shall again carefully examine the face of the petition to determine sufficiency and shall attach to the petition a certificate stating the findings. Immediately upon finding an original or amended petition sufficient, except in cities

over 500,000 population, the municipal clerk or school district clerk shall transmit the petition to the governing body or to the school board. Immediately upon finding an original or amended petition sufficient, in cities over 500,000 population, the board of election commissioners shall file the petition in its office.

(d) Promptly upon receipt of a certificate under par. (a), the governing body, school board, or board of election commissioners shall call a recall election. The recall election shall be held on the Tuesday of the 6th week commencing after the date on which the certificate is filed, except that if Tuesday is a legal holiday the recall election shall be held on the first day after Tuesday which is not a legal holiday.

(e) The official against whom the recall petition is filed shall be a candidate at the recall election without nomination unless the official resigns within 10 days after the date of the certificate. Candidates for the office may be nominated under the usual procedure of nomination for a special election by filing nomination papers or declarations of candidacy not later than 5 p.m. on the 4th Tuesday preceding the election and have their names placed on the ballot at the recall election.

(f) If more than 2 persons compete for an office, a recall primary shall be held. The names of the 2 persons receiving the highest number of votes in the recall primary shall be certified to appear on the ballot in the recall election, but if any person receives a majority of the total number of votes cast in the recall primary, a recall election shall not be held. If the incumbent receives a majority of the votes cast, the incumbent shall be retained in office for the remainder of the term. If another candidate receives a majority of the votes cast, that candidate shall be elected to serve for the residue of the unexpired term of the incumbent. Write–in votes are permitted only at a recall primary or at a recall election in which no primary is held.

(g) If a recall primary is required, the date specified under par. (d) shall be the date of the recall primary and the recall election shall be held on the Tuesday of the 4th week commencing after the recall primary or, if that Tuesday is a legal holiday, on the first day after that Tuesday which is not a legal holiday.

(h) All candidates for any town or village office, other than the official against whom the recall petition is filed, shall file nomination papers, regardless of the method of nomination of candidates for town or village office under s. 8.05.

(5) VOTING METHOD; ELECTION RESULTS. (a) The recall primary or election of more than one official may be held on the same day. If more than one official of the same office designation elected at large for the same term from the same district or territory is the subject of a recall petition, there shall be a separate election contest for the position held by each official. Candidates shall designate which position they are seeking on their nomination papers. Instructions shall appear on the ballot to electors to vote for each position separately.

(b) The official against whom a recall petition has been filed shall continue to perform the duties of his or her office until a certificate of election is issued to his or her successor. The person receiving a plurality of votes at the recall election or a majority of votes at a primary when authorized under sub. (3) (d) or (4) (f) shall be declared elected for the remainder of the term. If the incumbent receives the required number of votes he or she shall continue in office. Except as provided in sub. (4) (f), if another person receives the required number of votes that person shall succeed the incumbent if he or she qualifies within 10 days after receiving a certificate of election.

(6) LIMITATION ON RECALL ELECTIONS. After one recall petition and recall election, no further recall petition may be filed against the same official during the term for

which he or she was elected.

(7) PURPOSE. The purpose of this section is to facilitate the operation of article XIII, section 12, of the constitution and to extend the same rights to electors of cities, villages, towns and school districts.

9.20 Direct legislation. (1) A number of electors equal to at least 15% of the votes cast for governor at the last general election in their city or village may sign and file a petition with the city or village clerk requesting that an attached proposed ordinance or resolution, without alteration, either be adopted by the common council or village board or be referred to a vote of the electors. The individual filing the petition on behalf of the electors shall designate in writing an individual to be notified of any insufficiency or improper form under sub. (3). (2) The preparation and form of the direct legislation petition shall be governed by s. 8.40.

(2m) After the petition has been offered for filing, no name may be erased or removed. No signature may be considered valid or counted unless the date is less than 60 days before the date offered for filing.

(3) Within 15 days after the petition is filed, the clerk shall determine by careful examination whether the petition is sufficient and whether the proposed ordinance or resolution is in proper form. The clerk shall state his or her findings in a signed and dated certificate attached to the petition. If the petition is found to be insufficient or the proposed ordinance or resolution is not in proper form, the certificate shall give the particulars, stating the insufficiency or improper form. The petition may be amended to correct any insufficiency or the proposed ordinance or resolution may be put in proper form within 10 days following the affixing of the original certificate and notification of the individual designated under sub. (1). When the original or amended petition is found to be sufficient and the original or amended ordinance or resolution

is in proper form, the clerk shall so state on the attached certificate and forward it to the common council or village board immediately.

(4) The common council or village board shall, without alteration, either pass the ordinance or resolution within 30 days following the date of the clerk's final certificate, or submit it to the electors at the next spring or general election, if the election is more than 6 weeks after the date of the council's or board's action on the petition or the expiration of the 30–day period, whichever first occurs. If there are 6 weeks or less before the election, the ordinance or resolution shall be voted on at the next election thereafter. The council or board by a three–fourths vote of the members–elect may order a special election for the purpose of voting on the ordinance or resolution at any time prior to the next election, but not more than one special election for direct legislation may be ordered in any 6–month period.

(5) The clerk shall cause notice of the ordinance or resolution that is being submitted to a vote to be given as provided in s. 10.06 (3) (f).

(6) The ordinance or resolution need not be printed in its entirety on the ballot, but a concise statement of its nature shall be printed together with a question permitting the elector to indicate approval or disapproval of its adoption.

(7) If a majority vote in favor of adoption, the proposed ordinance or resolution shall take effect upon publication under sub. (5). Publication shall be made within 10 days after the election.

(8) City ordinances or resolutions adopted under this section shall not be subject to the veto power of the mayor and city or village ordinances or resolutions adopted under this section shall not be repealed or amended within 2 years of adoption except by a vote of the electors. The common council or village board may submit a proposition to repeal or amend the ordinance or resolution at any election.